Transport Law in Ukraine

Transport Law in Ukraine

Second Edition

Olena Bokareva
Denys Rabomizo
Vadym Shestakov
Yuliya Akimenko

This book was originally published as a monograph in the International Encyclopaedia of Laws/Transport Law.

General Editor: Roger Blanpain
Associate General Editor: Michele Colucci
Volume Editors: Marc Huybrechts, Eric Van Hooydonk

Wolters Kluwer
Law & Business

Published by:
Kluwer Law International
PO Box 316
2400 AH Alphen aan den Rijn
The Netherlands
Website: www.kluwerlaw.com

Sold and distributed in North, Central and South America by:
Aspen Publishers, Inc.
7201 McKinney Circle
Frederick, MD 21704
United States of America
Email: customer.service@aspenpublishers.com

Sold and distributed in all other countries by:
Turpin Distribution Services Ltd.
Stratton Business Park
Pegasus Drive, Biggleswade
Bedfordshire SG18 8TQ
United Kingdom
Email: kluwerlaw@turpin-distribution.com

ISBN 978-90-411-5428-6

This title is available on www.kluwerlawonline.com

The Authors

Olena Bokareva, born in 1982, holds a Master of Laws degree from National University 'Odessa Law Academy', Ukraine, and LLM degree in Maritime Law from Lund University, Sweden. She is currently a legal scholar at Lund University and a lecturer in Maritime Law.

Denys Rabomizo, born in 1982, holds a Master of Laws degree from Odessa National Maritime Academy, Ukraine, and LLM degree in Maritime Law from International Maritime Law Institute, Malta. He is a practising attorney-at-law in the fields of Maritime and Commercial Law and Arbitration and holds positions of the President of Ukrainian Maritime Bar Association and the Partner at Rabomizo Law Firm.

Vadym Shestakov, born in 1982, holds a Master of Laws degree in International Law from Kyiv National Economic University, Ukraine and LLM degree in Maritime Law from the University of Oslo, Norway. He is a practising lawyer in Kyiv, Ukraine, specializing in Maritime, Transport, Commercial Law and International Arbitration. Vadym is an author of numerous publications in the sphere of Maritime and Commercial Law.

The Authors

Yuliya Akimenko, born in 1984, holds a Master of Laws degree from National University 'Odessa Law Academy', Ukraine. She holds a Juris Doctor degree in EU Company Law from National University 'Odessa Law Academy', and also a lecturer at the same University. Yuliya is a practising lawyer in the field of Civil, Commercial and Administrative law.

Table of Contents

Table of Contents

List of Abbreviations

ADN	European Agreement concerning the International Carriage of Dangerous Goods by Inland Waterways, 2000
ADR	European Agreement Concerning the International Carriage of Dangerous Goods 1957
AIFF	Association of International Freight Forwarders of Ukraine
BALTIME 1939	BIMCO Uniform Time-Charter
BIMCO	Baltic and International Maritime Council
CIM	Uniform Rules Concerning the Contract for International Carriage of Goods by Rail
CIS	Commonwealth of Independent States
CIV	Uniform Rules concerning the Contract for International Carriage of Passengers and Luggage by Rail
CivPC	Civil Procedure Code of Ukraine
ComPC	Commercial Procedure Code of Ukraine
CLC	International Convention on Civil Liability for Oil Pollution Damage, 1969
CMNI	Budapest Convention on the Contract for the Carriage of Goods by Inland Waterways
CMU	Cabinet of Ministers of Ukraine
CMR	Convention on the Contract for the International Carriage of Goods by Road, 1956
COTIF	Convention Concerning International Carriage by Rail, 1980
COLREG	Convention on the International Regulations for Preventing Collisions at Sea, 1972
CVR	Convention on the Contract for the International Carriage of Passengers and Luggage by Road, 1973
ECAC	European Civil Aviation Conference
EEZ	Exclusive Economic Zone

List of Abbreviations

EU	European Union
EUROCONTROL	European Organization for the Safety of Air Navigation
FIATA	Federation of Freight Forwarders Associations
HR	Hague Rules, 1924
HVR	Hague-Visby Rules, 1968
GUAM- ODED	Organization for Democracy and Economic Development
IATA	International Air Transport Association
ICAO	International Civil Aviation Organization
ICJ	International Court of Justice
IMO	International Maritime Organization
ILO	International Labour Organization
ISF	International Shipping Federation
ISM	International Management Code for the Safe Operation of Ships and for Pollution Prevention, 1993
ISPS	International Ship and Port Facility Security Code, 2002
ITF	International Transport Federation
LLMC	International Convention Relating to the Limitation of Liability for Maritime Claims, 1976
MARPOL 73/79	International Convention for the Prevention of Pollution from Ships of 1973, modified by the Protocol of 1978
MLC 2006	Maritime Labour Convention, 2006
MSC	Merchant Shipping Code of Ukraine, 1995
MSCRF	Merchant Shipping Code of the Russian Federation
MSC USSR	Merchant Shipping Code of the Soviet Union, 1968
MTC	Ministry of Transport and Communication of Ukraine (from 1993 till 2004)
MTU	Ministry of Transport of Ukraine (from 2004 till 2010)
SAR	International Convention on Maritime Search and Rescue, 1979
SBU	Shipping Book of Ukraine
SCCU	Supreme Commercial Court of Ukraine
SCU	Supreme Court of Ukraine
SDR	Special Drawing Rights
SNK USSR	SOVNARKOM or Council of Peoples' USSR
SOLAS	Convention for the Unification of Certain Rules of Law Relating to Assistance and Salvage at Sea, 1974
SRU	State Shipping Register of Ukraine
STCW	International Convention on Standards of Training, Certification and Watchkeeping for Seafarers, 1978

TRACECA	Europe-the Caucasus-Asia corridor
UAH	Ukrainian Hryvnia
UMIC	Untaxed minimum of income of citizens of Ukraine (equal to UAH 17)
UN	United Nations Organization
UNCITRAL	United Nations Commission on International Trade Law
UNCLOS	United Nations Convention for the Law of the Sea, 1982
USSR	Union of Soviet Socialist Republics
Ukrainian SSR	Ukrainian Soviet Socialistic Republic
VTR	Vessel Traffic Regulation
SIWT	Statute of Inland Water Transport of the Soviet Union, approved by the Resolution of the Council of Ministers of USSR 1955
SMGS	Agreement on International Railway Cargo Transportation, 1951

List of Abbreviations

Preface

This volume represents a description and analysis of the Maritime and Transport Law of Ukraine. Since 1991, Ukraine has been developing its own maritime and transport legislation in accordance with the international standards. The text reflects the position as of 1 September 2013.

Odessa, September 2013
Olena Bokareva
Denys Rabomizo
Vadym Shestakov
Yuliya Akimenko

General Introduction

§1. General Background of the Country

I. Geography and Demography

1. Ukraine is the second largest country in Europe in terms of area (603,700 km^2) and the fifth in Europe in terms of population. Ukraine borders with Belarus to the North, Poland to the West, Slovakia, Hungary, Romania and Moldova to the Southwest, and Russia to the East and Northeast. Its southern territories are washed by the Black Sea and the Sea of Azov.

2. Ukraine is divided into twenty-four administrative regions and the Autonomous Republic of Crimea. Kyiv is the capital of Ukraine. The official language is Ukrainian, although Russian is largely spoken.

3. The Ukrainian citizens amount to 45,560,300 of the population.[1] The two largest ethnic communities are Ukrainians (73%) and Russians (22%), other ethnicities constitute 5% of the population.[2]

II. Political System

A. General

4. In July 1990, the Ukrainian Parliament – *Verkhovna Rada* – passed the Declaration of State Sovereignty and on 24 August 1991 proclaimed the independence in the Act of Declaration of the Independence of Ukraine. Due to that on 1 December 1991 the nationwide Ukrainian referendum was held and 92% of the population spoke in favour of the Independence Act.

5. The Ukrainian Constitution was enacted on 28 June 1996. According to the Constitution Ukraine is a unitary republic with presidential government. The system of the administrative and territorial structure of Ukraine is composed of the Autonomous Republic of Crimea, regions (*oblasts*), districts, cities, city districts, settlements and villages.

---

1. As on 1 Dec. 2012, www.ukrstat.gov.ua.
2. H.M. Kritzer (ed.), *Legal Systems of the World, a Political, Social & Cultural Encyclopaedia*, 1681 (Vol. IV, ABC CLIO 2002).

6. The Autonomous Republic of Crimea is an inseparable constituent part of Ukraine. Its competence is determined by the Constitution of Ukraine. The Autonomous Republic of Crimea has its own Constitution adopted by the *Verkhovna Rada* of the Autonomous Republic of Crimea and also approved by the *Verkhovna Rada* of Ukraine.

7. The state power is exercised by dividing it into legislative, executive and judicial branches. The bodies of legislative, executive and judicial power exercise their authority within the limits established by the Constitution and in accordance with the laws of Ukraine.

B. Legislative Power

8. In accordance with the Constitution, the *Verkhovna Rada* is a unicameral parliament and the sole legislative body of the country. The *Verhkovna Rada* of Ukraine has launched its functioning on 16 July 1990.

9. Four hundred and fifty national deputies comprise the *Verkhovna Rada* that are elected by secret ballot for four-year term through the general, equal and direct suffrage. Regular elections to the *Verkhovna Rada* take place on the last Sunday of March of the fourth year of the term of the *Verkhovna Rada's* authority. The Committees of the *Verkhovna Rada* perform the work of legislative drafting, prepare and conduct the preliminary consideration of issues ascribed to the authority of the *Verkhovna Rada*.

10. The *Verkhovna Rada* adopts laws, resolutions and other Acts by the majority of its constitutional composition except in cases envisaged by the Constitution. The *Verkhovna Rada* designates the Ukrainian referendum, approves the State Budget and controls its implementation, declares war and concludes peace. The main powers and tasks of the *Verkhovna Rada* also relate to appointment of the President's elections and acceptance of the nomination of the Prime Minister and the Prosecutor General by the President of Ukraine.

11. The right of legislative initiative in the *Verkhovna Rada* belongs to the President, the national deputies, the Cabinet of Ministers and the National Bank. The President signs the laws adopted by the *Verkhovna Rada* and signed by its Speaker. The President has also the right to veto the laws. A law enters into force in ten days from the day of its official promulgation, unless otherwise envisaged by the law itself, but not prior to the day of its publication.

12. The legal Acts of the *Verkhovna Rada* of the Autonomous Republic of Crimea and decisions of the Council of Ministers of the Autonomous Republic of Crimea shall not contradict the Constitution and the laws of Ukraine.

C. Institute of Presidency in Ukraine

13. The institute of presidency as the head of state is a comparatively new phenomenon in legal traditions and statehood of Ukraine. The functions of the head of state in the Ukrainian SSR until 1991 were performed by the *Verkhovna Rada* of the Ukrainian SSR, as a supreme body of state power.

14. The status of the President – who is the Guarantor of the Constitution – is defined in Article 102 of the Constitution. The President as a head of the State acts on its behalf. Under the Law of Ukraine on the President of the Ukrainian SSR[3] the President is proclaimed as a head of the executive power. He has an authority to suspend decisions of the governmental institutions and veto the laws passed by the *Verkhovna Rada*. Cooperating with all branches of power, the President appoints and dismisses members of the Government and heads of the executive power institutions; he can also participate in the Government's meetings and have his/her representatives at the Constitutional Court of Ukraine and the *Verkhovna Rada*.

15. The citizens of Ukraine elect the President of Ukraine for a five-year term on the basis of general, equal and direct suffrage by secret ballot. One and the same person cannot be the President of Ukraine for more than two consecutive terms.

16. The first elections of the President of Ukraine occurred on 1 December 1991. Then, Leonid Kravchuk was elected as a President through the direct elections. In 1994 Leonid Kuchma was elected as a President, being re-elected in 1999. On 26 December 2004 Viktor Yushchenko became a President. Viktor Yanukovych is a current President of Ukraine, elected on 7 February 2010.

D. Executive Power

17. The Cabinet of Ministers of Ukraine (CMU) is the highest body in the system of executive power. The Cabinet of Ministers is responsible to the President and is under the control of and accountable to the *Verkhovna Rada* within the limits envisaged in Articles 85 and 87 of the Constitution. The CMU exercises executive power directly and through the ministries,[4] other central executive authorities, the Council of Ministers of the Autonomous Republic of Crimea and local state administrations, directs, coordinates and controls their activity.

18. The CMU is composed of the Prime Minister, the First Vice-Prime Minister, three Vice-Prime Ministers and the ministers (Article 114 of the Constitution). The Prime Minister is appointed by the President with the consent of more than one-half of the constitutional composition of the *Verkhovna Rada*. The personal composition of the CMU is appointed by the President on the submission of the Prime Minister. The Prime Minister heads the CMU and directs its work. As provided by Article 117

3. Law of Ukraine on the President of the Ukrainian SSR dated 5 Jul. 1991, No. 1295-XII.
4. Law of Ukraine on the Central Executive Power dated 17 Mar. 2011, No. 3166-VI.

of the Constitution the CMU, within the limits of its competence, issues resolutions and decrees that are mandatory for execution. All Acts of the CMU are signed by the Prime Minister. The legal Acts of the CMU, ministries and other central bodies of executive power are subject to registration under the procedure established by the law. The Law on the CMU[5] governs organization, powers and activity of the CMU.

19. The executive power in regions (*oblasts*), districts, cities and in the cities of Kyiv and Sevastopol is exercised by State Administrations. Particular aspects of the exercise of executive power in the cities of Kyiv and Sevastopol are determined by special laws of Ukraine.

20. It is essential to add that an administrative reform is currently taking place in Ukraine. One of the elements of that reform is the reorganization of the central authorities of executive power. Decree of the President on Optimization of Central Authorities of Executive Power was enacted at the end of 2010 that changed the existed system of the central executive bodies.[6] The reasons for that reform as stated in the Decree is to optimize the system of central authorities of executive power, to eliminate overlap of competence, to ensure reduction of the administrative apparatus and to increase efficiency of the public administration.[7]

E. Judicial Power

21. Justice in Ukraine is administered exclusively by courts (Article 124 of the Constitution). According to the Constitution, courts constitute a self-sufficient authority functioning independently of other bodies or officials. The jurisdiction of courts extends to all legal relations arising in the State.

22. According to the Law on the Judicial System of Ukraine and Legal Status of Judges,[8] the judicial system of Ukraine consists of the courts of general jurisdiction, specialized jurisdiction and the court of constitutional jurisdiction.

F. The Constitutional Court of Ukraine

23. The Constitutional Court of Ukraine is the sole body of constitutional jurisdiction (Article 147 of the Constitution). It decides on the issues of conformity of laws and other legal Acts with the Constitution and provides an official interpretation of the Constitution of Ukraine and laws. It is composed of eighteen judges. The

---

5. Law of Ukraine on the Cabinet of Ministers of Ukraine dated 10 Oct. 2010, No. 2591-VI.
6. Decree of the President of Ukraine on Optimization of Central Authorities of Executive Power dated 9 Dec. 2010, No. 1085/2010.
7. See further at www.president.gov.ua/en/news/18926.html and www.kmu.gov.ua/control/.
8. Law of Ukraine on the Judicial System of Ukraine and Legal Status of Judges dated 7 Jul. 2010, No. 2453-VI, Art. 3.

President of Ukraine, the *Verkhovna Rada* of Ukraine and the Congress of Judges of Ukraine each appoints six judges to the Constitutional Court of Ukraine.

24. The Law on the Constitutional Court of Ukraine defines that Constitutional Court of Ukraine renders the decisions in the cases dealing with constitutionality of laws and other legal Acts of the *Verkhovna Rada*, the President, the CMU, and the *Verkhovna Rada* of the Autonomous Republic of Crimea; conformity of the current international treaties of Ukraine or those international treaties the consent on obligatory nature of which was given by the *Verkhovna Rada* of Ukraine to the Constitution of Ukraine; adherence to the constitutional procedure for investigation and consideration of cases on removing the President from the office following the impeachment procedure; official interpretation of the Constitution and laws.[9]

25. The Constitutional Court of Ukraine renders the decisions that are mandatory for execution throughout the territory of the country. They are final and shall not be appealed. The laws and other legal Acts, or their separate provisions deemed to be unconstitutional, shall be null and void.

G. Courts of General Jurisdiction

26. The system of courts of general jurisdiction is formed in accordance with the territorial principle and instance principle. This system consists of the following courts:

(1) local courts;
(2) appeal courts;
(3) Supreme Specialized Court of Ukraine on Civil and Criminal cases; and
(4) Supreme Court of Ukraine (SCU).

27. The Supreme Court is the highest judicial body in the system of courts of general jurisdiction.

28. The system of courts of specialized jurisdiction includes commercial courts and administrative courts. Among the specialized courts the highest judicial bodies are the Supreme Administrative Court of Ukraine and the Supreme Commercial Court of Ukraine (SCCU). In 2010, the Constitutional Court of Ukraine limited the power of SCU to review the decisions of supreme specialized courts (the Supreme Administrative Court and the Supreme Commercial Court).[10]

29. There are twenty-seven commercial courts (twenty-four local courts, commercial court of Kiev, Sevastopol, The Autonomous Republic of Crimea), eleven

9. Law of Ukraine on the Constitutional Court of Ukraine dated 16 Oct. 1996, No. 422/96-BP, Art. 13.
10. Dated 11 Mar. 2010, No. 1-1/2010.

appeal commercial courts and Supreme Commercial Court in Ukraine.[11] The system of administrative courts is contained of twenty-seven administrative local courts, nine appeal administrative courts and Supreme Administrative Court of Ukraine.

III. Legal System

30. The Ukrainian legal system follows a civil law model of the Germanic legal family which was mainly based on principles of the Roman law. The traditions of it are particularly reflected in many codes, legal education, judicial formation and jurisprudence.[12] Thus, like most countries of the continental Europe, Ukraine has adopted the Roman civil law traditions.

31. From October Revolution 1917, the Ukrainian legal system existed and developed within the Soviet Union's legal family. Notably, it still retains certain characteristics from the Soviet jurisprudence in current Ukrainian legal system. Despite declared freedom and autonomy of the Soviet Republics all the laws and decrees of the Soviet Union were in force for them, including Ukraine. The sources of law included not only codes, laws, decrees of the Presidiums of the Supreme Councils of the USSR, but also various legal Acts adopted by all-Union and Republic Ministries, including those adopted jointly with the Central Executive Committee of the USSR,[13] regulations, instructions, guiding materials, statutes, branch enactments and even revolutionary feeling of justice. The access to the legislation was restricted and the criteria of such restrictions were not defined because of the state policy depriving people of their individual rights and freedoms. In the field of civil law, all provisions pertaining to the property were removed from the Civil Code.

32. After the dissolution of the USSR and gaining its independence, Ukraine along with other ex-USSR States has started the development of its statehood and law, having democracy and rule-of-law state as its priorities. The promulgation of new legislation has begun with enactment of relevant norms, adoption of normative Acts in various spheres of social life and development of the large codification embracing all areas of law. Notably, the European integration is one of the principal in the Ukrainian state policy. Ukraine signed the Partnership and Cooperation Agreement with the European Union (EU)[14] in 1994. This Agreement was concluded for a ten-year period, and in March 2008 Ukraine and the EU have launched the negotiation process on a new agreement.

---

11. Decree of President on Optimization of System of Commercial Courts of Ukraine dated 12 Aug. 2010, No. 811/2010.
12. H. M. Kritzer (ed.), *Legal Systems of the World, a Political, Social & Cultural Encyclopaedia* 1683 (Vol. IV ABC CLIO 2002).
13. After 1938 – The Central Committee of the Communist Party of the Soviet Union.
14. Partnership and Cooperation Agreement between the European Communities and their Member States, and Ukraine in 1994 (came into effect on 1 Mar. 1998).

33. During the Soviet Union the Ukrainian SSR joined to the majority of international treaties signed by the USSR and deposited with the UN Secretary-General and third States. However, some of those treaties have been ratified by Ukraine after gaining the independence (e.g., United Nations Convention for the Law of the Sea (UNCLOS)). After the USSR dissolution, Ukraine declared itself as a successor of the States of the Soviet Union by enacting the Law of Ukraine on Succession of Ukraine dated 12 September 1991, No. 1543-XII.[15] Due to the lack of a unified treaty database in Ukraine the status of some of the treaties is not clear enough. Therefore, in case of uncertainty, a request for clarification should be made to the Ministry of Foreign Affairs of Ukraine.

34. In accordance with the Resolution of the *Verkhovna Rada* on the Procedure of Temporary Validity of Some Legal Acts of the Former USSR on the Territory of Ukraine[16] such Acts are still in force in some branches until the adoption of new legislation, provided that they do not contradict the Constitution and the laws of Ukraine.

35. By joining the Council of Europe in 1995, Ukraine has taken obligations to improve its legislation in regard to the human rights protection and to ensure the legal and judicial reform. In 1997, the *Verkhovna Rada* agreed on ratification of the Convention for the Protection of Human Rights and Fundamental Freedoms, 1950 (The European Convention on Human Rights)[17] and started a judicial reform in 2000. During the judicial reform the Law of Ukraine on the Judicial System of Ukraine[18] was enacted. This Law amended the existed judicial system. Before enactment of this law the principles of the judicial system, terminology, the legal status of judges and courts remained the same as in the USSR. The Law of Ukraine on Judicial System of 2001 was the first step forward in establishing of an independent and democratic judicial authority. In 2010, the *Verkhovna Rada* passed the new Law of Ukraine on the Judicial System and Legal Status of Judges dated 7 July 2010, No. 2453-VI.

36. The principal source of the Ukrainian law is the Constitution which has the highest legal force.[19] The norms of the Constitution are the norms of direct effect. The Constitution set that rights and freedoms of the individuals and citizens are guaranteed on its grounds. The laws and all other legal Acts should be adopted on its basis and in conformity with it. The Constitution is followed by various codes (Civil Code of Ukraine, Criminal Code of Ukraine Merchant Shipping Code, Subsoil Code of Ukraine, etc.), by laws of general and special nature. Laws (*zakon*) and

---

15. Certain international treaties mentioned in this monograph are in force for Ukraine as the successor of the USSR whereas the others were ratified by the independent Ukraine.
16. Resolution of the *Verkhovna Rada* on the Procedure of Temporary Validity of Some Legal Acts of the Former USSR on the Territory of Ukraine dated 12 Sep. 1991, No. 1545-XII.
17. Law of Ukraine on Ratification of the European Convention on Human Rights dated 17 Jul. 1997, No. 475/97-BP.
18. Law of Ukraine on the Judicial System of Ukraine dated 1 Jun. 2002, No. 3018-III.
19. The Constitution of Ukraine was adopted at the Fifth Session of the *Verkhovna Rada* of Ukraine on 28 Jun. 1996, the English translation is available at www.rada.gov.ua/const/conengl.htm.

subordinate regulatory Acts (*podzakonniy Act*),[20] issued on the basis of laws are the principal and the only sources of law in Ukraine.

37. The Constitution points out that important issues and relations are governed exclusively by the laws of Ukraine. The procedure for adoption of the laws is established by Article 94 of the Constitution as follows:

- The Chairman of the *Verkhovna Rada* of Ukraine signs a law and forwards it without delay to the President of Ukraine.
- Within fifteen days of the receipt of a law, the President of Ukraine signs it, accepting it for execution, and officially promulgates it or returns it to the *Verkhovna Rada* of Ukraine with substantiated and formulated proposals for repeat consideration.
- In the event that the President of Ukraine has not returned a law for repeat consideration within the established term, the law is deemed to be approved by the President of Ukraine and shall be signed and officially promulgated.
- If a law, during its repeat consideration, is again adopted by the *Verkhovna Rada* of Ukraine by no less than two-thirds of its constitutional composition, the President of Ukraine is obliged to sign and to officially promulgate it within ten days.[21]

38. The laws of Ukraine enter into force in ten days after their official promulgation, unless otherwise envisaged by those laws and Acts. The subordinate regulatory Acts include decrees (*ukaz*) and directives (*rozporyadzhennya*) of the President of Ukraine, resolutions (*postanova*) and decrees (*razporyadgennya*) of the Cabinet of Ministers, regulations, instructions and orders of ministries, state agencies and executive bodies. The Acts of the President and the Acts of the Cabinet of Ministers enter into force from the date of their issuance and publication.

39. The Decisions of the Supreme Court could be divided into two groups, namely decisions and judicial practice systematized in resolutions. Taking into account the fact that the court's decisions are not legal sources in Ukraine, they are obligatory only for persons, legal entities and state bodies to whom they are addressed. Although in practice, courts usually take into account some important decisions since they reflect an official opinion of the Supreme Court of Ukraine (SCU).

40. It should be observed that the so-called dualism of private law is inherent to the Ukrainian legal system. Its meaning is expressed in parallel existence of the Civil and Commercial Codes which could lead to difficulties in application of law having overlapping provisions. Apparently, ideas of having two codes that regulate similar relationships were rejected in a number of the European countries as well as

20. The legislation of Ukraine can be found at portal.rada.gov.ua/rada/control/en/index, including short annotations in English for Codes and major laws.
21. See further at www.rada.gov.ua/const/conengl.htm.

in the former USSR countries. As it will be seen further, the provisions on carriage of goods sometimes are similar or even identical in both codes.[22]

41. After the proclamation of independence, Ukraine has a tendency to the priority of international law which is evidenced by the Declaration on State Sovereignty of Ukraine Part X, and further in the Laws on the International Treaties of Ukraine adopted in 1991, 1993 and 2004 respectively. On the constitutional level such a provision is enshrined in Article 9 of the Constitution. It stipulates that:

(1) International treaties that are in force, agreed to be binding by the *Verkhovna Rada*, are part of the national legislation of Ukraine.
(2) Conclusion of international treaties that contravene the Constitution is possible only after introducing relevant amendments to the Constitution.

Article 19 of the Law of Ukraine on International Treaties of Ukraine[23] (hereinafter – Law on International Treaties) provides that:

(1) The current international treaties of Ukraine the consent on the obligatory nature of which is given by the *Verkhovna Rada* constitute a part of the national legislation of Ukraine and applied in the manner provided for the provisions of national legislation.
(2) If an international treaty which has become valid in due course contains the provisions different from the Ukrainian legislative Act, the international treaty shall prevail.

42. The international treaties of Ukraine shall be registered in the Secretariat of UN upon submission of the Ministry of Foreign Affairs of Ukraine in compliance with the UN Statute. They shall also be registered in the Ministry of Foreign Affairs of Ukraine and included into the Unified State Register of Normative Acts.

43. The Law on International Treaties sets the procedure for concluding, implementation and termination of the international treaties of Ukraine for the proper ensuring of national interests, fulfilment of goals, tasks and principles of foreign policy of Ukraine set in the Constitution and legislation of Ukraine. Pursuant to Article 3 of the Law on International Treaties, an international treaty shall be concluded by the President of Ukraine or by his Decree on behalf of Ukraine; by the CMU or by its Order on behalf of the Government of Ukraine; by ministries and other central bodies of executive power, State bodies on behalf of the ministries, other central bodies of executive power and local State bodies.[24]

44. Article 6 of the Law on International Treaties defines the authorities that can hold negotiations and sign the international treaties of Ukraine:

---

22. Read further A. Biryukov, '*The Doctrine of Dualism of Private Law in the Context of Recent Codifications of Civil Law: Ukrainian Perspectives*', Annual Survey of Intl. Comp. L. 8 (2002).
23. Law of Ukraine on International Treaties of Ukraine dated 3 Aug. 2004, No. 1906-IV.
24. Law of Ukraine on International Treaties of Ukraine Art. 3, s. 1.

- as regards to international treaties concluded on behalf of Ukraine – by the President;
- as regards to international treaties concluded on behalf of the Government of Ukraine – by the Cabinet of Ministers;
- as regards to interdepartmental treaties – under the procedure set by the Cabinet of Ministers.[25]

45. The Law on International Treaties in Article 13 states that the consent of Ukraine to the binding nature of international treaty may be granted by signing, ratification, approval, adoption of treaty and accession thereto. The consent of Ukraine to the binding nature of international treaty may be granted in other way as agreed by the parties.

46. Ukraine belongs to dualistic countries when it comes to the relationship of international law with national law which implies a formal ratification and enactment of a law on ratification. The International treaties of Ukraine shall be ratified by adoption of the law on ratification. The text of an international treaty is translated into Ukrainian and included in the Law. On the basis of the law, signed and officially published by the President, the Speaker of the *Verkhovna Rada* shall sign the instrument of ratification to be certified by the signature of the Minister of Foreign Affairs, if a treaty provides for exchange of instruments of ratification. The following international treaties of Ukraine shall be subject to ratification:

- political, territorial and those related to the state borders delimitation of exclusive (maritime) economic zone and continental shelf of Ukraine, peaceful treaties;
- related to human rights, freedoms and duties of a person and a citizen;
- general economic, regarding general financial questions, granting of loans and economic aid by Ukraine to foreign States and international organizations, as well as on receipt of loans by Ukraine which are not stipulated by the State Budget of Ukraine, from foreign States and international organizations;
- on Ukraine's participation in interstate unions and other interstate associations, systems of collective security;
- on military aid and sending units of the Armed Forces of Ukraine to other States or admission of units of foreign States' armed forces to the territory of Ukraine, conditions of their temporary stay in Ukraine;
- related to transfer of historical and cultural values of Ukrainian people, as well as objects of Ukraine's State property right;
- whose implementation cause changes to the laws of Ukraine or adoption of new laws of Ukraine;
- other international treaties whose ratification is stipulated by international treaty or law of Ukraine.[26]

25. Law of Ukraine on International Treaties of Ukraine Art. 6, s. 4.
26. Law of Ukraine on International Treaties of Ukraine Art. 9, s. 2.

47. The Law of Ukraine on Private International Law[27] sets the procedure for the regulation of private legal relations connected through at least one of their elements with one or some legal orders different from the Ukrainian legal order.

48. The Acts issued by the authorized bodies of foreign states according to the set form shall be valid in Ukraine in case of their legalization unless otherwise is envisaged by the laws or the international treaties ratified by Ukraine. The courts of Ukraine shall consider the cases with the participation of foreigners provided that:

- real estate under dispute is located on the territory of Ukraine;
- both parties to the case regarding legal relations between parents and children reside in Ukraine;
- in the case on inheritance the testator is the citizen of Ukraine that resided in it;
- the dispute is connected with the registration of intellectual property that requires registration or issue of certificate (patent) in Ukraine;
- the dispute is connected with the registration of liquidation on the territory of Ukraine of foreign legal entities, natural persons – entrepreneurs;
- the dispute relates to the authenticity of records in the State Register, Cadastre of Ukraine;
- the debtor was established according to the legislation of Ukraine in the cases on bankruptcy;
- the case relates to the issue or destruction of securities registered in Ukraine;
- the case relates to the adoption that was performed or is being performed on the territory of Ukraine;
- in other cases determined by the laws of Ukraine.[28]

49. Decisions of the foreign courts that entered into force may be recognized and enforced in Ukraine. They concern the following range of cases:

- cases arising during civil, labour, family and commercial legal relations;
- criminal cases in the part related to the compensation of damages and caused losses;
- arbitration and other bodies of foreign states that consider civil and commercial cases.[29]

§2. General Introduction Relating to Transportation

I. Introduction

50. Transport is one of the most important sectors of economy in Ukraine. Being a maritime country with strong seafaring traditions, these days Ukraine is also

27. Law of Ukraine on Private International Law dated 1 Sep. 2005, No. 2709-IV.
28. Law of Ukraine on Private International Law dated 1 Sep. 2005, No. 2709-IV, Art. 77.
29. Law of Ukraine on Private International Law Art. 81.

known as a manning supply country since a number of the Ukrainian seafarers working on ships under the foreign flag is increasing every year. All types of transport exist in Ukraine, including railway, motor, maritime, air, inland waterway and pipeline transport. The railway transport plays a leading role in transport communications. It accounts for a major part of cargo and passenger transportation.

51. Ukraine occupies beneficial geopolitical position in Europe and serves as a transit territory for numerous countries. The access to the Black Sea and the Sea of Azov and through the Black Sea Straits to the Mediterranean Sea makes Ukraine very attractive in term of export, import and transit of goods, carriage of goods and passengers.

52. In 2012 foreign trade was carried out with partners from 213 States.[30] The biggest export deliveries were to Commonwealth of Independent States, including the Russian Federation – 36.9% of all goods, to EU Countries – 24.5%. The main goods are mineral products, semi-precious metals, mechanical and electric cars, products of chemical industry.

53. In 2012, 772.8 million tonnes of goods were carried by transport enterprises, where rail transport is taking the leading role. Approximately 6.8 billion passengers used transport in 2012.[31]

II. Inland Waterways and Ports

54. Inland waterway transport has been playing an important role in Ukraine since ancient times. The beneficial geographical location and favourable environmental conditions create advantageous basis for the development of maritime and inland water transport in Ukraine. The Black Sea and the Sea of Azov provide Ukraine with an access to the Mediterranean through the straits of Bosporus and Dardanelles. The total length of the coastal line exceeds 2,000 km. Regular maritime transportation started back in the eighteenth century and its development continues today.

55. There are about 23,000 rivers in Ukraine with a total length of nearly 180,000 km.[32] The major navigable rivers are Danube, Dnieper and Dniester. The Danube has an international importance in the sphere of goods and passengers carriage. The total length of inland waterways is 2,240 km in Ukraine; about 42% can be attributed to the river Dnieper which was developed for hydropower and high capacity inland shipping after World War II.[33]

30. Social Economic State of Ukraine in 2012, see at www.ukrstat.gov.ua.
31. Social Economic State of Ukraine in 2012, see at www.ukrstat.gov.ua.
32. I. Stebelsky & I.Teslia, *The Internet Encyclopaedia of Ukraine*, vol. 4 (1993) wwwencyclopedia ofukraine.com/land.asp.
33. Declaration of the International Transport Forum 'Inland Waterways of Eurasia', Informal document, No. 1, Agenda, item 5 Presented by Ukraine (Odessa, 12 Oct. 2004).

56. Today the Black Sea coast is divided among Ukraine, Russia, Georgia, Turkey, Bulgaria and Romania. The Black Sea is connected to the Oceans via the Mediterranean Sea through Istanbul, Canakkale and Gibraltar Straits and with the Sea of Azov in the northeast through the Kerch Strait. The total coastal line of the Black Sea is 4,340 km, of which 1,628 is the Ukrainian coastline.[34] The Sea of Azov is a shallow branch of the Black Sea connected to it by the Kerch Strait. It is located between mainland Ukraine in the North, the Crimea in the West and the Kuban region in the East.[35]

57. At present time Ukraine actively reforms the port sector of the economy after the adoption of the Law of Ukraine on Sea Ports of Ukraine dated 17 May 2012, No. 4709-VI, which entered into force on 13 June 2013. First of all, this law sets the new approach to the definition of the term *seaport*. Notably, it is no longer defined as a *state-owned transport company*, as it was stipulated by Article 73 of the MSC, but as 'defined by the limits territory and water area equipped for the servicing of vessels and passengers, carrying freight, transport, and forwarding activity, as well as other related economic activities'. Such definition points out that a seaport is not a kind of monopoly of the state and thus, it does not violate the freedom of entrepreneurship and does not limit competition in the field of merchant shipping.

According to the law the further operation and development of seaports shall be based on principles established by law. Among these principles the following should be mentioned:

– separation of administrative functions in relation to the safety of navigation and supervision (control) of the safety of navigation and the economic (commercial) activities;
– separation of functions concerning support of the safety of navigation and supervision (control) of the safety of navigation.

58. In order to implement these principles, in accordance with the Resolution of the Cabinet of Ministers[36] and the Order of the Ministry of Infrastructure,[37] adopted in March 2013, 18 seaports, State Enterprise 'Delta-Pilot' and State shipping company 'Kerch ferry' shall be reorganized to establish on their basis the State Enterprise 'Administration of Seaports of Ukraine'.

59. Administration of Seaports of Ukraine shall ensure mainly the operation of seaports, maintenance and use of port infrastructure, owned by the state, the safety of navigation. At the same time the harbormaster's service will continue to exist,

34. See at www.blacksea-commission.org/_geography.asp.
35. SeeI.Stebelsky&I.Teslia, *The Internet Encyclopaedia of Ukraine*, vol.4 (1993) wwwencyclopedia ofukraine.com/land.asp.
36. Resolution of the Cabinet of Ministers on Approval of Proposals for the Reorganization of State-Owned Enterprises of Maritime Transport, dated 4 Mar. 2013, No. 133-p.
37. Order of the Ministry of Infrastructure on Measures of Reorganization of the State-Owned Enterprises of Maritime Transport and the Establishment of the State Enterprise 'Administration of Seaports of Ukraine', dated 4 Mar. 2013, No. 163.

providing supervision of navigation in the seaport. In every seaport the conditions for the activities of the various entities and the Council of the Port as a permanent advisory and consultative body to coordinate matters related to the development and operation of the seaport shall be established. The law provides that property used to carry out activities in the port, as well as plots of land within the territory of seaports can be in the state, municipal and private property.

60. According to the provisions of the Law of Ukraine on Sea Ports of Ukraine, the state guarantees the right to private ownership of the port infrastructure, including hydrotechnical constructions acquired legally before the law came into force. In accordance with Article 26 of the Law of Ukraine on Sea Ports of Ukraine, private investment in objects of seaport infrastructure, owned by the state, shall be carried out on the basis of concession agreements, joint venture agreements, lease agreements, and other types of investment agreements concluded on the basis of special procedures defined by the laws of Ukraine.

61. The largest Black Sea ports are Odessa, Illichivsk, Sevastopol and Kherson and the largest ports at the Sea of Azov are Mariupol, Berdyansk and Kerch. The Odessa Port and the Port of Illichivsk are located at the junction of intensive marine and river transport international communications that makes powerful transport transit potential of the region.

62. Odessa Commercial Sea Port[38] is one of the largest ports of the Black Sea Azov range. The Port of Odessa is situated in the northwest part of the Black Sea on the historically founded trade routes between East and West. The technical facilities of the port allow processing of more than 18 million tonnes of dry cargoes and 25 million tonnes of liquid cargoes annually.[39] Developed infrastructure allows delivering cargoes by motor, rail, maritime and inland water transport. The container terminal has a capacity of more than 500,000 containers per year. The Oil Harbour of the Port, being the largest functioning oil harbour in Ukraine, services handling of all kinds of export-import oil products and condensed gas.

63. Sea Commercial Port of Illichivsk is situated on the North coast of the Black Sea. Its importance is determined by its key position at the crossroads of main transport routes between Europe and Asia, North and South, Central and Eastern industrially developed regions of Ukraine, Russia, Kazakhstan and the shipping routes running across the Mediterranean Sea into the Atlantic and Indian oceans. At present the port has international relationships with almost 100 countries of the world.

64. Mariupol Sea Commercial Port[40] is one of the leading ports in the Sea of Azov and one of the oldest ports of Ukraine. The capacities of the port give the possibility to handle more than 15 million tonnes of cargoes per year.

---

38. See www.port.odessa.ua, 1 Sep. 2013.
39. *Ibid.*
40. See at www.marport.net, 1 Sep. 2013.

65. Port of Izmail, as one of the major ports in the Black Sea region part of Danube, is located on crossing of the corridor No. 7 and the Balkan branch of the transport corridor No. 9 which plays an important role and serves as a link between Ukraine and other EU countries.

66. There are also ferry routes operating on a regular basis: Illichivsk (Ukraine) – Varna (Bulgaria), Illichivsk (Ukraine) – Poti/Batumi (Georgia). The sea and river merchant fleets transported about 7.8 million tonnes of cargo in 2012.[41]

67. Passenger traffic. The Odessa passenger terminal accepts cruise ships with up to 300m in length and up to 11.5m draught. Throughput of the Passenger Terminal is 4 million people per year. The marine passenger terminal in Sevastopol is equipped with two moorings at 135m and 200m and has the capacity to accommodate passenger cruises with a draught of 4m and 8m respectively.[42] Yalta Sea Trade Port annually services about 700 big passenger ships under the flags of different countries of the world. About 7.6 million passengers used water transport in 2012.

68. Shipyards and shipping companies. The independent shipping companies established in Ukraine are Ukrrichflot, Ukrferry, Ukrship, Ukrreefer, Ukrtanker. A number of shipyards and several shipbuilding companies are operating in various cities of Ukraine. Among the largest can be named Wadan Yards Ocean, Black Sea Shipyard and 61 Kommunar Shipyard in Mykolaiv, Zaliv Shipyard in Kerch, Sevastopol Shipyard, Kherson Shipyard, etc.

III. Railways

69. A well-developed network of the Ukrainian railways is more than 22,000 km long. Two-thirds of the Ukrainian railways service eighteen ports of the Black Sea and the Sea of Azov.[43] The Ukrainian rail transport system ranks fourth in the world after Russia, the United States and Canada. Ukraine is linked via railways with many countries of the world.[44] The main transit cargo is coal, oil and oil products, iron ore, ferrous metals, fertilizers, chemicals and grain. About 4,325 million tonnes of cargo were carried by Ukrainian railways in 2012. In 2012 rail transport carried 426.6 million passengers.[45]

IV. Road System

70. Seven important international automobile transport corridors cross Ukraine. The length of roads in the areas of transport corridors constitutes 5,240 km.[46] The network of public highways stretches for 169,100 km of which 20,100 km are of

41. Social Economic State of Ukraine in 2012, see at www.ukrstat.gov.ua.
42. See at www.morport.sebastopol.ua/index_en.html, 5 Jul. 2010.
43. See further at www.uz.gov.ua.
44. www.ukraine-gateway.org.ua/gateway/gateway.nsf/webcontent/05020600, 22 Dec. 2010.
45. Social Economic State of Ukraine in 2012, see at www.ukrstat.gov.ua.
46. www.ukravtodor.gov.ua.

national importance. The motor transport enterprises carried 179.0 million tonnes of cargo in 2012. The motor transport was used by 3.5 billion passengers in 2012.[47]

V. Airports

71. The air transport connects Ukraine with many countries and interlinks nearly all major cities of Ukraine. The main airports of Ukraine are Kiev-Borispol International Airport, Donetsk Airport, Lviv Airport, Odessa Airport and Simferopol Airport. The air transport carried 114.9 thousand tonnes of cargo and 8.1 million passengers in 2012.[48]

VI. Pipelines

72. The pipeline transport system plays an important role in the transport of oil and natural gas as Ukraine is a key transit country for energy resources from Russia to the EU, particularly for gas and, in the future, for oil.[49] Part of them are trans-European mainlines transporting oil, petrochemicals, natural gas and other products. Ukraine's geographic location enables it to be engaged in various oil supply routes from Azerbaijan, Kazakhstan, Turkmenistan, the Near and the Middle East countries, etc. The main pipeline in Ukraine and one of the longest in the world is *Druzhba* (Friendship) pipeline which starts in central Russia and connects the West Siberian oilfields to major refineries in Europe. The pipelines transported 128.4 million tonnes of cargo in 2012.[50]

VII. State Authorities Responsible for Transport Policy

73. The Ministry of Transport and Communications of Ukraine was reorganized into the Ministry of Infrastructure of Ukraine in the course of the administrative reform as mentioned above.[51] Furthermore, the mentioned Decree of the President determines a scheme of organization and interaction between the central authorities of executive power. Hence, the Cabinet of Ministers through the Vice Prime Minister of Ukraine – a Minister of Infrastructure of Ukraine – directs and coordinates an activity of various authorities in the sphere of transport. According to this Decree and other legal Acts, the following new state authorities subordinated to the Ministry of Infrastructure are formed:

- State Aviation Service of Ukraine;
- State Motor Transport Service of Ukraine;

47. Social Economic State of Ukraine in 2012, see at www.ukrstat.gov.ua.
48. Social Economic State of Ukraine in 2012, see at www.ukrstat.gov.ua.
49. See at ec.europa.eu/energy/international/bilateral_cooperation/ukraine_en.htm, 1 Sep. 2013.
50. Social Economical State of Ukraine in 2012, see at www.ukrstat.gov.ua.
51. Decree of the President of Ukraine on Optimization of the Central Executive Authorities System dated 9 Dec. 2010, No. 1085/2010.

– State Communications Service of Ukraine;
– State Inspectorate of Ukraine for Maritime and Inland Water Transport Safety.[52]

74. The functions of realization of the tourism state policy are also assigned to the Ministry of Infrastructure. The State Administration of Rail Transport of Ukraine (*UkrZaliznytsya*) was not mentioned in the Presidential Decree. It is assumed that its legal status has not been changed. It is to be noted that there are other executive bodies which can partially deal with transport matters and cooperate with other state authorities (Tax Administration, Customs Service, etc.).

A. *Ministry of Infrastructure of Ukraine*

75. The Ministry of Infrastructure is the principal body in the central executive system on the implementation of the state policy on motor, rail, maritime, inland water and air transportation and usage of airspace of Ukraine, ensuring safety of navigation and hydrographical support of navigation, merchant shipping, radio frequency resource of Ukraine, etc.[53] In case of necessity and to the extent the ministry is authorized, it issues orders, which are binding for central executive powers, their territorial authorities and local state administrations, authorities of the Autonomous Republic of Crimea, municipal governments, enterprises, institutions and organizations of all form of ownership and citizens.

B. *State Aviation Service of Ukraine*

76. A new period in the history of civil aviation of Ukraine started with the establishment of the state body regulating aviation (*Ukraviatsiya)* in October 1992, which coincided with the launch of the market relations in civil aviation. It was the beginning of creation of new national airlines of different forms of ownership. Under the Presidential Decree on System of the Central Executive Bodies in 1999[54] *Ukraviatsiya* was reorganized into the State Department of Air Transport. It was governed by Regulation on State Department of Air Transport.[55]

77. In 2006 the State Department of Air Transport was further reorganized into the State Air Administration of Ukraine which was further reorganized into State Aviation Service of Ukraine in 2010.[56]

---

52. Decree of the President of Ukraine on Optimization of the Central Executive Authorities System dated 6 Apr. 2011, No. 370/2011.
53. Decree of the President of Ukraine on Regulation of the Ministry of Infrastructure of Ukraine dated 12 May 2011, No. 581/2011.
54. Decree of the President of Ukraine on System of the Central Executive Bodies of Ukraine dated 15 Dec. 1999, No. 1573.
55. Decree of the CMU on Regulation of State Department of Air Transport dated 29 Mar. 2000, No. 573.
56. Decree of the President of Ukraine on Optimization of the Central Executive Authorities System dated 9 Dec. 2010, No. 1085/2010.

78. The main novelty is that the Head of the State Aviation Service of Ukraine shall be appointed by the President. It functions according to the Regulation[57] and is responsible for:

- implementation of the state policy in the area of Civil Aviation: aircraft operations, aerial works and services, airports, financial, technical, investment and social policy;
- safety oversight and aviation security;
- registration and certification of Civil Aviation activities;
- promotion of safe, efficient and cost effective air navigation services;
- elaboration of National Civil Aviation regulations;
- international activity and representation of the Ukrainian Civil Aviation in international organizations.[58]

C. State Motor Transport Service of Ukraine

79. The State Motor Transport Service has the same history of establishment as the State Aviation Service. Based on the Presidential Decree, the State Department of Motor Transport was established in 1999. The legal status of that Department was regulated by the Cabinet of Ministers.[59] The State Motor Transport Department (*Ukravtotrans*) was a state body in the field of motor transport that operated within the Ministry of Transport and was subordinated to it. The State Motor Transport Department was reorganized in 2008 into the State Administration of Motor Transport.[60] This Regulation is still in force for the State Motor Transport Service of Ukraine. The main objectives of the State Motor Transport Service are participation in implementing the governmental policy on motor transport and realization of regulatory and registration functions.

80. The State Motor Transport Service:

- organizes work to fulfil the requirements of legislation on road safety;
- summarizes legislative practice on motor transport, elaborates proposals for its improvement;
- ensures state regulation of motor transport;
- develops draft regulations related to motor transport, etc.

57. Decree of the President on Approval of Regulation on State Aviation Service of Ukraine dated 6 Apr. 2011, No. 398/2011.
58. See at www.avia.gov.ua.
59. Regulation on Creation of the State Department of Motor Transport approved by the Decree of the CMU dated 30 Mar. 2000, No. 586.
60. Regulation on State Administration of Motor Transport approved by the Decree of the CMU dated 3 Sep. 2008, No. 771.

D. State Communications Service of Ukraine

81. In 2004, the Decree of the President approved the establishment of Ministry of Transport and Communications[61] by integration of the Ministry of Transport of Ukraine (MTU) and the State Committee on Communications and Information. The Ministry of Transport and Communications of Ukraine (now the Ministry of Infrastructure) is a successor of the rights and responsibilities of the MTU and the State Committee for Communications and Information of Ukraine. The State Department on Communications (*Ukrzvyazok*) is subordinated to the Ministry of Infrastructure and existed separately from it since 2004.[62] This Department was reorganized into the State Administration on Communications[63] and subsequently into the State Communications Service of Ukraine in 2010. In 2011, the State Communications Service was liquidated and its functions were performed by the Ministry of Infrastructure[64].

E. State Inspectorate of Ukraine for Maritime and Inland Water Transport Safety

82. State Inspectorate of Ukraine for Maritime and Inland Water Transport Safety (*Ukrmorrechinspektsiya*) is a central executive authority, established to ensure the implementation of the state policy in the field of safety of maritime and inland water transport. Its activity is directed and coordinated by the Cabinet of Ministers through the Vice Prime Minister – Minister of Infrastructure.

The main tasks of the State Inspectorate are as follows:

(1) implementation of the state policy in the field of maritime and inland water transport;
(2) fulfilment, according to the law, of state supervision (control) of maritime and inland water transport safety;
(3) making suggestions concerning formation of the state policy on maritime and inland water transport;
(4) rendering of administrative services in the field of maritime and inland water transport.

61. Decree of the President of Ukraine on Establishment of the Ministry of Transport and Communications of Ukraine dated 16 Jul. 2004, No. 811/2004.
62. Regulation on State Department on Communications approved by the Decree of the CMU dated 8 Sep. 2004, No. 1186.
63. Regulation on State Administration of Communications approved by the Decree of the CMU dated 22 Sep. 2004, No. 1264.
64. Decree of the President on Optimization of the Central Executive Authorities System dated 6 Apr. 2011, No. 370/2011.

83. According to these tasks, the State Inspectorate, except for other powers, stipulated in the section 4 of the Regulation on State Inspectorate of Ukraine for Maritime and Inland Water Transport Safety:[65]

(1) keeps a record of and analyses maritime and inland water transport accidents;
(2) certifies transport conditions of dangerous goods on maritime and inland water transport;
(3) keeps a record of fires of transport facilities on maritime and inland water transport;
(4) grants a license for carrying of commercial activity to transport passengers, dangerous goods, luggage by means of maritime and inland water transport, as well as exercise control over compliance with licence provisions;
(5) exercises control over conclusion of the agreements of the compulsory insurance of the liability of persons, who transport dangerous goods by means of maritime and inland water transport;
(6) exercises state supervision (control) over compliance with the law and standards on the maritime and inland water transport;
(7) carries out certification on maritime and inland water transport;
(8) registers vessels in the State Registry of Ukraine, granting Ukrainian flag certificate (certificate of registry), and in the Ship Register Book of Ukraine, granting ship's letter, and issues deletion certificates;
(9) keeps a register of vessels (except fishing vessels), registered in the State Registry of Ukraine and in the Ship Register Book of Ukraine;
(10) exercises state supervision over conditions of sea routes;
(11) exercises flag and port state controls;
(12) exercises control over training, retraining, advanced training and certification of crews of maritime, inland water and craft vessels, workers of coastal enterprises of maritime and inland water transport, who deal with ensuring of safety navigation and prevention of environmental pollution from vessels;
(13) supervises the operation of services of vessel traffic regulation and pilotage;
(14) grants according to the law vessel documents;
(15) carries out other powers, stipulated by the law of Ukraine imposed on the State Inspectorate by the President of Ukraine.

84. The State Inspectorate is chaired by the Chairman, who shall be appointed upon the recommendation of the Prime Minister, submitted by the Vice Prime Minister – Minister of Infrastructure, and dismissed by the President of Ukraine.

F. State Administration of Rail Transport of Ukraine (UkrZaliznytsya)

85. UkrZaliznytsya is a state body subordinated to the Ministry of Infrastructure[66] which manages the system of rail transport of Ukraine and function

65. Regulation on State Inspectorate of Ukraine for Maritime and Inland Water Transport Safety, approved by the Decree of the President of Ukraine of 8 Apr. 2011, No. 447/2011.
66. Regulation on State Administration of Rail Transport approved by the Decree of the CMU dated 29 Feb. 1996, No. 262.

as a legal entity with an independent balance, bank accounts, official seal, etc. *UkrZaliznytsya* comprises six railways: Donetsk, Lviv, Odessa, South, South-Western and Dnieper. One of the major spheres of activity of *UkrZaliznytsya* is development of transit cargo transportation. *UkrZaliznytsya* provides centralized control for both domestic and international traffic and regulates the economic activity of the railways.

86. The main tasks of *UkrZaliznytsya* are:

- organization and coherence of railway enterprises to satisfy the needs of the industry and population in transportation;
- ensuring the efficient operation of railway rolling stock, its repair and renewal;
- elaboration of the concepts of development of railway transport.

87. *UkrZaliznytsya* according to its tasks:

(1) carries out operational activities related to:
  (a) directions of rolling stock according to the plans of transportation;
  (b) drafting of the coordinated timetables of trains;
  (c) formulation and implementation of a uniform tariff and pricing policy on the railways;
  (d) development and introduction of new routes for cargo and passenger transportation both in domestic and international directions;
  (e) organizing and conducting settlements of accounts with foreign railways for international transportation;
  (f) development of technical requirements for new types of rolling stock and railway equipment;
  (g) upon approval of the Ministry of Infrastructure sets the tariffs for railway transportation of cargoes in transit through Ukraine;

(2) develops plans for railway transportation in direct, mixed and international traffic;

(3) takes measures to ensure safety of trains, investigates the causes of accidents, develops safety standards in accordance with the international standards and laws of Ukraine.

88. *UkrZaliznytsya* issues orders within its competence binding for railways and enterprises that are managed by railways, and organizes and supervises their implementation. *UkrZaliznytsya* is headed by the General Director appointed by the Cabinet of Ministers. The General Director of *UkrZaliznytsya* has the First Deputy and other Deputies appointed by the CMU upon recommendation of the Minister of Infrastructure.

Part I. Introduction

Chapter 1. Transport and Maritime Law

89. The transport legislation in Ukraine contains the legal provisions related to motor, rail, maritime, inland waterway, air and pipeline transport. The division on such chapters in this monograph reflects the same structure. The authors include an analysis of legal provisions related to carriage of goods and passengers, transport documents, insurance, liability and settlement of disputes.

90. The Ukrainian law distinguishes *international maritime law* and *international private maritime law*. The former one includes the law of the sea based on international conventions and national legislation defining the maritime zones, the regime of state border, passage in the internal waters of foreign ships, limitations and other issues. The *international private maritime law* includes the carriage of goods and passengers by sea, insurance, liability and limitation of liability, issues on the ownership, vessel, crew, towage, salvage and others. This division is conditional since it is not always possible to draw a line between different legal relationships arising in shipping. It is worth mentioning that curriculum of educational institutions does not always include a thorough course on maritime law, limiting it with basic understanding of law of the sea and UNCLOS provisions, its relations with national legislation and basic concepts of the private maritime law. The extensive English case law dealing with admiralty law and shipping is not considered. However, the international conventions and their comparison with national legislation are brought to the attention.

91. The root of word maritime is derived from Latin and means 'of pertaining to the sea'. It is defined as:[67]

- connected with or situated near the sea;
- of or relating to sea navigation or commerce.

92. The maritime law is defined as follows:

> the body of law governing marine commerce and navigation, the carriage at sea of persons and property, and marine affairs in general; the rules governing

67. B.A. Garner (ed.), *Black's Law Dictionary*, 1054.

contract, tort, and workers' compensation claims or relating to commerce on or over water.[68]

93. In the common law jurisdiction it is also referred to *admiralty* or *admiralty law*. It is well acknowledged that many aspects of commercial maritime law are in fact derived from the *lex mercatoria*. Article 1 of the Merchant Shipping Code of Ukraine[69] (MSC) defines *merchant shipping* as an activity related to use of seagoing vessels for transportation of cargoes, passengers, baggage and mail, fishing and other sea trades, exploring and mining or minerals, conducting tow, ice-breaking and rescue operations, laying cables, as well as for other commercial, scientific and cultural purposes.

94. The provisions of the MSC apply to seagoing vessels during their sailing on seaways, as well as rivers, lakes, reservoirs and other water routes, unless provided otherwise and inland vessels when sailing on seaways, as well as rivers, through lakes, reservoirs and other water routes when carrying out transportation with calling to a foreign port.

95. With respect to the transport law, a number of law faculties in Ukraine do not include transport law as a separate subject in their curriculum, whereas the transport contracts are mainly considered during the courses in civil and commercial law and partially in administrative law.

96. There is an extensive system of inland waterways in Ukraine. The inland water transport is governed by the Statute of Inland Water Transport of the USSR[70] (SWIT) and the Water Code of Ukraine.

97. The multimodal transportation neither constitutes a separate part of the transport law nor legislation; nevertheless, it plays an important role in Ukraine.

98. The legal provisions related to the insurance including marine insurance are not considered as a self-contained branch of law. The main legal Acts are the Law of Ukraine on Insurance, the MSC, the Civil Code of Ukraine and other subordinate regulatory Acts.

---

68. B.A. Garner (ed.), *Black's Law Dictionary*, 1055.
69. Merchant Shipping Code of Ukraine dated 23 May 1995, No. 176/95 BP.
70. Statute of Inland Water Transport of the Soviet Union approved by the Resolution of the Council of Ministers of the USSR dated 15 Oct. 1955, No. 1801.

Chapter 2. History of Transport Law

§1. Maritime Law

I. Introduction

99. Since antiquity transport and shipping played a vital role in life and social development of every state. In ancient time people used the advantages of waterways to trade and exchange the goods with neighbouring countries. There is historical evidence that sea trade flourished in the ancient civilizations of India and in the Middle East.

II. Antiquity

100. The earliest recorded mention of maritime law is in the Babylonian Code of Hammurabi which dates back to the period between 2000 BC and 1600 BC. The Code contained rules with respect to maritime collisions, the practice of bottomry and leases of ships.[71] As early as 400 B.C., the Greek law included many maritime provisions ranging from substantive matters to procedural matters such as jurisdiction of the maritime court.[72] It is said that the Rhodians developed and compiled the first comprehensive set of sea laws known as the Sea Code or *Maritime Code of Rhodes*.

III. Medieval Maritime Law

101. In the Middle Ages the relevant maritime laws and codes included *Consolato del Mare* of Barcelona which contained the customs and practices of maritime law. It is held to be the earliest general code of maritime law preserved and carried into modern Europe. The *Laws of Wisby* named after the town on the Island of Gotland shall be mentioned as well, and the *Roles d'Oleron* which are considered to be the most distinguished of the medieval maritime codes. They said to be the basis of latter-day modern European maritime codes.[73]

IV. Establishment of the Kievan Rus and the First Ukrainian Codifications

102. Slavic tribes were largely engaged in trade since old times. They benefited from numerous rivers and seaways to transport their goods, to accomplish military

71. See further P.K. Mukherjee, *Maritime Legislation* 11–20 (WMU Publications, 2002).
72. *Ibid.*
73. See further P.K. Mukherjee, *Maritime Legislation* 11–20 (WMU Publications 2002).

campaigns on ships and to explore the new territories. A well-known transcontinental path 'Great Silk Road' went out on flat area between the South Ural and the Caspian Sea. This path functioned from the last decade of two thousand BC,[74] until the events, traditionally named as Mongolian invasion. Further this path led to the Genoese colony with a centre in Sudak, located on the coast of the Black Sea, that carried out the role of major geopolitical factor of geographical division of continent (through Poltava and Lubny) – in Kyiv, and already from it – to Zhytomyr and Lviv. The geographical position of the Kievan Rus played an important role on the political map of Europe. Economic growth of Byzantium stipulated the necessity of forming the new way – 'from Varangians to Greeks'. Ethnic natural borders became significant for consolidation of the East Slavic tribes and of the Kievan Rus along trading this path.

103. Already in the tenth century the Kievan Rus entered into treaties with the Byzantium Empire and other states. The earliest of them were four peace treaties concluded in or about the years 907, 911, 944 and 971 between the Grand Prince (*Velikiy Knyaz)* of the Kievan Rus and Byzantium. The treaties evidence that the maritime relationships existed between the two states. In particular the treaties of 911 and 944 included the norms of maritime law. According to them Byzantium accepted a right of merchants from the Kievan Rus to visit Constantinople and trade there during summer months. The Treaty of 911 included provisions regarding the safety of maritime connections and ships in distress, protection of seafarers and their property which evidences the development of early maritime law of those States. The treaties reflected the high level of merchant shipping as well as high level of legal thought.[75]

104. The zenith of the Kievan Rus came during the reigns of Grand Prince Vladimir (978–1015) and Grand Prince Yaroslav the Wise (1019–54).[76] The power of the then Slavic Navy was indicated by particular campaigns which were accomplished by Princes. It is submitted that a number of treaties were concluded with Greeks and Byzantium. To enhance their power, Vladimir married the sister of the Byzantium Emperor, and Yaroslav arranged marriages for his sister and three daughters to the kings of Poland, France, Hungary, and Norway. Vladimir's greatest achievement was the Christianization of the Kievan Rus, a process that began in 988.[77] He built the first great edifice of the Kievan Rus, the *Desyatinnaya* Church in Kiev. An early compilation of the Russian Laws, the *Pravda Russkaia* (*Russian Truth)*, is believed to have been composed in the reign of Yaroslav the Wise (1015–1054).[78] This code was heavily influenced by Byzantium and the Christian principles and was based on mercy, forgiveness and restoration of the individual.

74. See further F. Wood, *The Silk Road* (California University Press 2002).
75. A.N. Shemyakin, *Morskoe Pravo* 51 (2nd ed., VMV 2006).
76. 'Kievan Rus in the Reign of Knyaz Yaroslav', www.ukrmap.kiev.ua/ index.php?id=974&lang=en.
77. G.E. Curtis (ed.), *Russia: A Country Study* (Washington, DC: Federal Research Division of the Library of Congress, 1996), www.shsu.edu/~his_ncp/Kievan.html, 22 Dec. 2010.
78. Vernadsky, *Medieval Russian Laws* (1947), see at W.E. Butler, *Russian Law* 16 –17 (3d ed., Oxford U. Press 2002).

The Kievan Rus in the form of thirteen separate principalities became the part of the Moscow principality in the middle of the fourteenth century.

105. The Ukrainian *Cossacks* appeared on the territory of Ukraine by the end of the fifteenth century. They were armed men which protected trade caravans travelling the steppe routes against Turks and Tatar.[79] *Cossacks* established settlements located in Zaporizhye and later on they began to conduct their own external policy independently from the government and frequently contrary to its interests. A significant historical interest presents the norms of the Treaty of 1649 between Zaporizhye and a Turkish sultan. Pursuant to this treaty the Zaporizhye merchants obtained a right to enter all ports of Turkey, sail through the Black Sea Straits to the Mediterranean Sea as well as other privileges. In the seventeenth century the port of Khortytsya became an important centre of *Cossacks'* maritime trade. *Cossacks'* boats *(seagulls)* moved along rivers into great lakes and seas.

V. Ukrainian SSR

106. Being a part of the Russian Empire the development of transport and maritime law of Ukraine was conducted in the frames of the Empire. However, there are also specific maritime norms, inherent only to Ukraine. For nearly three-quarters of the twentieth century the fundamentals of Marxism-Leninism penetrated all the disciplines in the former Soviet Union universities and secondary-level studies, including law.[80]

107. After the formation of the USSR, the first codification of maritime law was reflected in the Merchant Shipping Code of the USSR in 1929. Although it did not contain the definition of *merchant shipping,* its application included not only merchant shipping but also related issues. The following codification developed in the Merchant Shipping Code of the USSR 1968 and consequently in the MSC in 1995.

§2. Transport Law

108. In contrast to maritime transport, other transport modes became regulated in the nineteenth century. Taking into account the sizes of the Russian Empire (CIS countries, Estonia, Latvia, Lithuania, as well as Finland, Eastern Poland and some lands of modern Turkey and China), transportation played an important role.

109. For a long time, the railways in Russia were only used for transporting passengers, in particular the troops. Under the reign of Emperor Nicholas I the Trans-Siberian Railway was built, as well as the Chinese Eastern Railway in the territory of neighbouring China. The building was unprofitable, but it did not prevent the development of international rail traffic, as the Russian Empire was interested in

79. www.encyclopediaofukraine.com/pages/C/O/Cossacks.htm, 1 Sep. 2013.
80. W.E. Butler, *Russian Law* 37 (3d ed., Oxford U. Press 2002).

entering new markets in the Asia-Pacific region. It is also worth mentioning that the width of the Russian railways is wider than the European one. It is called 'Russian Gauge' and has a width of 1,520 mm (5 feet). The Russian track is extended to all post-Soviet space. The Europeans use a little narrower track – 1,435 mm. There is a theory that the difference in tracks was made in order to prevent the speedy advancement of troops in case of war between the Soviet Union and the European countries and vice versa. The difference in the rut has a significant impact on the implementation of international rail traffic between Russia and European countries.[81]

110. The first city shuttle bus for eight passengers went on the line in Germany in 1895. The Minister of Transport of the Russian Empire and the Government signed a Decree on the procedure and conditions of carriage of loads and passengers on the highway of the Office of Communications in the self-propelled carriages. 11 September 1896 should be considered the beginning of regular passenger services within cities and between cities in the Russian Empire.[82]

111. Before the October Revolution 1917, the Russian civil law did not regard the contract of carriage as a separate contract for services (Laws of the Russian Empire, Article 1738).[83]

81. See at statehistory.ru/1286/ZHeleznye-dorogi-v-dorevolyutsionnoy-Rossii, 1 Sep. 2013.
82. See at www.luxautocom.com.ua/html/history.php?lang=1, 1 Sep. 2013.
83. See at statehistory.ru/1286/ZHeleznye-dorogi-v-dorevolyutsionnoy-Rossii, 1 Sep. 2013.

Chapter 3. Sources of Transport Law

§1. Introduction

112. The legal regulation of transport in Ukraine is divided into three groups of legal Acts:

- international treaties ratified by the *Verkhovna Rada*;
- laws and codes;
- subordinate regulatory Acts.

113. After the USSR dissolution, the legal regulation of transport in Ukraine has been changed considerably. A wide range of new laws, codes and subordinate regulatory Acts have been adopted, the Law on Transport, the Merchant Shipping Code, the Water and Air Codes. In addition, the new Civil and Commercial Codes of Ukraine have been adopted.[84] As it has been already mentioned, some legal Acts originating from the Soviet Union are still in force in Ukraine. They mostly include the rules regulating carriage of goods and passengers by specific transport modes.

114. The main legal Acts, governing the legal relationships associated with the carriage of goods in Ukraine are the Civil and Commercial Codes of Ukraine. The latter sets the legal grounds for commercial activity based on the variety of legal entities of different ownership forms. It defines the fundamentals of commercial activity in Ukraine and regulates commercial relations arising in the process of exercising commercial activity between legal entities, as well as between them and other participants of relations in the sphere of commercial activity. It includes general conditions of carriage of goods and conditions of contract of carriage which are defined not only in the Commercial Code of Ukraine, but also in the Civil and other transport codes of Ukraine.

115. The special rules, conditions of carriage of cargo, passengers, standards of safety and health standards are issued in the form of subordinate regulatory Acts by the authorities in charge (services, agencies, etc.). Those rules are to be complied with by all entities and individuals.

116. The Law of Ukraine on Transport[85] governs the general issues related to transport in Ukraine and defines the legal, economic, organizational and social grounds of transport activity. According to the Law the unified transport system of Ukraine consists of the public transport (motor, rail, maritime, inland water, air transport, as well as city electric transport and underground), industrial rail transport, departmental transport, pipeline transport system and public communication.

---

84. The Commercial Code of Ukraine dated 1 Jan. 2003, No. 436-IV.
85. Law of Ukraine on Transport dated 10 Nov. 1994, No. 232/94-BP.

§2. Maritime Law

117. It should be noted that Ukraine is not a party to any of the conventions in the field of carriage of goods by sea, such as the Hague Rules, the Hague-Visby Rules, the Hamburg Rules, and the Rotterdam Rules. However, some provisions on bill of lading are contained in the MSC.

118. Regarding the passenger carriage, Ukraine has acceded to the Athens Convention Relating to the Carriage of Passengers and their Luggage by Sea and Protocol 1976.[86]

119. Ukraine joined the International Convention on Standards of Training, Certification and Watchkeeping for Seafarers 1978 (STCW). There are also a number of bilateral agreements between Ukraine and other countries concerning the maritime law.

120. The Merchant Shipping Code (containing eleven Parts) has been adopted in 1995 with further amendments. The MSC deals with private shipping law, regulating such issues as vessels, crew, sea port, carriage of goods and passengers, charter parties, towage, marine insurance, marine causalities, limitation of liability, claims and suits.

121. Moreover, a separate Law of Ukraine on Seaports of Ukraine has been adopted in 2012.

122. There are also the rules emanating from the USSR concerning particular issues on carriage of goods and passengers. The sources of maritime law will be discussed in details in the respective chapters.

§3. Other Transport Law

123. Ukraine is a party to the Convention on the Contract for the International Carriage of Passengers and Luggage by Road (CVR) concluded for the purpose of unification the conditions governing the contract for the international carriage of passengers and luggage by road. This Convention applies to any contract of carriage of passengers and, in appropriate cases, their luggage in vehicles if the contract states that the carriage is in at least two countries and that the point of departure or destination, or they both are in one of the contracting countries. Additionally, Ukraine has joined the Convention on the Contract for the International Carriage of Goods by Road (CMR) which applies to any contract of road transport of goods for consideration by vehicles, if the point and place of delivery specified in the contract are located in two different countries, of which at least one must be a Party to the Convention. There is a Law on Motor Transport and the Statute of Motor Transport in Ukraine.

86. Law of Ukraine on Accession to the Athens Convention dated 15 Jul. 1994 No. 115/94-BP.

124. Ukraine is a party to the Convention Concerning International Carriage by Rail 1980 (COTIF), including its annexes the Uniform Rules Concerning the Contract for International Carriage of Goods by Rail (CIM) and the Uniform Rules Concerning the Contract for International Carriage of Passengers and Luggage by Rail (CIV). The Protocol 1999 includes a new version of the Convention that introduces the revised uniform rules regulating the content of international rail contracts and that makes provision for the validation of technical standards applicable to railway material intended to be used in international traffic, and the technical admission of such material. The Statute of the Railways[87] is effective in Ukraine, in addition to the Law of Ukraine on Rail Transport. Some various rules are also adopted with regard to the carriage of goods and passengers.

125. With respect to the carriage by air, Ukraine has joined to the Convention for the Unification of Certain Rules Relating to International Carriage by Air (Warsaw Convention) and the Convention for the Unification of Certain Rules for International Carriage (Montreal Convention). The Montreal Convention has amended provisions of the Warsaw Convention and is focused on liability of a carrier and compensation for the victims of air disasters. The Montreal Convention introduces the concept of 'unlimited liability of airfreight carriers' and aims to protect passengers and consumers financially in case of potential accidents in air freight which take place in the signatory states. Ukraine has its own Air Code of Ukraine.[88]

126. Ukraine has acceded to the European Agreement concerning the International Carriage of Dangerous Goods by Inland Waterways (ADN). There are also the Water Code[89] and the Statute of Inland Waterway Transport (SIWT) of the USSR.

87. Dated 6 Apr. 1998, No. 457.
88. Dated 19 May 2011, No. 3393-VI.
89. Dated 6 Jun. 1995, No. 213/95BP.

Chapter 4. Jurisdiction and Courts

§1. General Maritime Cases

127. Pursuant to Article 8 of the MSC, property disputes related to merchant shipping and referred to the competence of the Maritime Administration Commission at the Chamber of Commerce and Industry of Ukraine (Maritime Arbitration Commission) shall be considered by this Commission upon consent of the parties. A property dispute related to merchant shipping in which a foreign legal entity or natural person participates may be transferred to consideration of a foreign court or arbitration upon consent of the parties.[90]

I. Maritime Arbitration Commission

128. The Maritime Arbitration Commission (further – Commission) as a separate permanent arbitration institution (intermediate court) is regulated by the Law of Ukraine on International Commercial Arbitration.[91] The Law (section 2) enshrines that the Commission solves the disputes of merchant shipping, regardless of whether the parties are subjects to the Ukrainian or foreign law. The list of disputes includes the disputes arising out of the relationships on: charter parties, carriage of goods by sea, combined carriage of goods (sea-river), towage of ships and other floating objects; maritime insurance and reinsurance, sale and purchase of ships, mortgages and ship repair, pilotage and ice pilotage, agency and servicing the seagoing ships, inland ships and others. The Commission also accepts and solves the disputes concerning the sailing of seagoing ships and inland ships along international rivers, and also the disputes arising out of performance of foreign transportation by inland ships. The Commission initiates proceedings upon the agreement between the parties. The parties fulfil the Commission's decision voluntarily within the set terms.

II. The Marine and Inland Water Transport Bodies

129. Article 225 of the Code on Administrative Offences of Ukraine[92] endows with competence the marine and inland water transport bodies. It includes the hearing of cases on the following administrative offences: violations of rules of public order and safety on maritime transport, rules of use of sea transport's means, regulations for the protection of order and safety on inland water transport and low dimensional ships; rules on ship registration, rules ensuring the operational safety of vessels on inland waterways, registration rules of merchant ships, fire safety regulations on maritime and inland water transport, etc.

---

90. The maritime cases can also be considered in the courts of general jurisdiction as will be shown in Chapter on Arrest of Ships.
91. Law of Ukraine on International Commercial Arbitration dated 24 Feb. 1994, No. 4002-XII.
92. The Code on Administrative Offences of Ukraine dated 6 Jul. 2005, No. 2747-IV.

130. Depending on the administrative offence, the penalty can be imposed by the Head of the State Inspectorate of Ukraine for Maritime and Inland Water Transport Safety and his substitutes, by harbourmasters, heads of marine passenger terminals and their substitutes and the courts.[93]

§2. OTHER TRANSPORT LAW CASES

I. Jurisdiction and Courts

131. Nowadays the judicial system of general jurisdiction in Ukraine consists of local courts, twenty-four regional courts, appeal courts and courts for Autonomous Republic of Crimea and the cities of Sevastopol and Kyiv.

132. The system of commercial courts is an independent body responsible for reviewing and solving the contractual disputes among the legal entities. All the disputes in commercial courts are adjudicated under the ComPC.[94] The amendments to this Code are introduced by the Law of Ukraine on Judicial System and Legal Status of Judges and particularly provides for:

(1) implementation of an automatic system of document circulation aiming at, *inter alia*, the automatic assignment of judges to consider the cases. Any breach of this automatic order of assignment of the judge to a case will be the ground for challenging such judge's competence over the particular dispute;
(2) possibility for an interested party to change the subject matter and/or the grounds of the dispute only before the commencement of the consideration of the dispute on the merits;
(3) possibility for the respondent in the dispute to file its counter-claim against the plaintiff only before the commencement of the consideration of the dispute on the merits;
(4) exhaustive list of the court rulings subject to further appeal separately from the court decision;
(5) possibility of challenging the decisions of the first instance court with the SCCU only after their review in the appellate procedure;[95]
(6) restriction of the authority of the SCU to review decisions of the SCCU only in the cases:[96]
    (a) where there exists a different application by the cassation instance court of the same substantive rules in similar relations which results in rendering of different decisions in similar cases; or

93. Regulation on State Inspectorate of Ukraine for Maritime and Inland Water Transport Safety approved by the Decree of the President of Ukraine dated 8 Apr. 2011, No. 447/2011.
94. The Commercial Procedure Code dated 6 Nov. 1991, No. 1798-XII.
95. Since the adoption of the Law there has not been such a practice, see para. 28.
96. *Ibid.*

(b) where an international judicial institution, recognized by Ukraine, establishes a violation by Ukraine of its international obligations while considering the dispute.

133. Ukraine is a party to the Hague Conventions, namely the Convention on the Taking of Evidence Abroad in Civil or Commercial Matters dated 18 March 1970 and Convention on the Service Abroad of Judicial and Extrajudicial Documents in Civil or Commercial Matters dated 15 November 1965. According to their provisions and regulations of the Ukrainian legislation, the judgment creditor can enforce a foreign judgment in Ukraine. Bilateral treaties between Ukraine and foreign countries may also serve as legal grounds for enforcement of foreign judgments and for rejection in their enforcement. Sometimes those treaties are ad hoc agreements. A foreign judgment may be enforced within three years from the date when the judgment becomes effective.

134. Ukraine is also a party to the New York Convention on the Recognition and Enforcement of Foreign Arbitral Awards, 1958. The United Nations Commission on International Trade Law (UNCITRAL) Model Law on International Commercial Arbitration dated 21 June 1985 is the basis of the Law of Ukraine on International Commercial Arbitration dated 24 February 1994. The Rules of the International Commercial Arbitration Court at the Ukrainian Chamber of Commerce and Industry is attached as an Annex to this Law. Those instruments contain the most important rules that regulate the process of the international arbitration in Ukraine.

135. Any dispute could be submitted to the international commercial arbitration, except certain cases: disputes with respect to invalidation of statutory and non-statutory Acts; disputes arising from conclusion, amendment, termination or performance of commercial contracts related to the state needs, and disputes of exclusive jurisdiction of the state courts, such as: related to immoveable property located in Ukraine; concerning relationships between children and parents, where all parties are residents of Ukraine; if the testator in a probate case was a citizen and resident of Ukraine; arising from intellectual property rights secured by registration or patent certification in Ukraine; relating to registration or dissolution of foreign companies, non-governmental organizations, charitable foundations or other associations, or legal entities in Ukraine; related to the validity of records in one of the Ukrainian State Registers, including the Unified State Register of Legal Entities and Register of Immoveables; if the debtor in an insolvency case was incorporated under the Ukrainian legislation; involving the issue or cancellation of securities officially registered in Ukraine; in which an adoption took place or is taking place in Ukraine; and other cases where the Ukrainian law provides that the courts take precedence.[97]

97. Law of Ukraine on International Private Law dated 23 Jun. 2005, No. 2709-IV.

II. State Immunity: International Law

136. The public international law provides that the visit of warships of friendly States to the national ports requires the recognition of the ships' immunity from local jurisdiction.[98] The International Convention on Jurisdictional Immunities of States and their Property was adopted by the UN General Assembly in 2004 although is not in force yet.[99] Article 5 reiterates that a state enjoys immunity, in respect of itself and its property, from the jurisdiction of the courts of another state subject to the provisions of the present Convention. Ukraine has not signed the Convention.

137. The specific provisions appertaining to the ships owned or operated by a State are enshrined in Article 16 of the Convention. They provide *inter alia* that the warships, or naval auxiliaries, and other vessels owned or operated by a state and used, for the time being, only on government non-commercial service can invoke the immunity from jurisdiction before a court of another state.

138. The Ukrainian legislation contains the similar provision in Article 18 of the MSC. It reads that the vessels belonging to a state cannot be arrested or imposed a penalty without consent of a body that administers the property belonging to the State property, if these vessels are used exclusively for performing the state service.

---

98. M.D. Evans, *International Law* 344 (3d ed., Oxford U. Press 1996).
99. See at http://treaties.un.org/pages/ViewDetails.aspx?src=TREATY&mtdsg_no=III13&chapter=3&lang=en, 1 Sep. 2013.

Part II. Maritime Law

Chapter 1. Waterways

§1. Introduction

139. In this chapter the authors highlight the legal issues pertaining to the regime of the waterways' use from the international and the national perspective. The regime of internal waters and territorial sea, the status of international rivers and straits, delimitation, Exclusive Economic Zone (EEZ), continental shelf and the rules governing the passage under the Ukrainian law are submitted. Additionally, the case concerning delimitation in the Black Sea decided by the International Court of Justice (ICJ) is mentioned in this Chapter.

§2. Law of the Sea

I. Law of the Sea Convention

140. The main principles of usage of waterways are enshrined in the international law. There are a number of international conventions regulating the regime of high seas, territorial sea and contiguous zone, continental shelf and fisheries. Most of these legal regimes were codified in the United Nations Convention on the Law of the Sea in 1982 (UNCLOS). It received a wide application worldwide. Ukraine has ratified and implemented UNCLOS by means of the Law of Ukraine dated 3 June 1999 on Ratification of the UN Convention on the Law of the Sea 1982 and Implementation Agreement, Part XI of the Convention. Upon ratification (26 July 1999), Ukraine made the reservations concerning the settlements of disputes and chose an arbitral tribunal constituted in accordance with Annex VII as the principal means for settlement of the disputes concerning the interpretation or application of this Convention. For consideration of the disputes concerning the interpretation or application of the Convention in respect of questions relating to fisheries, protection and preservation of the marine environment, marine scientific research and navigation, including pollution from vessels and by dumping, Ukraine chooses a special arbitral tribunal constituted in accordance with Annex VIII. Ukraine recognizes the competence, as stipulated in Article 292 of the Convention, of the International Tribunal for the Law of the Sea in respect of questions relating to the prompt release of detained vessels or their crews.[100]

141. International law of the sea is a part of the general international law or law of the nations. The father of modern international law is considered a Dutch lawyer Hugo Grotius. His well-known book *De mare liberum* published in 1609 upheld the doctrine of the freedom of the seas, and was seen as threatening contemporary British claims to control the seas around Great Britain.[101]

142. The sources of modern law of the sea as well as international law in general are enshrined in Article 38 of the ICJ Statute. They include *inter alia* international conventions, international custom, as evidence of a general practice accepted as law, the general principles of law recognized by civilized nations, judicial decisions and legal doctrine.

143. The first international conventions dealing with the law of the sea were four Geneva Conventions on the territorial sea and contiguous zone, on the high seas, continental shelf and on fishing and conservation of living resources of the high seas all adopted in 1958. The first three conventions were ratified by a number of States and were mainly based on customary international law. In the 1970s it was agreed to revise the law of the sea and adopt a convention which would embrace all the issues that did not find its expression in the four Geneva Conventions.[102] The new convention was adopted in 1982, also known as the Oceans' Constitution and it has 166 States Parties, including other entities (e.g., EU).[103]

II. Zones Recognized under UNCLOS

A. Internal Waters

144. Waters on the landward side of the baseline of the territorial sea form part of the internal waters of the State.[104] Internal waters are subject to the national legislation of the coastal States but with consideration of the international law commitments. Pursuant to Article 3 of UNCLOS every State has the right to establish the breadth of its territorial sea up to a limit not exceeding twelve nautical miles, measured from baselines. Two types of baselines are known, these are normal baselines and straight baselines. The normal baselines for measuring the breadth of the territorial sea is the low-water line along the coast as marked on large-scale charts officially recognized by the Coastal State. The straight baselines are normally used

---

100. For a complete list or reservations made by Ukraine, see at www.un.org/Depts/los/index.htm.
101. R.R. Churchill & A.V. Lowe, *The Law of the Sea* 5 (3rd ed., Juris Publishing, Manchester U. Press, 1999).
102. Read further Churchill, *Law of the Sea* (1999).
103. As on 9 Aug. 2013, see www.un.org/Depts/los/index.htm.
104. UNCLOS, Art. 8.

if the coastline is deeply intended and cut into, or if there is a fringe of islands along the coast in its immediate vicinity. The rules on how to measure the baselines are dealt with in Part II, section 2 of UNCLOS. Straight baselines shall not be drawn to and from low-tide elevations, unless lighthouses or similar installations which are permanently above sea level have been built on them.[105]

145. According to the Law of Ukraine on the State Border of Ukraine dated 4 November 1991, No. 1777-XII the state border is determined by the laws of Ukraine and also by the international treaties ratified by Ukraine. Article 6 of that Law enshrines that internal waters of Ukraine include:

- marine waters situated on the landward side of the straight baselines adopted for the measurement of the width of the territorial sea of Ukraine;
- such waters of the ports of Ukraine as are bounded by a line passing through the permanent port structures which extend farthest seaward;
- the waters of bays, bights, inlets and estuaries, harbours and roadsteads whose shores belong in their entirety to Ukraine, out to a straight line drawn from one shore to the other at the point where one or several passages are first formed from the seaward side, provided that the width of each of them is not more than twenty-four nautical miles;
- the waters of bays, bights, inlets and estuaries, seas and straits historically belonging to Ukraine;
- the waters of those rivers, lakes and other bodies of water out to the line of the State Border whose shores belong to Ukraine.

146. The Treaty for Cooperation on Using of the Sea of Azov and the Kerch Strait between Ukraine and the Russian Federation was signed in 2003 and ratified by Ukraine in 2004.[106] The Treaty states that the Parties, guided by relationships of friendship and cooperation between the people of Ukraine and Russia, agreed that the Sea of Azov and the Kerch Strait are internal waters of Ukraine and the Russian Federation and that the Sea of Azov is demarcated by the state border pursuant to the Treaty between the Parties. Further, it is stated that the ships flying flags of the Parties which are used in non-commercial purposes shall enjoy freedom of navigation, while ships of other states will be able to enter the Azov Sea and pass the Kerch Strait only upon invitation of one of the Parties and upon permission of the other one.

147. Pursuant to the Water Code of Ukraine all waters on the territory of Ukraine are the national wealth of the Ukrainian citizens, one of the natural grounds for their economic development and social welfare. All waters on the territory of Ukraine form the water fund of Ukraine. It includes surface waters (natural ponds (lakes), water flows (river, wells), artificial water reservoirs (storage ponds (lakes)) and channels; underground waters, wells, internal waters and territorial sea. The

105. UNCLOS, Art. 7(4).
106. Dated 20 Apr. 2004, No. 1682-IV.

Code also enshrines that water fund is exclusive property of the Ukrainian people which is granted only for use.

148. There are trade, fishing and other specialized ports in Ukraine. In 2012 the Law of Ukraine on Sea Ports of Ukraine has been adopted. According to this law, all seaports of Ukraine and some state enterprises are currently under reform.

149. At present, the legal status of the Ukrainian sea ports is defined in the MSC, Chapter 4 and in the Law on Sea Ports of Ukraine. Some legal issues related to sea ports of Ukraine have been discussed in paragraph 'Inland Waterways and Ports' (II, § 2, General Introduction).

B. Territorial Waters

150. UNCLOS gives a right to every State to establish the breadth of the territorial sea up to a limit not exceeding twelve nautical miles, measured from baselines.[107] The term *territorial sea* was first introduced at the first UN Conference on the Law of the Sea in 1958, resulted by adoption of four international conventions.

151. The Law of Ukraine on the State Border of Ukraine, Article 1, defines the state border of Ukraine as 'a line and the vertical surface passing through that line which determines the limits of the territory of Ukraine – land, water, mineral resources and airspace'. Article 3 of this Law further determines the order of establishment of the state borders. It provides that at sea the borders are established along the outer limit of the territorial sea of Ukraine. This Article also deals with the method of establishing the state borders on navigable rivers.

152. Article 5 of this Law states that the territorial sea of Ukraine includes the coastal marine waters having a width of twelve nautical miles measured from the line of minimum low tide both on mainland and on islands belonging to Ukraine, or from the straight baselines joining the corresponding points. The geographical coordinates of the stated points shall be confirmed by a procedure established by the Cabinet of Ministers. The Law of Ukraine on the State Border of Ukraine also deals with the rules on innocent passage through the territorial sea of Ukraine which will be illustrated below.

C. Straits Used for International Navigation and International Rivers

153. The importance of straits for Ukraine is self-evident. The Black Sea Straits are the only natural exit of Ukraine to the world ocean and the Kerch Strait has significance for Ukraine.

107. UNCLOS, Art. 3.

154. In the international law a passage includes stopping and anchoring insofar as this is incidental to ordinary navigation or rendered necessary by force majeure or distress.[108] Article 35(3) of UNCLOS enshrines that nothing affects the legal regime of straits in which passage is regulated in whole or in part by long-standing international conventions in force specifically relating to such straits.

D. Black Sea Straits

155. The Black Sea Straits comprise 'the Strait of the Dardanelles, the Sea of Marmara and the Bosphorus'. Turkey started to officially use the term 'Turkish Straits' in its domestic legislation, for example, 'Maritime Traffic for the Turkish Straits'.[109] However, Ukraine and few more states prefer to use the wording of the 'Straits' or the 'Black Sea Straits'. The Black Sea Straits do not only have geopolitical and strategic significance, but also rapidly increasing importance for the international transportation, both for the Black Sea and for the whole world.

156. The first attempts to regulate the legal regime of the Straits go back to the fourth century B.C. and have a long history of political fights among different states.[110] The conference to replace for the previously existed Lausanne Straits Convention was held in Monteux in 1936. The new Convention was signed by the State Parties on 9 November 1936. It regulates the passage and navigation of commercial and naval vessels through the straits in times of peace and war, and during times when Turkey considers itself under threat of imminent war. It gives a right to merchant vessels in time of peace to 'enjoy complete freedom of transit and navigation in the Straits, by day and night, under any flag and with any kind of cargo'. The Convention makes a distinction in the transit of warships of littoral states and other states. The provisions dealing with warships are more precise.

157. Turkey undertook several times one-sided actions aimed at change of the legal regime of the Straits, in particular to improve the safety of navigation and environment. On 1 May 1982, Turkey spreads on a part of Bosporus the Regulation of Port Istanbul in one side, establishing by its national legislation several limitations on transit of vessels. One of the reasons was an increasing vessel traffic through the Straits that affects Istanbul.[111] From 1 July 1994 the National Regulation of Shipping covers the Straits.

E. Danube River

158. The regime of rivers establishing the rights for riparian and non-riparian states usually is regulated by the international treaties. The Danube River Basin is

108. UNCLOS, Art. 18(2).
109. Y. Inan, '*The Current Regime of the Turkish Straits*' VI J. Intl. Aff. (2001).
110. Shemyakin, 269.
111. See Y. Inan, '*The Current Regime of the Turkish Straits*', VI J. Intl. Aff. (2001).

the European second largest river basin. It is the world's most international river basin as it includes the territories of nineteen countries. Three sub-basins of the Danube are partly located in Ukraine, as well as part of the Danube Delta.

159. The principle of freedom of navigation on the Danube River was enshrined in the Paris Congress in 1856. The Versailles Peaceful Treaty proclaimed Danube an international river in 1919. The Convention regarding the Regime of Navigation on the Danube was signed in Belgrade on 18 August 1948 (Belgrade Convention). It states in Article 1 that the navigation on the Danube shall be free and open for the nationals, vessels of commerce and goods of all States, on a footing of equality in regard to port and navigation charges and conditions for merchant shipping. The foregoing shall not apply to traffic between ports of the same State.

160. According to the Convention, eleven Member States including Ukraine undertake to maintain their sections of the Danube in a navigable condition for river-going and, on the appropriate sections, for seagoing vessels and to carry out the works necessary for the maintenance and improvement of navigation conditions and not to obstruct or hinder navigation on the navigable channels of the Danube as provided in Article 3 of the Convention. Having a purpose to supervise the implementation of the Convention and dealing with other matters concerning the shipping on the Danube, the Danube Commission has been established.

F. Contiguous Zone

161. The *contiguous zone* is a zone of sea contiguous to its territorial sea in which the coastal States may exercise the control necessary to prevent infringements of its customs, fiscal immigration or sanitary laws and regulations within its territory or territorial sea, punish infringement of the above laws and regulations committed within its territory or territorial sea. The contiguous zone may not extend beyond twenty-four nautical miles from the baselines from which the breadth of the territorial sea is measured.[112]

162. The *Verkhovna Rada* is considering a Draft Law on Contiguous Zone of Ukraine. It is expected that a new Law will include provisions on delimitation of contiguous zone, prevention of offences and research on archaeological and historical objects of cultural heritage in contiguous zone and issues on liability.

G. Continental Shelf and Economic Zone

163. The *continental shelf* of a coastal state comprises the sea-bed and subsoil of the submarine areas that extend beyond its territorial sea throughout the natural prolongation of its land territory to the outer edge of the continental margin, or to

112. UNCLOS, Art. 33.

a distance of 200 nautical miles from the baselines from which the breadth of the territorial sea is measured where the outer edge of the continental margin does not extend up to that distance.[113] Islands are entitled to their own EEZ and continental shelf [114] save for rocks which cannot sustain human habitation or economic life of their own.[115]

164. The provisions on *EEZ* are enshrined in Part V of the UNCLOS. Article 55 defines it as an area beyond and adjacent to the territorial sea, subject to the specific legal regime under which the rights and jurisdiction of the coastal State and the rights and freedom of other States are governed by the relevant provisions of the UNCLOS. It shall not extend beyond 200 miles from the baselines from which the breadth of the territorial sea is measured, the coastal State enjoys a number of rights concerning the exploitation of natural recourses, jurisdiction in some matters, with the consideration of the rights and duties of third States and other rights and duties provided for in UNCLOS.

165. The Law of Ukraine on Exclusive (Maritime) Economic Zone dated 16 May 1995, No. 162/95-BP constitutes in Article 2 that the breadth of the EEZ of Ukraine extends up to 200 nautical miles. The Law is dealing with delimitation, sovereign rights over the living and non-living resources, jurisdiction with regard to artificial islands, installations and structures, protection of the marine environment and the conduct of marine scientific research.

H. Maritime Delimitation

166. The provisions on delimitation of the EEZ of Ukraine are enshrined in Article 3 of the Law of Ukraine on Exclusive (Maritime) Economic Zone. It provides that the delimitation of the EEZ between Ukraine and States with coasts opposite or adjacent to the coast of Ukraine shall be effected, taking into consideration the legislation of Ukraine, by agreement on the basis of principles and criteria generally recognized under the international law, in order to achieve an equitable solution.

167. There are very few islands in the Black Sea and they are located close to the coasts. The Black Sea is bordered by six countries, following the fragmentation of the former Soviet Union in 1991. The Ukraine and Georgia have agreed with Turkey that they will accept the relevant sections of the 1987 Soviet-Turkish maritime boundary.[116] Ukraine confirmed to Turkey by Note dated 30 May 1994 its agreement to the former Continental Shelf Agreement 1978.[117]

113. UNCLOS, Art. 76.
114. UNCLOS, Art. 121(2).
115. UNCLOS, Art. 121(3).
116. Agreement between the Government of the Republic of Turkey and the Government of the Union of Soviet Socialistic Republics concerning the Delimitation of the Continental Shelf between the Republic of Turkey and the Union of Soviet Socialist Republics in the Black Sea dated 23 Jun. 1978.
117. See at www.blacksea-commission.org, 1 Sep. 2013.

168. Ukraine and the Russian Federation share a maritime border in the Sea of Azov and the Black Sea. One factor complicating the relationship between Ukraine and the Russian Federation is the status of Crimea which forms part of Ukraine, but sought a larger measure of autonomy from Ukraine and closer ties with the Russian Federation.[118] In 2010, the issue on status of the Sea of Azov and Kerch Strait became an agenda for two countries.

169. On 3 February 2009, the ICJ rendered its judgment on the merits in the case concerning Maritime Delimitation in the Black Sea between Romania and Ukraine. The dispute concerned the delimitation of the continental shelf and the EEZ between both States.

170. During the proceedings several bilateral treaties and agreements between Romania and Ukraine in respect of their State border including the territorial sea were taken into account. A number of these instruments had been concluded between Romania and the USSR before the independence of Ukraine in 1991. Among them the 1949 instruments make no reference to the EEZ or the continental shelf within the meaning of UNCLOS, Articles 74 and 83. The only Agreement between the parties expressly dealing with delimitation of the EEZ and the continental shelf is the Additional Agreement 1997 to the Treaty on Good Neighbourliness and Cooperation dated 2 June 1997. It does not establish boundary but rather a process for arriving at one which is reaching its culmination in these proceedings. However, no delimitation agreement has been reached since that time.[119]

171. One of the most difficult delimitation issues in the Black Sea was the Ukraine's Island *Zmeinyy* (Serpent's Island) on the maritime boundary between Ukraine and Romania[120] which is situated in the north-western part of the Black Sea, approximately twenty nautical miles to the East of the Danube delta. The status of the island arose in two contexts in this delimitation case. In particular, the Court stated that Serpents' Island lying alone some twenty nautical miles away from the mainland is not one of a cluster of fringe islands constituting the coast of Ukraine. Another issue concerned the status of Serpent's Island, in particular whether it falls under the definition of an 'island' within the meaning of Article 121(2) of the UNCLOS or constitutes a 'rock' that cannot sustain habitation and economic life of its own. However, the Court disregarded Serpent Island in drawing the provisional equidistance line.

118. A.G. Oude Elferink, '*Russian Federation Maritime Boundary Delimitations*', 11 Int'l J. Marine &Coastal L. 563 (1996).

119. ICJ Judgment, para. 18.

120. V. Prescott & C. Schofield, *The Maritime Political Boundaries of the World* 383 (2d ed., Martinus Nijhoff Publishers 2005).

I. High Seas

172. Convention on the High Seas defines the notion *high seas* as 'all parts of the sea that are not included in the territorial sea or in the internal waters of a State'. Freedom of the high seas included freedom of navigation, freedom of overflight, freedom to lay submarine cables and pipelines, freedom of fishing. The provisions on the high seas are also contained in Part VII of the UNCLOS which applies to all parts of the sea that are not included in the EEZ, in the territorial sea or in the internal waters of a State, or in archipelagic waters of the archipelagic State. UNCLOS, Article 86, provides that the high seas are open to all States, whether coastal or land-locked. UNCLOS in Article 87 added additional freedoms, such as freedom to construct artificial islands and other installations permitted under international law and freedom of scientific research.

III. Domestic Rules

A. Internal Waters

173. A right of innocent passage through the territorial sea to ships of all states, whether coastal or land-locked is granted by UNCLOS, Article 17. The meaning of *passage* and *innocent passage* are further specified in UNCLOS, Articles 18 and 19. Passage means navigation through the territorial sea without entering internal waters or calling at a roadstead or port facility outside international waters or proceeding to or from internal waters or a call as such roadstead or port facility. Additionally, a passage should be continuous and expeditious. Passage is considered innocent so long as it is not prejudicial to the peace, good order or security of the coastal State.

174. Article 13 of the Law of Ukraine on the State Border of Ukraine enshrines that innocent passage through the territorial sea of Ukraine shall be engaged in for the purposes of crossing it without entering the internal waters and the ports of Ukraine, or else for the purpose of leaving them and entering the open sea. Passage shall be deemed innocent if the peace of Ukraine and the law and order or security of Ukraine is not violated thereby. Foreign non-military vessels and warships may exercise the right of innocent passage through the territorial sea of Ukraine in accordance with the legislation of Ukraine and with the international treaties concluded by Ukraine.

175. Foreign warships and underwater means of transport shall engage in innocent passage through the territorial sea of Ukraine in the manner established by the Cabinet of Ministers. The conditions and limitations concerning the transit and sailing of foreign warships in inland waters, territorial sea and seaport are established in the Rules on Navigation and Stay of Foreign Warships in the Territorial Sea, Internal Waters, in Roadsteads and in Ports of Ukraine.[121] The Rules determine the procedure for foreign warships, as well as foreign submarines of innocent passage through the territorial waters of Ukraine and procedure of their entering and stay in the roadsteads and in the ports of Ukraine. Foreign warships during its voyage and stay in the territorial sea, internal waters, in the roadsteads and in the ports of Ukraine must bear its naval or state flag. In case a foreign warship, its craft, aircraft or crew members fail to comply with the laws and regulations of Ukraine during the voyage and stay in the territorial sea and internal waters, in the roadsteads and ports of Ukraine, a foreign warship commander is requested to observe the laws and regulations of Ukraine. In case of ignorance of those requests, the competent authorities can demand an immediate leave of a warship from the territorial sea of Ukraine.

B. Pilotage

176. For ensuring safety of shipping at the approaches to the sea ports, within waters of these ports, as well as between the sea ports, regardless of the state flag which the ship flies and ownership form of the ship, the ship shall be sailed by the sea pilots. Article 94 of the MSC defines compulsory and non-compulsory pilotage of ships. The pilotage fee is charged in this case. The legal regulation pertaining to pilotage in Ukraine will be further discussed in Chapter 13.

C. Vessel Traffic Regulation (VTR)

177. By virtue of Article 110 of the MSC the Vessel Traffic Regulation (VTR) Service is created by the Ministry of Infrastructure in the regions of intensive shipping (harbour and coastal waters, narrows, intersection of navigational routes) to carry out radiolocation service operation for the vessels. The service area and the order of traffic of vessels shall be established by the rules of navigation in this area, which shall be approved by the central executive power, who is responsible for ensuring of formation of state policy in the field of transport.

The radiolocation service operation means the control of the safety of navigation, vessel traffic regulation, radiolocation guiding, vessel assistance at the time of rescue operations, reporting of vessel traffic, conditions of aids to navigation, hydrometeorology and other factors, which have an impact on the safety of navigation. The list of services which have to be rendered by each VTR Service, the degree of obligation of some kinds of the radiolocation service operation shall be notified in the compulsory regulation for port, sailing directions and Notices to mariners. Beyond the limits of the territorial sea of Ukraine the VTR Service shall serve the vessels only under the request of the master.

---

121. These Rules were approved by the Decree of the CMU dated 16 May 1996, No. 529.

178. Article 111 of the MSC stipulates that the VTR Service shall act in accordance to the Model regulation, approved by the central executive power, who is responsible for ensuring of formation of state policy in the field of transport. Thus, the MTU has issued the Order On Approval of the Regulation of Vessel Traffic Service, dated 28 May 2001, No. 340, registered at the Ministry of Justice on 25 June 2001, No. 545/5736. According to section 3.4 of the Regulation of the Vessel Traffic Service, the VTR Services depending on zones are divided into:

– port VTR Service that services the vessels in port harbour and on the approaches to it;
– regional (coastal) – services the vessels in coastal waters and narrowness or in adjacent waters of several maritime and river ports.

The VTR Service serves vessels in the following sequence:

– vessels in distress and vessels stood towards to provide an aid;
– ferry and passenger vessels stood towards according to timetable;
– vessels with perishable goods;
– vessels with dangerous goods;
– liners;
– other vessels – according to receipt of requests and established traffic schedule.

179. Vessels using the services of the VTR Service shall pay a fee, stipulated by the Ministry of Infrastructure[122]. It is also stipulated in Article113 of the MSC that the pilot of the VTR Service is able to refuse to continue the radiolocation guiding of the vessel if the master of the vessel, guided by the pilot of the VTR Service, does not follow its recommendations. Such refusal shall be fixed by means of technical facilities. However, even after the refusal in radiolocation guidance the pilot of the VTR Service shall be on call with the vessel, and, if the master needs any information, necessary for the safety navigation, he shall provide it. The liability of the VTR Service is limited to by its disaster fund, created by 10% of deductions from the amounts of fees received in the calendar year passed before the incident.

D. Port Dues

180. Article 22 of the Law of Ukraine on Sea Ports of Ukraine stipulates the following port dues:

– the tonnage dues shall be paid to the user of harbour as well as to the owner of the operating water area of berth, build before coming into force of the Law of Ukraine On Sea Ports of Ukraine;

122. Order of the MTU dated 15 Dec. 2000, No. 711 on Amendments and Supplements to Charges and Fees for Services Rendered to Vessels in Sea Ports of Ukraine registered at the Ministry of Justice of Ukraine dated 10 Jan. 2001, No. 5/5196.

- the birth dues shall be paid to the owner of the birth, and if the birth is in use – to the user of the birth;
- anchor dues;
- channel dues shall be paid to the owner of the channel;
- light dues which shall be paid to the public institution responsible for organization and performance of navigational and hydrological support of shipping;
- administrative dues; and
- sanitary dues.

The rates of these dues shall be established by the national commission responsible for state regulation in the field of transport.

The procedure for payment, accounting and application of funds received from the port dues, except for the use of funds from the administrative dues, shall be stipulated by the Ministry of Infrastructure. Use of funds from administrative dues shall be done according to the law.

Chapter 2. Vessels

§1. Definition and Legal Status of a Vessel

181. According to Article 15 of the MSC a commercial vessel is a floating self-propelling or not self-propelling construction which is used for the following purposes:

- transportation of goods, passengers, luggage or post, fishing or other offshore operations, exploration and production of natural resources, life-saving or salvage of vessels at sea, towing of other vessels or water-crafts, hydro engineering, lifting of sunken property;
- carrying out of public duties (protection of fishing, sanitary and quarantine service, protection of sea from pollution, etc.);
- scientific, educational and cultural purposes;
- sporting purposes;
- other purposes.

182. The key term encompassed by the definition stipulated in Article 15 of the MSC is a 'floating construction'. Thus, the vessel can only be 'the construction'; that is, artificially and purposefully constructed entity, not just a random natural object located at sea. Further, the vessel is a 'floating construction' which means that it is purposefully constructed for floating.

183. Fishing vessels can be defined as any commercial crafts used for fishing or other offshore operations. The means used for the purposes of fishing or for other offshore operations are deemed to be inseparable parts of the vessel and in this regard all the maritime events connected with the damage of such means are qualified as collision of vessels.

184. The definition of a nuclear vessel is also given by the MSC, according to which a nuclear vessel is a vessel equipped by a nuclear power installation. Nuclear vessels are subject to a specific legal regime in Ukraine, thus, a nuclear vessel can only be in the ownership of the state and cannot be a subject of the mortgage involving natural persons and private legal entities.

§2. Registration and Nationality of Vessels

I. Registration and a Right to Fly the Ukrainian Flag

185. The rules which apply to registration of vessels in Ukraine and which regulate the right of vessels to fly the Ukrainian flag are stipulated by Chapter 2 of the MSC (Articles 26–34).

186. Ukrainian vessels surveyed by classification societies are to be registered in the State Shipping Register of Ukraine (SRU) according to the current Ukrainian legislation. All other vessels which are not subject to registration in the SRU of Ukraine have to be registered in the Shipping Book of Ukraine (SBU).

187. It has to be clarified that Article 22 of the MSC provides that technical survey of the maritime vessel is conducted by classification society chosen by the ship owner. Classification societies conduct technical survey of:

(1) passenger vessels, tankers, vessels designated for transportation of dangerous cargo as well as tugs regardless the main engine's capacity and gross tonnage;
(2) self-propelling vessels not mentioned in section 1 with main engine's capacity 55 kW and more;
(3) vessels not mentioned in sections 1 and 2 with gross tonnage 80 units and more.

188. The above-mentioned list of vessels (subject to registration in the SRU) is also indicated in Article 12 of the Decree of the CMU dated 26 September 1997, No. 1069 on Approval of the Procedure of Keeping of the SRU and of the SBU (hereinafter – Procedure). The vessels, not mentioned in sections 1–3 above, are, accordingly, subject to registration in the SBU.

189. According to the said Procedure, the general control over the process of registration of the vessels in Ukraine and keeping of the SRU and SBU is conducted by the Ministry of Transport and Infrastructure of Ukraine. Registration of the vessels in SRU is conducted by the harbourmasters upon approval of the Inspectorate of Ukraine for Maritime and Inland Water Transport Safety (hereinafter – Inspectorate). Registration of fishing vessels is conducted upon approval of the Inspectorate and the State Agency of Fisheries of Ukraine.[123]

190. Ukrainian legislation allows for the temporary registration of the vessel in the SRU or SBU in cases when the vessel is bareboat chartered to the Ukrainian charterer, but not more than for the period of validity of the charter party agreement. Such temporary registration is only possible if the vessel has not been registered in a register of any other state at the time of chartering or if such registration was suspended, in which case the ship owner should submit the certificate of the suspension of the registration to the Ukrainian registration authorities.

191. The vessel can be registered in the SRU or SBU only in one seaport of Ukraine. The port of registration can be changed on request of the ship owner.

192. Registration in the SRU is evidenced by the Certificate of the right to fly the state flag of Ukraine (ship patent), and the registration in the SBU is evidenced by the ship letter. The registration fee is defined by the Ministry of Infrastructure and should be paid to the Ukrainian registration authorities.

123. Decree of the President of Ukraine on State Agency of Fisheries of Ukraine dated 16 Apr. 2011, No. 484/2011.

193. From the moment of registration of the vessel in the SRU or SBU all previous records regarding such vessel in all other foreign shipping registers are deemed invalid. In the same manner the vessel cannot be deemed registered with the foreign shipping register unless the vessel is deleted from the SRU or SBU.

194. According to the MSC, the vessel is subject to deletion from the SRU or SBU in the following cases:

- the vessel is qualified as unfit for further exploitation and repairing;
- the vessel loses a right to fly the state flag of Ukraine;
- the vessel is lost.

The Procedure also contains additional reasons for temporary deletion of the vessel from, which are the end of the period of bareboat charter of the foreign vessel; changing of the registered ship owner or charterer under the bareboat charter.

195. The owner of the vessel or the charterer should notify the shipping registration authority on any change of relevant information concerning the vessel within two weeks upon such change.

196. The MSC contains the definitions of 'Ukrainian vessel' or 'vessel of Ukraine' which means the vessel which falls under the jurisdiction of Ukraine. The national identity of the vessel is defined by its state registration in Ukraine (by its right to fly the Ukrainian flag). Regarding the right to fly the Ukrainian flag, the MSC contains a very special provision according to which such right can be given only to a vessel being in the state ownership, in the ownership of a natural person citizen of Ukraine or a legal entity established under the laws of Ukraine by Ukrainian owners only. The right to fly the Ukrainian flag can also be given (on the temporary basis) to a vessel chartered by the aforementioned entities/persons. The right to fly the Ukrainian flag is granted upon the registration of the vessel in the SRU or SBU.

197. The mentioned provision deprives of the possibility to register the ships in Ukraine not only foreign natural persons and legal entities, but also ship owning companies with foreign capital (regardless of the size of such capital).The effect of such provision is that each year the number of vessels flying the Ukrainian flag is substantially decreasing. According to the statistical information the total number of vessels flying the Ukrainian flag in 2010 is five times smaller than in 1991.

198. The Ukrainian ship owners give preference to register the ships elsewhere due to the general unattractiveness of the Ukrainian flag which is also the reason of decreasing of the Ukrainian merchant fleet. At the moment the right to sail under the Ukrainian flag does not give any privileges even in domestic ports. The last privilege for the vessels flying the Ukrainian flag – 20% discount on tonnage dues in the Ukrainian ports – was abolished in 2004.[124] The only benefit which still exists now is that the Ukrainian vessel can actually sail in inland waters which are as a

124. *Dzerkalo tyzhnya,* No. 24 (552) dated 25 Jun.–1 Jul. 2005, www.dt.ua/2000/2241/50433.

rule closed for foreign vessels (sailing in inland waters of Ukraine for foreign vessels is allowed only by special permission).

199. A discussed ship registration reform in Ukraine would allow registration of foreign vessels, simplify the registration procedures and reduce tax and fiscal burden on owners of the vessels. Undoubtedly, increase of the vessels flying the Ukrainian flag will result in increasing flows to budget in a form of registration fees from the vessels and profit tax from the seafarers working on board (taking into account the fact, that Ukraine at the moment occupies the fifth place in the world by the number of seafarers). Despite such potential benefits, the policy of registration of vessels in Ukraine remains unchanged.

200. In case the vessel is acquired abroad the right to fly the Ukrainian flag can be obtained if a temporary certificate of the right to fly the Ukrainian flag is issued by the Consul of Ukraine in the state of acquisition. Such a temporary certificate is valid until the vessel is actually registered in the SRU or SBU but not more than for one year.

201. The liability for flying the Ukrainian flag without the prior registration is provided for by Article 339 of the Criminal Code of Ukraine. The Article makes clear that the penalty for committing such a crime may be up to six months of arrest and/or a fine.

202. If the owner of Ukrainian vessel charters it out to a foreign natural person or legal entity on the conditions of bareboat charter the right to fly the Ukrainian flag can be temporarily withdrawn from the vessel if the consent of the Ministry of Infrastructure is obtained, provided that:

- the legislation of the foreign state does not prohibit change of the flag;
- the owner of the vessel agrees to transfer the vessel temporarily under the flag of the foreign state;
- the consent of mortgagees of the vessel for the temporary transfer under the flag of the foreign state is obtained.

II. Vessel Documents

203. Chapter 3 of the MSC provides the list of the documents to be on board the vessel. In accordance with Article 35 of the MSC, the vessel should possess the following documents:

(1) certificate on the right to fly the Ukrainian flag (ship patent or ship letter);
(2) certificate of ownership on the vessel;
(3) classification certificate;

(4) tonnage certificate (for the vessels surveyed by the classification society only);
(5) minimum safe manning certificate;
(6) list of crew members;
(7) list of passengers on board;
(8) ship's log;
(9) engine log (for the vessels with engine);
(10) sanitary log;
(11) shipping sanitary certificate;
(12) passenger certificate if there are more than twelve persons on board;
(13) permission for the use of shipping radio station (radio service record);
(14) certificate of load line;
(15) log of registration of measures taken to avoid sea pollution.

204. If a vessel sails abroad it should possess additional documents stipulated by the international treaties as well. The certificate on the right to fly the state flag and the certificate of ownership are issued by the harbourmaster where the vessel is registered in the SRU. The ship letter is issued by the authority carrying out the registration in the SBU. The permission for the usage of the radio station is given by the Ministry of Infrastructure. Other documents are obtained from the classification society surveying the vessel (for the vessels subject to survey by classification societies). All the originals of the documents mentioned above should be kept on board except for the certificate of ownership on the vessel and the ship letter which can be kept as the certified copies.

§3. Acquisition and Ownership of the Vessels

205. According to Article 16 of the MSC the vessels may be subject to all forms of ownership unless otherwise is provided by the current legislation of Ukraine. Nuclear vessels are subject to the state ownership only.

206. All vessels under the state ownership cannot be arrested without a prior consent of the authority managing the state property if such vessels are used for the purposes of public service.

207. The right of property on the vessel under construction is regulated by the law of the country where such vessel is located, unless otherwise provided by the shipbuilding contract. The right of property and other related rights to the vessel located outside the borders of Ukraine as well as origin, alteration and termination of such rights are regulated by the law of the country of the vessel's flag.

208. The definition of a ship owner is given in Article 20 of the MSC. It provides that the ship owner is a legal entity or natural person who operates the vessel on its own behalf regardless of whether it is an owner of the vessel or operates it under other legal grounds (e.g., on the basis of the bareboat charter party). The owner of a vessel is a person to whom the vessel belongs based on the right of property. The concepts of the ship owner and the owner of the vessel provided for in the MSC match with the similar notions existing in the maritime law of the traditional maritime countries.

209. According to the provisions of the MSC the vessel should have its own name which must be assigned to it by the owner of the vessel. Any vessel possessing communication equipment is assigned a call sign and, depending on the vessel's technical facilities, identification number of a satellite station and ship's radio call number. The procedure for assigning to the vessel of the name, call sign, identification number and ship's radio call number is stipulated by the Ministry of Infrastructure.

§4. Vessel Safety

210. Inspectorate of Ukraine for Maritime and Inland Water Transport Safety has been established to carry out the state supervision over safety on sea and river transport and is controlled by the Ministry of Infrastructure.[125] The main tasks of the abovementioned Inspectorate is the state supervision over safety of shipping at sea and river ports, territorial sea, inland waters, on the vessels flying the Ukrainian flag. Its competence also includes control of compliance with the legislation and the international treaties of Ukraine concerning the safety of shipping and carrying out of measures on prevention of environmental pollution from vessels. It organizes investigation of accidents and disasters connected with merchant shipping, examines vessels at any time, as well as legal entities on their compliance with the safety of shipping.

211. The Code on Administrative Offences of Ukraine establishes the administrative liability for violations of the rules on protection and safety on sea transport, the rules of using the sea transport means, the rules of merchant ships' registration and the rules that ensure the safety of exploitation of vessels on inland waterways. It should be observed that the imposed liability is in the form of a fine.

212. The Regulation on Management Safety System of Navigation on Sea and River Transport[126] defines organization of work on prevention of emergency situations on maritime and inland water transport, tasks, functions, departments, subjects and objects of navigational safety management and also determines forms of enforcement activities connected with navigational safety. The described System covers:

- human protection – life, health, property, rights pertaining to the use of territorial sea, internal waters and other water objects for work, recreation, sport, use of water resources including those for navigation;

---

125. Regulation on State Inspectorate of Ukraine for Maritime and Inland Water Transport Safety approved by the Decree of the President of Ukraine dated 8 Apr. 2011, No. 447/2011.
126. Order of the MTC dated 20 Nov. 2003, No. 904, registered at the Ministry of Justice on 19 Dec. 2003. No. 1193/8514.

- protection of environment – protection from negative impact of navigation;
- vessels – their status, conditions of sailing and staying of people on board;
- waterways – their suitability for use and conditions of their voyages;
- coastal objects – their compliance with navigational safety standards, readiness and reliability.

213. According to the Order of the Ministry of Infrastructure on Regulation on Harbourmaster and the Service of the Harbourmaster dated 27 March 2011, No. 190 this body carries out the state supervision over the safety of navigation in the port. The charges collected for its services such as pilot services, vessel traffic regulation, as well as ships' charges are primarily directed to ensure the safety of navigation. The Service of the Harbourmaster supervises over the compliance with the legislation and the rules of navigation, international treaties ratified by Ukraine related to merchant shipping, registration of vessels calling into and leaving the port in the manner prescribed by the Ministry of Infrastructure, revision of the vessel's documents, diplomas and qualification certificates of crew members, examination and record of the documents containing information on cargo, with the purpose of its safe carriage by sea for the vessels loaded in the port. The Regulation also governs the vessel traffic regulation in the port harbour, the approach channels and ditches in ports where the traffic vessel control is not provided.

214. The Rules on Fire Safety on Maritime Vessels of Ukraine[127] set the general requirements of the fire safety and apply to all types of maritime vessels of Ukraine, including floating cranes, floating decks and other floating structures, as well as vessels of mixed navigation (river-sea) which perform navigation by seaways, at all stages of their exploitation regardless of ownership forms, and are obligatory for ship owners, ships' crew and all other persons on board a vessel. The Rules do not apply to the fishing vessels, warships and auxiliary military vessels, ships and auxiliary ships of the State Border Service of Ukraine.

127. Approved by the MTC dated 24 Feb. 2007, No. 159, registered at the Ministry of Justice on 12 Jul. 2007, No. 806/14073.

Chapter 3. Mortgages and Other Real Rights

§1. Maritime Liens

I. Maritime Liens: General Concept

215. The current Ukrainian legislation (not taking into account international treaties) does not contain the classical definition of such a well-known and peculiar notion of maritime law as *maritime lien*. In order to understand the peculiarities of legislative regulation of the maritime liens in Ukraine it is necessary to give a short description of the maritime liens and their basic characteristics how they are understood in the countries with the well-developed maritime law tradition.

216. The maritime lien is a lien on a vessel given to secure a specific claim of a creditor which arises out of the vessel's use and associated with this vessel.[128] Claims which give rise to maritime liens are usually exclusively listed in the legislation of a given country in a specific order in which they are prioritized. It must be noted, that characteristics of maritime liens can slightly vary from country to country, though the basic features remain the same and they are the following:

- maritime lien arises by operation of law – it does not need to be registered or in any other way made valid;
- maritime liens arise when the law prescribes it – maritime lien has a priority over all other encumbrances – it is ranked higher than registered mortgage on a ship, etc.;
- maritime claim secured by a maritime lien on a ship must not necessarily be against the registered owner of such ship – a claim can be against demise charterer, manager or operator of such ship or against anyone to whom the ship owner has delegated his/her functions;
- maritime lien is attached to a ship and travels with it – if the ownership of a ship is changed, the maritime lien continues to encumber it;
- maritime lien has a short limitation period.

217. All the named features are as a rule reflected in the national legislation and in the international Acts regulating the notion of maritime liens. The most recent international act in force which concerns maritime liens is the International Convention on Maritime Liens and Mortgages of 1993 (hereinafter – Maritime Liens Convention or the Convention) entered into force on 5 September 2004. There are not many ratifications yet, though the basic provisions of the Maritime Liens Convention are generally reflected in the national law of many maritime countries. This speaks for the fact that the Convention reflects the main features of maritime liens and how they are understood in the maritime world.

128. T. Falkanger, H. Jacob Bull & L. Brautasset, *Scandinavian Maritime Law*, 118 (2d ed., Universitetsforlaget 2008).

218. Ukraine is a party to the Maritime Liens Convention to which it acceded on 22 November 2002 when the *Verkhovna Rada* enacted the Law of Ukraine on the Accession of Ukraine to the 1993 International Convention on Maritime Liens and Mortgages, No. 240-IV. However, the national legislation of Ukraine, including the MSC has not been brought in conformity with it. As a result, the provisions of MSC contradict the Convention and also general recognized understanding of what a maritime lien actually is.

II. Preferred Claims versus Maritime Liens: Terminological and Legal Conflict in the Ukrainian Legislation

219. The first issue which is worth paying attention is the terminology used in the MSC that stems from the Soviet era and is generally outdated. The MSC does not contain a notion *maritime lien* at all. The notion contained in the Code and which is in principle most closely related (though by its nature is not completely equivalent) to the notion of *maritime lien* is *a preferred claim.*

220. It must be mentioned that sometimes in legal literature the notion used in the MSC is translated into English as *maritime lien* though such translation cannot be considered as completely correct. There is a separate notion for *maritime lien* in the Ukrainian language used in the Ukrainian translation of the Maritime Liens Convention and which is *morska zastava*. This notion can be translated into English as *maritime lien*. The notion used in the MSC is *pryvylejovana vymoga* which in English refers to the *preferred claim.*

221. Notably the above approach is supported by the example that can be found in the legislation of the Russian Federation that has very similar legal tradition with Ukraine. The Merchant Shipping Code of the Soviet Union dated 17 September 1968, which was also valid in Russia for some years, did contain the notion of preferred claim. When the Russian Federation joined the Maritime Liens Convention and the new Merchant Shipping Code of the Russian Federation (MSCRF) was adopted on 30 April 1999, the mentioned notion was excluded from the Russian legislation and substituted with the maritime lien while the provisions of the Convention were incorporated into Chapter XXII of the MSCRF.[129] Amending of the national legislation of the Russian Federation upon accession to the Maritime Liens Convention constitutes an example of successful legislative implementation of the notion *maritime lien* into national law which can be taken over by Ukraine.

222. The difference between the notion *maritime lien* in conventional understanding and notion *preferred claim* in the understanding of the MSC is more than purely terminological – in their legal nature these notions have as many differences as they have similarities.

129. P. Falillev, 'Commentary to the Chapter XXII of CMSRF', www.fortisjuris.ru, 10 Mar. 2011.

223. The statutory basis of the preferred claim in the Ukrainian law is contained in Chapter 2 (Preferred Claims) of Part X (Limitation of Liability of the Ship Owner) of the MSC (Articles 358–363).

224. Article 358 of the MSC sets up a list of claims considered as preferred claims and which have priority before all other claims, including those secured by mortgage (a characteristic feature of a maritime lien). Article 358 gives the general list of preferred claims listed by priority which are as follows:

(1) claims arising out of the employment relations, claims in respect of loss of life or personal injury, as well as claims connected with social security payments as long as they relate to a specific vessel;
(2) claims regarding the nuclear damage, pollution of the sea as well as elimination of the consequences of the pollution;
(3) claims for canal and port dues;
(4) claims for reward for the salvage of the vessel and regarding general average contribution;
(5) claims regarding the damages incurred as a result of collision between vessels or other incident at sea, damages of port installations and other property, as well as of navigational equipment;
(6) claims arising out of actions of the master performed on the basis of his authority with an aim of saving the vessel or continuation of voyage;
(7) claims regarding the reimbursement of damages of cargo or luggage;
(8) claims regarding the freight and other payments payable for cargo transportation;
(9) claims regarding the port services are equally ranked with subsections 7 or 8 depending on the account of which property they are reimbursed.

225. It has to be underlined that the above list of preferred claims includes the claims which give rise to maritime liens in accordance with Article 4 of the Maritime Liens Convention, though there are a number of inconsistencies between the provisions of the Convention and of the MSC in this respect, among which can be named:

- claims contained in sections 2, 6, 7, 8 above are not included into the list of claims secured by maritime liens in the Convention;
- claims for the canal and port dues ranked after claims for reward for salvage in the Maritime Liens Convention.

226. According to Article 6 of the Convention a State Party may, under its law, grant other maritime liens on a vessel to secure claims other than those referred to in Article 4, provided that such liens:

(1) shall be subject to the provisions of Articles 8, 10 and 12 of the Convention;
(2) shall be extinguished:

(a) after a period of six months from the time when the claims secured thereby arose unless, prior to the expiry of such period, the vessel has been arrested or seized, such arrest or seizure leading to a forced sale; or
(b) at the end of a period of sixty days following a sale to a bona fide purchaser of the vessel, such period to commence on the date on which the sale is registered in accordance with the law of the State in which the vessel is registered following the sale, whichever period expires first; and

(3) shall rank after the maritime liens set out in Article 4 and also after registered mortgages, 'hypotheques' or charges which comply with the provisions of Article 1 of the Convention.

227. As it can be clearly seen from the provisions of MSC, additional claims which are included into Article 358 do not rank after the list of claims mentioned in Article 4 of the Convention. Moreover, all mentioned preferred claims (Article 363 of the MSC) are extinguished after one year except for the claims stipulated in section 6 of Article 358 of the MSC, which becomes extinguished after six months from the day when the claim arose. Therefore, a clear contradiction between Article 358 of the MSC and Article 4 of the Convention can be traced.

228. Another important difference between preferred claims in the MSC and maritime liens in the Convention is the property which is subject to lien: claims, mentioned in the Convention are secured by a maritime lien on the vessel (and not any other property/payments/dues, etc.), but the preferred claims can be reimbursed on the cost of different types of property/payments/contributions. Namely, Article 359 of the MSC stipulates preferred claims which are reimbursed on the vessel's cost. According to the mentioned Article, the claims stipulated in sections 1–7 of Article 358 are reimbursed from:

(1) value of the vessel;
(2) freight and payment for carriage of passengers and their luggage payable for the voyage during which a basis of the claim arouse;
(3) general average contributions payable to the ship owner regarding the vessel in question;
(4) reimbursements payable to the ship owner for the loss of hire and for the damages incurred by the vessel and not yet restored;
(5) reward payable to the ship owner for the salvage which took place before the end of the voyage except of the sums which must be paid by the ship owner in accordance with Article 336 of the MSC (procedure of salvage reward distribution).

229. Article 360 of the MSC stipulates claims which are reimbursed on the cargo's cost. Namely, preferred claims stated in sections 2, 4, 6 and 8 of Article 358 of the MSC are reimbursed from:

(1) value of the cargo not delivered to the consignee;
(2) reimbursement payable for the damaged cargo;
(3) general average contributions payable to the cargo owner.

230. According to Article 361 of the MSC the claims (Article 358) are reimbursed in order of priority of sections and within each section proportionally to the size of the claim. Though claims stipulated in sections 4 and 6 of Article 358 of the MSC are reimbursed within each section in order, reverse to the order of their appearance. The claims arising in connection with one accident/casualty are considered as arisen simultaneously.

231. Article 362 of the MSC stipulates the principle of reimbursement for the last voyage. According to this principle the claims which are attributed to the last voyage are reimbursed before the similar claims which have arisen during the previous voyages. However, the claims stipulated in section 1 of Article 358 of the MSC which are attributed to several voyages are equal to the same claims for the last voyage.

232. As it can be seen from above, a preferred claim within the MSC has the following features, similar to a maritime lien: it arises by operation of law, has a priority over all other encumbrances and has a short limitation period. Due to such similarities it can be considered as a vague analogy of a maritime lien. Nevertheless, it lacks the following crucial features of a maritime lien.

233. First, it is an ability to enforce the maritime lien against anyone to whom the ship owner has delegated his/her functions (demise charterer, manager or operator). Part I of Article 4 of the Convention which contains the list of claims secured by a maritime lien in the vessel provides that the listed claims secured by a maritime lien on the vessel can be directed against the owner, demise charterer, manager or operator of the vessel. The MSC or other Ukrainian legislation in force (except for international treaties) does not provide for a possibility to enforce a lien over the property which is not owned by a debtor (person who bears responsibility for a specific claim). Therefore, in accordance with the literal reading of the provisions of MSC or other Ukrainian legal Acts it is not possible to enforce a preferred claim against any other person than a registered owner of the vessel or other property, on the cost of which the preferred claim is to be reimbursed (cargo, sums of rewards and contributions, etc.).

234. Second, it is 'attachment' to a vessel notwithstanding the fact of changing of ownership or flag. Article 8 of the Convention provides that maritime liens follow the vessel despite any change of ownership or of registration or of flag. The MSC does not contain such provisions, thus, a preferred claim cannot be enforced against a new owner of the vessel.

235. Basing on the abovementioned a conclusion can be made that the notion of a preferred claim stipulated in the MSC does not match together with the notion of maritime lien provided in the Maritime Liens Convention. As both the MSC and the Maritime Liens Convention constitute the Ukrainian legislation in force, such inconsistency can create legislative confusion which can result in incorrect application of the legislative norms by Ukrainian courts and ignoring the notion of a maritime lien as such in the Ukrainian legal environment.

III. Maritime Liens in Ukraine: Legislative Framework and Practical Application

236. As it has already been mentioned above, the Maritime Liens Convention was acceded by Ukraine on 22 November 2002 and it came into force on 5 September 2004. Therefore, the Convention constitutes an integral part of the national law of Ukraine and its provisions may be directly applied by the parties to commercial relations as well as by the courts and official authorities. Moreover, in parts, where the Convention conflicts with the provisions of the MSC, provisions of the Convention shall prevail over the provisions of MSC.

237. Thus, while considering the disputes when one of the parties claims its right on a vessel based on a maritime lien, the courts of Ukraine shall be governed by the provisions of the Maritime Liens Convention hence directly, as it is not incorporated into any other Ukrainian legal Acts.

238. The *Primorskiy* Court of the city of Odessa passed the Decision in the case No. 2-7562/07 dated 11 December 2007 where one of the parties (claimant) made an attempt to enforce a claim 'in rem' which he directed against a vessel for the damage of the cargo which was on board that vessel. First, the court denied the possibility of directing the claim against the vessel (in rem action) as the Ukrainian legislation does not provide for the possibility of directing a claim against the property. This is fair enough taking into consideration the fact that in rem actions are a characteristic feature of the common law countries while being unknown to the majority of the civil law jurisdictions.

239. Moreover, the court indicated that due to the fact that the owner of the vessel which carried the damaged cargo subsequently changed, the claim could not be directed against the vessel or against the present owner of the vessel, as he had nothing to do with the damage to the cargo. The court applied the general procedural norms of the Ukrainian legislation while indicating that the claim was directed against the wrong defendant and, thus, should be dismissed. The Decision in the first instance was subsequently upheld in the appeal court.

240. As damage to cargo is excluded from the scope of the Maritime Liens Convention (Article 4(1)(e)) the court in the above-mentioned case made a right decision by not allowing a claim to 'follow the vessel'. Nevertheless, neither the court of the first instance, nor the appeal court in the named case referred to the issue of a maritime lien or to the Convention at all, though the case in principle was very closely related to the concept of a maritime lien, as the claimant acted in a way as if he wanted to enforce a maritime lien against the vessel for the damage to cargo carried on such vessel. It is hard to say how would the court have acted in this case if the claim was secured by the maritime lien according to the provisions of the Convention.

241. In another case, No. 2-434/2010 dated 23 April 2010 claimants were the crew members of a vessel owned by a company-defendant. The claim concerned the unpaid amounts of salary payable to the crew members and the claimants sought the satisfaction of their claims on the account of the vessel owned by the defendant. The court ordered to satisfy the claims on the account of the vessel. In its reasoning the court directly referred to subsection 1(a) of the Maritime Liens Convention stating that the claims regarding the amounts of salary and other sums which belong to the master, crew members or other members of the staff of the vessel are secured by a maritime lien. Based on this the court recognized that the claims are secured by a maritime lien in the vessel belonging to the debtor. Thereafter the court referred to Article 348 of the MSC according to which the ship owner is liable for his obligations with the property belonging to him and on which a penalty can be imposed in accordance with the Ukrainian legislation in force. Moreover, the court underlined that the claim is a preferred claim and must be satisfied before all other claims in accordance with subsection 16, Article 42, Part II of Article 358 of the MSC.

242. The actual circumstances of the case appeared to be quite simple (the vessel subject to lien was actually owned by a debtor) and the court based its decision on the Maritime Liens Convention. Therefore, there was no conflict between the Convention and other procedural or material legislation of Ukraine (i.e., with Article 348 of the MSC, which was also applied by the court). Thus, it is unclear how the court would have decided if the vessel was sold to another ship owner and did not belong to the debtor anymore. Presumably in such case the conflict would have placed between the Convention that allows the maritime lien on such vessel and legislation of Ukraine, allowing imposition of sanctions exclusively on the property belonging to the debtor.

243. Scarce judicial practice on the matter does not allow making a clear conclusion regarding the Ukrainian court's vision of the matter. However, it can be surmised that the legislative collision connected with the notion of maritime lien in the Ukrainian legislation does really exist. Until the collision is properly settled, there is a high risk that the courts would apply the general procedural legislation of Ukraine and the MSC without taking into consideration the provisions of the Maritime Liens Convention.

244. A good example of adequate bringing of national legislation in compliance with the provisions of the Maritime Liens Convention can be found in legislation of the Russian Federation (already described above). Chapter XXII of MSCRF literally restates many provisions of the Convention. In particular, the notion 'maritime lien', as well as its key characteristics like ability to secure a claim against demise charterer, manager or operator of such ship and its 'attachment to a ship' are reflected there. Thus, the maritime liens as they are understood in the rest of the maritime world were enforceable in Russia even before the Convention came into force in 2004.[130] As it has been repeatedly mentioned above, the current MSC still contains outdated provisions of the old Soviet code on preferred maritime claims while the notion of maritime lien is absent.

130. P. Falillev, 'Commentary to the Chapter XXII of CMSRF', www.fortisjuris.ru, 10 Mar. 2011.

§2. SHIP MORTGAGES

I. General Legal Framework for Ship Mortgages in Ukraine

245. Ship mortgage is a specific kind of mortgage to which general provisions on mortgage provided by general legislation of Ukraine, as well as specific provisions of maritime legislation apply.

246. The basis of regulatory framework of ship mortgages in Ukraine at the moment encompasses the following legal Acts: the Civil Code, the Law of Ukraine on Mortgage dated 5 June 2003, No. 898-IV (hereinafter – Law on Mortgage), the MSC, the International Convention on Maritime Liens and Mortgages of 1993 (hereinafter – Maritime Liens Convention or the Convention).

247. Taking into consideration the general provisions of the Ukrainian legislation on pledge and mortgages, it shall be noted that a ship mortgage is a separate type of securing the principal obligation. Thus, it has the same features as the pledge – it is dependent upon the principal obligation, it is accessory to the principal obligation and it can secure only valid obligation or satisfaction of a claim that might appear in future arising out of a valid contract.

248. After the Law of Ukraine on Mortgage dated 5 June 2003 came into force in January 2004, section II of the Law of Ukraine on Pledge dated 2 October 1992, No. 2654-XII related to the mortgages became inapplicable. Generally, the Law on Mortgage applies to the mortgage of immovable property. Nevertheless, according to Article 1 of the said Law its provisions also apply to the mortgage of marine vessels, aircrafts, and space crafts as well as to the mortgage of the mentioned objects under construction – the objects with a special status within the mortgage legislation. A ship or a ship under construction which is registered in the SRU or in the SBU can be a subject to mortgage.[131]

249. As it has been mentioned before, along with the general norms regulating the mortgages of different kinds of property, there are also special norms related specifically to maritime vessels – norms of the MSC (Chapter 3 of Part X, Articles 364–378). Being not untypical for the Ukrainian legislation, special and general norms do not always coincide with each other and in some cases even contradict. Moreover, existence of the Maritime Liens Convention being directly applicable in Ukraine as a ratified international Act, but which was not incorporated into the Ukrainian legislation, makes it a difficult task to structure the legislative framework for ship mortgages.

131. Definition of a vessel is given in Art. 15 of MSC, regarding the SRU and SBU see *supra* §2, Ch.

II. Mortgage Agreement: Parties, Essential Elements and Form

250. The definition of maritime mortgage is provided by Article 364 of the MSC. According to the aforementioned Article any vessel registered in the SRU or in the SBU can be mortgaged according to the legislation in force by a ship owner (mortgagor) in order to secure an obligation before a creditor (mortgagee). Any legal entity or natural person of Ukraine or of any foreign state to whom the vessel could be transferred according to the legislation of Ukraine can act in the capacity of a mortgagee.

251. According to the MSC, the rights and obligations of the parties to the mortgage agreement as well as the procedure of its registration are stipulated by the law of the country of the mortgagee unless otherwise provided by the agreement between the parties. It is difficult to define how can a mortgage agreement regarding a ship flying the Ukrainian flag be governed by foreign legislation. Therefore, the mortgage agreement under Ukrainian law will be subject to analysis. In such a case, provisions of the MSC on ship mortgages shall be read together with the Law of Ukraine on Mortgage and the Civil Code.

252. Article 365 of the MSC provides that the mortgage agreement must be concluded in writing stating a name of the vessel, requisites of the parties, their location, claims secured by the mortgage, the size of the mortgage and time limit of execution of the obligation, assessment and location of a vessel and other terms and conditions. It has to be underlined, that the essential elements of the mortgage agreement, non-compliance with which may lead to declaring of the mortgage agreement invalid, are stipulated in Article 18 of the Law of Ukraine on Mortgage and are in principle similar to those provided in Article 365 of the MSC. Though the list of requirements in Article 18 is more detailed, therefore, it has to be taken into account when concluding a ship mortgage agreement.

253. The mortgage does not mean a transfer of the vessel to the mortgagee, as well as it does not mean that the mortgagor loses its right of property for the vessel. The marine vessel which is a subject to the mortgage is kept by the mortgagor or by a third party. Thus, the mortgagor's right to possess and exploit the vessel is maintained. The rights and obligations of the mortgagor are stipulated by Articles 8–10 of the Law of Ukraine on Mortgage, among which is an obligation to take measures for safeguarding the object of mortgage, to insure the object of mortgage on his own expense, etc. The rights of the mortgagee, including the right to demand from the mortgagor taking measures for safeguarding the object of mortgage, are stipulated by Article 10 of the Law of Ukraine on Mortgage.

254. According to Article 366 of the MSC the mortgage agreement shall be certified at the place of the vessels registration. SRU has its territorial divisions in each Ukrainian port where the ship can be registered. Therefore, in order to properly conclude the mortgage agreement of a marine vessel the parties (mortgagor and mortgagee) shall travel to the city – port of the vessel's registration to have the mortgage agreement certified by the local notary. Non-compliance with the requirement of notarization of the mortgage agreement results in nullity of the agreement. It is needless to say that such requirement creates unnecessary complications for the parties.

III. Registration of the Ship Mortgage

255. Like in legislation of many other countries, absence of state registration does not in itself make a mortgage agreement invalid. Nevertheless, the mortgagor's unregistered right does not have a priority before similar registered rights of other parties, even if they appeared later (Article 4 of the Law of Ukraine on Mortgage). Therefore, in order to obtain the full protection of its right on the object of mortgage, one must search for registering it in accordance with the procedure prescribed by the legislation.

256. Ship mortgage registration under the Ukrainian legislation is a quite controversial issue. In most maritime countries there is one register for a ship mortgage registration – a shipping register, where the ship itself is registered. This makes not only registration of a ship mortgage easier, but also simplifies the procedure of checking the status of ship by a potential buyer, charterer, mortgagee, etc. The situation in Ukraine is quite different – due to imprecise legislative definition of the nature of a marine vessel, ship mortgage can, in principle, be registered in several different registers at the same time.

A. *Book of Mortgages*

257. The MSC prescribes for a special Book of Mortgages where all mortgages are to be registered by the mortgagor. It is provided that the Book of Mortgages is to be kept by a mortgagor and a deed of mortgage should be recorded in it within three days from the moment of its certification by a notary. The mortgagor is liable for making timely and accurate records in the Book of Mortgages and is obliged to reimburse to the mortgagee or to the third party all the damages caused by inaccurate, incomplete or incorrect records in the Book of Mortgages as well as by failure to provide it for review. It shall be noted that the MSC stipulates that the form and terms of keeping of the Book of Mortgages shall be prescribed by the law.

258. The requirement regarding the Book of Mortgages keeping is an example of one of the numerous outdated provisions of the MSC, because at the moment there is no law in Ukraine, which provides the form and terms of keeping of the Book of Mortgages. The Law of Ukraine on Pledge provided the procedure for keeping of the Book of Pledges (which by analogy could be applied to the Book of Mortgages), but in 2006 the Law was abolished. Nevertheless, MSC still contains the provisions on the Book of Mortgages.

B. State Shipping Register of Ukraine and Shipping Book of Ukraine

259. The MSC does not contain any other (except of registration in the Book of Mortgages) provisions related to registration of the mortgage, including registration of the mortgage in the SRU or in the SBU. Nevertheless, a ship mortgage can be registered in one of the mentioned registers and such possibility is provided by the Procedure for Maintenance of SRU and of the SBU, adopted by the Resolution of the CMU dated 26 September 1997, No. 1069. Thus, when the vessel is registered for the first time in one of the registers, the ship owner, among other documents, is obliged to submit a document certifying existence or absence of mortgages or any other encumbrances over the vessel.

260. The application form which has to be filled in order to include the information about the vessel into one of the registers contains a box named 'Encumbrances over the vessel', where the information on a ship mortgage can be stated. There is no explicit obligation to submit information about subsequent (which happened after the vessels registration) encumbrances over the vessel to any of the registers. However, a mortgagee may insist on including of the information about the mortgage into the shipping register or book. Along with the registration of a mortgage in the register or the book a ship mortgage may be registered in other registers that are considerably more formal and secure.

C. State Register of Encumbrances over Movable Property

261. In connection with the administrative reform which is ongoing in Ukraine, the procedure of state registration of ship mortgages has been substantially changed. Before the reform a ship mortgage could be registered, except for the Book of Mortgages and SRU and SBU, in at least three other registers. Starting from September 2012 there is only one state register in Ukraine for registration of ship mortgages – the State Register of Encumbrances over Movable Property.

Before the reform this Register was commonly used for registration of tax encumbrances over any property – movable or immovable. At the moment it also contains information on the mortgages over seagoing vessels. This Register is obligatorily checked by the notary upon certification of a deal whose subject-matter is the ship. A ship mortgage, as well as sale or other alienation will not be certified if any encumbrances are registered with respect to the ship in question. The Register is administered by the Ministry of Justice of Ukraine.

IV. Convention on Maritime Liens and Mortgages and the Ukrainian Legislation

262. As it has been already mentioned above, Ukraine is a party to the Maritime Liens Convention, which provisions prevail over the provisions of national legislation. In this regard it is relevant to analyse the provisions of the Convention concerning the maritime mortgages with a view of verifying compliance of the Ukrainian legislation with the provisions of the Convention.

A. *Public Accessibility of the State Registers*

263. In order to establish international uniformity in the field of maritime liens and mortgages, the Convention provides, *inter alia*, that mortgages, 'hypotheques' and charges over sea vessels will be recognizable and enforceable in the States parties to the Convention, provided that such instruments have been effected and registered in accordance with the laws of the state in which the vessel is registered.

264. One principal distinction between the Convention and the Ukrainian legislation is connected with an accessibility of the Registers of Mortgages of the vessels by the general public. Thus, Article 1 of the Convention provides that the mortgages are to be registered and the registers are open to public inspection, and that extracts from the register and copies of such instruments are obtainable from the registrar.

265. With this regard it has to be underlined that the State Register of Prohibitions of Alienation of Immovable Property – a register which as it has been clearly shown above, would most probably contain the information about the existing encumbrance over the ship, is not always available for access.

266. According to section 3.1 of the Regulation on the State Register of Prohibitions approved by the Order of the Ministry of Justice of Ukraine dated 9 June 1999, No. 31/5 official extract from this Register can be obtained by any natural person or legal entity upon filing a specific request. In principle, this norm fully complies with the provisions of the Convention regarding public accessibility. In practice, such requirement is often neglected by many notaries, who have a right to access the Register and give official extracts from it. One can face the situation when a notary denies issuing the official extract from the Register claiming that official extract can be obtained only by the owner of the vessel or by a person holding the power of attorney from the owner of the vessel (not taking into consideration the official requests from the competent state authorities). Notaries in such case justify their position by the provisions of the Law of Ukraine on Notarial Actions and Notarial Instruction that prohibit disclosure of the notarial secrets. It is always possible to obtain an official extract from the State Information Centre established within the Ministry of Justice that officially administers the State Register of Prohibitions, though the described position of some notaries considerably hinders the adequate level of openness prescribed by the Convention.

267. Moreover, the information from the SRU and the SBU is not available to the general public at all. Granting adequate public access to the named Registers should be a matter of concern for the Ukrainian legislators.

B. Other Provisions of the Convention and Their Implementation in Ukraine

268. The Convention provides that any deregistration of vessels or change of ownership for the vessel registered in the States party to the Convention will be permitted only if all registered mortgages, 'hypothèques' and charges have been previously deleted or the written consent of all holders of such mortgages, 'hypothèques' or charges is obtained.

269. Furthermore, the Convention provides that in the event of a forced sale, a notice will be provided to: (a) the registration authorities, (b) all of the holders of registered mortgages, 'hypothèques' and charges, (c) all of the holders of maritime liens, and (d) the registered owner, of the vessel. The MSC stipulates by Article 372 as well that the notice of the sale should be sent to the registration authorities and to the holders of registered mortgages and liens, but Article 372 does not preclude sending of such notice to the owner of the vessel. The Law of Ukraine on Mortgage by Article 38 provides that sending of notification of sale to the mortgagor and to all interested parties is an obligation of a mortgagee and if he fails to send such notification he is liable for all damages caused to the third parties.

270. The Convention defines the effects of the forced sale that are similar to those cases provided by the MSC where a right of retention may be granted in respect of a vessel and defines the legal consequences of a temporary change of flag with respect to maritime liens, mortgages, 'hypothèques' and charges.

V. Satisfaction of Claims from the Subject of the Mortgage

271. Article 367 of the MSC stipulates that if the subject of a mortgage is a vessel which has already been in a mortgage, the right of the *first mortgagee* remains in force. The claims of all subsequent mortgagees are to be satisfied from the cost of the vessel remaining after all the claims of the *first mortgagee* are satisfied.

272. According to the provisions of MSC, mortgagees' prerogative rights for indemnification in case of subsequent mortgage of the same marine vessel are observed depending on the time and date of registration of the mortgages in the Book of Mortgages in rotation. The mortgagor is obliged to notify all subsequent mortgagees on all existing mortgages as well as on the substance and the size of the obligations secured by the mortgages. The mortgagor shall reimburse all the damages caused by failure to fulfil the aforementioned obligation.

273. As it has already been mentioned above, the provisions regarding the Book of Mortgages in the MSC do not have a practical effect anymore; therefore, the time and date of registration of the mortgage in the Book of Mortgages cannot be taken into account while defining the prerogative rights on the mortgaged ship. Instead, the provisions of Article 3 of the Law of Ukraine on Mortgage shall be used. In accordance with it the priority right of a mortgagee appears from the moment of the registration of a mortgage (in the State Register of Encumbrances over Movable Property – see above). The registered rights and claims are subject to satisfaction in rotation depending on the time of their registration.

274. If the mortgagor performs the principal obligation secured by the mortgage, the mortgagee is obliged by Article 375 of the MSC to provide duly certified documents as evidences of the performance on request of the mortgagor.

275. Further, the MSC stipulates the right of a mortgagee to satisfy his claim out of the mortgaged vessel if the obligation secured by the mortgage is not performed in due time, unless otherwise stipulated by the legislation or by the mortgage agreement between the parties. The same right of the mortgagee is provided by Article 3 of the Law of Ukraine on Mortgage – a right to have all his claims satisfied out of the subject of the mortgage in case of debtor's non-performance of obligations predominantly before other persons whose claims related to the subject of the mortgage were not registered or were registered after the state registration of the mortgage.

276. Limits of collection are set forth by Article 369 of the MSC stating that the mortgagee is entitled to have his claims satisfied from the subject of the mortgage in full size including interests, damages caused by late performance and penalties in cases established by the law or by the mortgage agreement.

277. Expenses of the mortgagee related to the satisfaction of claims secured by the mortgage can also be compensated. Except as otherwise provided by the law or by the mortgage agreement, the following expenses can also be satisfied:

- expenses related to presenting the claim related to the principal obligation and collecting the mortgaged property;
- expenses relating to keeping and securing the subject of the mortgage;
- expenses related to the insurance of the subject of the claim;
- damages caused by the non-performance of the principal obligation of the mortgage agreement (Article 7 of the Law of Ukraine on Mortgage).

VI. Foreclosure of the Subject of the Mortgage

278. The mortgaged vessel may be collected under a court decision, commercial court decision or a decision of the Maritime Arbitration Commission, unless otherwise stipulated by the legislation of Ukraine.

279. The court decision (or the decision of the commercial court, the Maritime Arbitration Commission) on sale of mortgaged vessel or a vessel under construction should be published in one of the specialized newspapers within three subsequent days and the publication should contain:

(1) the name of the court adjudicating, date when the decision was issued;
(2) grounds for the sale;
(3) method, place and time of a sale;
(4) information about the vessel or about the vessel under construction;
(5) invitation to all the creditors to submit their claims connected to the vessel within sixty days starting from the moment of publication;
(6) other relevant information.

Together with the publication the court (commercial court, the Maritime Arbitration Commission) should within at least thirty days before the date of sale of the vessel send a notification about the time and place of the sale by a registered letter to:

– the authority that has registered the vessel or the proprietary right on the vessel under construction;
– all interested mortgagees.

280. A person who made a claim on forced sale of the vessel should submit an extract from the respective register/registers stating the list of names and addresses of all mortgagees to the court.

VII. Forced Sale of the Mortgaged Vessel

281. A sale of the mortgaged vessel is carried out in accordance with the current legislation of Ukraine unless otherwise stipulated by the mortgage agreement. The mortgaged property can be sold through the auctions (public bidding) or otherwise according to the agreement of the parties. The method of sale of the mortgaged property should in any case be stipulated in the mortgage agreement. The method of sale depends mainly on characteristics of the mortgaged property, its type and properties. A difficulty of the procedure of sale through the auction (public bidding) should be taken into consideration.

282. The procedure for carrying out the public bidding of the mortgaged (pledged) property is provided by Regulation on the Procedure for Carrying Out the Auctions (Public Bidding) for Realization of the Pledged Property enacted by the Resolution of the CMU dated 22 December 1997, No. 1448. The realization through the auction is carried out by the officials of the State Enforcement Service on the basis of the enforcement order of a judge or an order of a judge of the commercial court.

283. One more important notice should be made with regard to the distribution of revenue from the sale of the vessel. Thus, according to Article 374 of the MSC all the expenses caused by arrest or detention of the vessel by subsequent sale of the vessel including the expenses connected with maintenance of the vessel during the period of arrest or detention, repatriation of a crew, and the distribution of the revenue itself should be covered from the revenue obtained from the sale of the vessel prior to all other claims. The remainder of the revenue should be distributed in order to cover existing claims as stipulated by Article 358 of the MSC (preferred claims).

284. In case of forced sale of the mortgaged vessel all the maritime mortgages except those accepted by a buyer of the vessel, lose their effect provided that:

(1) at the moment of sale of the vessel or the vessel that is being constructed is situated within the territory of Ukraine;
(2) the sale was carried out according to the legislation of Ukraine and Articles 371 and 372 of the MSC prescribing the procedure for forced sale.

285. If all the conditions are met the court, commercial court or the Maritime Arbitration Commission on request of the buyer issues a certificate stating that the aforementioned vessel is not the subject of any mortgage anymore. In case when the certificate is issued the authority registering the vessels is obliged to delete all the mortgages and maritime claims burdening the vessel (except of those accepted by the buyer) from the SRU and the SBU as well as from other registers.

286. If the buyer of the mortgaged vessel is a legal entity or natural person being a resident of Ukraine, he shall be registered as an owner of the vessel. If the buyer is a foreign legal entity or natural person the registration authority issues a certificate stating that the vessel is deleted from the SRU or the SBU or the Certificate stating that the right of property for the ship that is being constructed belongs to the person for subsequent registration in a foreign register.

287. The maritime mortgage should also be deemed terminated if the principal obligation losses its validity or if the general conditions provided by the Law of Ukraine on Mortgage are fulfilled. If the maritime mortgage is terminated the appropriate notice should be made in the register where the mortgage is registered.

VIII. Assigning the Claim Secured by a Mortgage to Third Parties

288. According to Article 377 of the MSC, in case when the mortgagee assigns his claim secured by the mortgage to the third party or in case when the mortgagor transfers his debt arising from the principal obligation to the third party, the mortgage itself remains valid. Upon presentation of the duly certified document evidencing the assignment of the claim by the mortgagee or the transfer of the debt by the mortgagor to the third party, the respective records/changes are to be introduced into the respective registers.

289. It has to be underlined that the mortgagee can assign his/her claim secured by the mortgage to the third party without obtaining mortgagor's consent, unless otherwise provided by the mortgage agreement. Assignment of rights under the mortgage agreement is deemed to mean assignment of the claim under the main obligation, unless otherwise proved. The mortgagee is obliged to inform the mortgagor about the assignment in writing within five days from the date of assignment. The Agreement on Assignment is subject to notarial certification and state registration (Article 24 of the Law of Ukraine on Mortgages).

Chapter 4. The Arrest of Ships

§1. General

290. The notion 'maritime claim' was as such absent in the Ukrainian legislation before the MSC was enacted in 1995. Chapter 4 of Part II of the MSC is called 'Arrest of Ships' and contains specific rules on arrest of ships in Ukraine. The list of maritime claims for which the ship can be arrested is contained in Article 42 that practically restates the list of maritime claims contained in Article 1 of the International Convention on the Arrest of Ships (hereinafter – the Geneva Convention) which came into force on 14 September 2011. Ukraine has not ratified the Geneva Convention, though the representatives of Ukraine took part in the Diplomatic Conference on Arrest of Ships, in Geneva in 1999, and signed its Final Act that was the mentioned Convention. Article 1 of this Convention (that corresponds to Article 42 of the MSC) has an exhaustive list of maritime claims giving rise to the right of arrest. As compared to the corresponding provisions of the International Convention Relating to the Arrest of Sea-Going Ships 1952 (hereinafter – the Brussels Convention), the list of maritime claims is longer (new claims include environmental damages; vessel sale and purchase contract disputes; wreck removal; port, harbour and canal dues; and insurance claims). Ukraine has acceded to the Brussels Convention by the Law of Ukraine dated 7 September 2011, No. 3702-VI and became effective on 16 May 2012. Ukraine made a reservation upon accession that it will not apply the Convention to the warships and the state-owned ships exploited for non-commercial purpose. The accession to the Brussels Convention implies that as a general rule, Ukrainian vessels could be arrested in the contracting states under maritime claims only, as well as vessels of the Contracting States could be arrested under maritime claims only in the ports of Ukraine. Nevertheless, there could be a number of exceptions from the conventional arrest regime. Notably, in Ukraine, along with the Brussels Convention, there are several other sets of legal rules based on which an arrest of a vessel can be decreed. These are the following:

- The legal rules of the MSC to secure a maritime claim, stipulated by this code;
- General procedural rules of the CivPC and ComPC to secure a claim as provisional remedy.

Each of the above-mentioned legal regimes will be considered below.

§2. The Brussels Convention Regime

291. Starting from 16 May 2012 the Brussels Convention became effective in Ukraine. This enabled to arrest a vessel in Ukrainian port based on a maritime claim, defined in the Convention, and on a maritime claim only if the conventional regime is applicable. Following Ukraine's accession to Brussels Convention, jurisdiction rules in CivPC and ComPC were slightly amended and supplemented with a jurisdiction rule that the arrest of a vessel based on a maritime claim shall be exclusively decreed either by the Ukrainian court in the place where the vessel is or by the court at the place of the vessel's registration. Therefore, for those who have a maritime claim it would be possible to apply to the court at the place where the vessel is and arrange arrest based on the conventional regime (provided that the vessel flies a flag of the Contracting State).

§3. MSC Regime

292. Article 14(1) of the MSC stipulates that arrest rules in the MSC apply only to ships flying the Ukrainian flag which makes them inapplicable to foreign vessels. Thus, arrest rules in MSC which differ from the arrest rules in the Brussels Convention (even the list of maritime claims is different), can be applicable only to Ukrainian vessels. According to Article 42 of the MSC, arrest means any detention or restriction on removal of a ship to secure a maritime claim during ship's presence in a sea port of Ukraine, but does not include measures for execution of valid judgments of a court or commercial court. Article 42 of the MSC also provides that arrest of a vessel or release of a vessel from arrest can be based only on the decision of a general court, commercial court[132] or the Head of the Maritime Arbitration Commission.[133]

As already mentioned above, Article 42 of MSC also contains a list of maritime claims, based on which a vessel flying Ukrainian flag can be arrested, which restates the list of maritime claims contained in Article 1 of Geneva Convention.

293. Article 43 of the MSC provides the conditions under which the ship can be arrested (restating the provisions of Article 3 of the Geneva Convention). The ship can be arrested for a maritime claim if at least one of the following conditions is satisfied:

- the claim is secured by a preferred claim (stipulated by sections 1,2, 3–5 and 7 of Article 358 of the MSC);
- the claim is based upon a mortgage or a charge of the same nature on the ship;
- the claim relates to the ownership or possession of the ship;
- the person who owned the ship at the time when the maritime claim arose is liable for the claim and is owner of the ship when the arrest is effected;
- the bareboat charterer of the ship at the time when the maritime claim arose is liable for the claim and is bareboat charterer or owner of the ship when the arrest is effected.

132. The courts of general jurisdiction in the court system of Ukraine are divided basing on the types of cases that they consider, in the general courts, commercial courts and administrative courts. The general courts deal with civil and criminal cases, usually involving the natural persons (with some exclusions). The commercial courts deal mainly with disputes involving the legal entities and private entrepreneurs (with some exclusions) having the commercial nature.

133. Permanent arbitration body under the Chamber of Commerce of Ukraine which deals with maritime cases. However, there are no procedural legal rules in Ukraine which entitle the Maritime Arbitration Commission to grant the writs of seizure of the vessel.

294. Arrest is also permissible of any other ship (*sister ship*) or ships which, when the arrest is effected, is or are owned by the person who is liable for the maritime claim and who was, when the claim arose, the owner of the ship in respect of which the maritime claim arose or bareboat charterer, time charterer or voyage charterer of that ship. This provision does not apply to the claims in respect of ownership or possession of a ship.

295. Other provisions of Chapter 4, Part II of the MSC regulate release from the arrest upon posting the security (Article 44 of the MSC resembles Article 4 of the Geneva Convention), right of re-arrest and multiple arrest (Articles 45 and 5 respectively), protection of owners and bareboat charterers of arrested ships (Articles 46 and 6) and arrest of the state-owned ships (Article 47).

296. The amendments of the MSC on arrest of ships in compliance with the Geneva Convention (to be more precise – with its earlier drafts) as internationally recognized arrest rules were introduced, but they cannot be considered successful due to the reasons explained below.

297. One of the reasons can be found in Article 14, section 1 of the MSC stipulating that arrest rules in the MSC apply only to ships flying the Ukrainian flag which makes them inapplicable to foreign vessels. Apparently, a ship flying foreign flag theoretically cannot be arrested in the Ukrainian ports. Notwithstanding this fact, many foreign ships are arrested in Ukraine since the MSC does not contain any procedural rules whatsoever on arrest of ships.

As seen from the description of arrest rules in MSC above, they are based on Geneva Convention and are quite sound. This means that if the Ukrainian vessel is arrested in the Ukrainian port, a quite clear set of rules is applicable. In addition to rules on jurisdiction provided in CivPC and ComPC, the Brussels Convention contains a jurisdiction rule that the arrest of a vessel based on a maritime claim shall be exclusively decreed either by the Ukrainian court in the place where the vessel is or by the court at the place of the vessel's registration. This provides a rather clear regime of arrest of Ukrainian vessels in the Ukrainian ports. In other words, if there is a maritime claim prescribed by MSC against the Ukrainian ship owner – the MSC arrest rules are applicable and the court can decree an arrest where the vessel is situated or registered. However, one should be cautious that the list of maritime claims in MSC is based on the Geneva Convention and thus, is different from the list of maritime claims set in the Brussels Convention ratified by Ukraine.

The question arises in this respect whether the Brussels Convention regime can be used for arresting a Ukrainian ship in Ukraine, and not the MSC regime taking into account that Ukraine is a party to Brussels Convention. In theory, the answer can be given in the positive since the international treaties supersede national legislation. However, it cannot be guaranteed that Ukrainian courts will apply Brussels Convention instead of MSC, as these two Acts do not fully coincide. Such legislative ambiguity can create the situation in which the Ukrainian judges would have to be convinced every time to use the Brussels Convention regime instead of MSC. It is submitted that such ambiguity can only be solved by amending the relevant provisions in the MSC and bringing it in line with the Brussels Convention.

§4. General Procedural Rules of the CivPC and ComPC

298. As seen from above, in case a vessel flying a flag of a state party to the Brussels Convention needs to be arrested in the Ukrainian port, the Brussels Convention is applicable. If this is a Ukrainian vessel, then the MSC regime or the Brussels Convention regime might be applicable. If the vessel that needs to be arrested in the Ukrainian port is neither a Ukrainian nor flying a flag of the state party to the Brussels Convention then the general procedural rules of the CivPC and ComPC become applicable.

According to the general jurisdiction rules the arrest can be decreed only by the court that has jurisdiction to decide the underlying claim on the merits.

There are two possible instances and two possible sets of procedural rules that can be used to decree arrest of a ship as movable property of a debtor before the basis of enforcement of claim is obtained:

- General Court, based on procedural rules of the CivPC.
- Commercial Court, based on procedural rules of ComPC.

299. As has been already mentioned above, the Ukrainian courts have a right to decree arrest when they have jurisdiction to decide the underlying claim on the merits.

300. When arrest is sought of a ship, flying a foreign flag of a country that is not a party to the Brussels Convention, jurisdiction of general or commercial court on the merits is established by the special jurisdiction provisions of CivPC (regarding general courts), ComPC (regarding commercial courts), as well as of Law of Ukraine on International Private Law dated 18 March 2004, No. 1618-IV (hereinafter – the Law on International Private Law) which contains the rules of jurisdiction of the Ukrainian courts (both general and commercial) in cases with foreign element (i.e., when the defendant is foreign).

301. According to the mentioned Acts, Ukrainian courts (general or commercial) will have jurisdiction on the merits in the following cases:[134]

(1) if the parties to the dispute have chosen a Ukrainian court as a dispute resolution venue (Article 76, section 1 of the Law on International Private Law). General or commercial court will have a jurisdiction in such case. Not long ago, the SCCU (court of cassation instance in the system of commercial courts) refused to recognize this as a ground for jurisdiction of commercial courts in the disputes with foreign element, as general jurisdiction rules of the ComPC do not stipulate it.[135] However, the SCU, which is the highest judicial body in the system of courts of general jurisdiction, has recently changed this position.[136] According to the position of the SCU, Article 76 of the Law on International

134. V. Mallayev, *Ship Arrest in Ukraine.*
135. SCCU Explanation dated 31 May 2002, SCCU Rulings dated 27 Feb. 2007 and 20 Mar. 2007.
136. See the SCU Rulings dated 22 May 2007 and 17 Apr. 2007.

Private Law can establish jurisdiction for commercial courts and they do not have a right to withdraw a case, if the parties have chosen Ukrainian court as a dispute resolution venue. Naturally, the same must apply for general courts – their jurisdiction also can be established by Article 76 of Law on International Private Law;

(2) if there are several defendants, any claims if one of the defendants is domiciled in Ukraine (Article 15, section 3 of ComPC, Article 113 of CivPC). General or commercial court in the district of domicile of the defendant will have jurisdiction;

(3) claims regarding possession, title or ownership of a ship or a share in a ship (Article 16, section 2 of ComPC). Commercial court in the district of Ukraine where the ship is situated will have exclusive jurisdiction;

(4) claims arising out of the contracts of employment with ship's crew if a claimant is domiciled in Ukraine (Article 110, section 1 of CivPC). General court in the place of domicile of the claimant will have jurisdiction;

(5) claims arising out of the collisions and compensation for salvage (Article 110, section 11 of CivPC). General court of the place in Ukraine where the ship is situated will have jurisdiction;

(6) claims arising out of the loss of life or personal injury to a person who is domiciled in Ukraine or if the accident took place in Ukraine (Article 110, section 3 of CivPC, Article 76 section 3, section 5 of Law on International Private Law). General court in the place of domicile of the claimant or in the place of accident will have jurisdiction;

(7) claims arising out of the damage caused in Ukraine to property of private persons or legal entities as a result of operation of a ship (Article 110, section 6 of CivPC, Article 76, section 3 of Law on International Private Law). General court in the place where the damage was caused will have jurisdiction, if CivPC provisions are applied. The Law on International Private Law can establish jurisdiction for commercial court as well;

(8) claims arising out of any contract to be executed in Ukraine (Article 110, section 8 of CivPC). General court in the place of enforcement will have jurisdiction;

(9) any claims if the debtor owns any movable or real property which can be seized in the process of enforcement of judgment, that is, located in Ukraine or if the foreign debtor has a representation office or affiliated company in Ukraine (Article 76, section 2 of the Law on International Private Law). This is a very important provision that in cases involving foreign element, as soon as the ship (property) is in Ukraine and it is owned by debtor, Ukrainian courts will have jurisdiction to decide the case on its merits.

302. It has to be mentioned, that not so long ago the Ukrainian commercial courts did not tend to apply provisions of the Law on International Private Law to establish jurisdiction (see above in paragraph 1). As has been mentioned above, such approach was changed by the SCU and now is clearly accepted by the SCCU in the Ruling dated 18 March 2008. The Ruling related to the case of arrest of a foreign ship REEF in the Ukrainian port to secure a debt in connection with a contract of purchase and sale of the named ship. The SCCU provided that the presence of the vessel owned by a foreign debtor in the Ukrainian port gave a ground for jurisdiction of the Ukrainian commercial court in accordance with Article 76(2) of the Law on International Private Law. The named Ruling of the SCCU is clearly progressive providing more favourable conditions of arrest of foreign ships in Ukraine. Though it must be borne in mind that Ukraine is a civil law country, where precedents do not have a binding force. Therefore, the named Ruling cannot guarantee analogous application of the provisions of the Law on International Private Law by all commercial courts of first instance (not speaking of general courts). Though such application now seems to be very probable.

303. According to the general provisions on arrest of property in the CivPC (Article 152) and ComPC (Article 43-2, Article 67), objects of arrest can only be the property owned by a debtor. Therefore, it is not possible to arrest a ship that is not owned by the debtor (though Article 43 of the MSC provides that a bareboat chartered vessel can be arrested if the bareboat charterer is liable for the claim, but provisions of the MSC, as has been shown above, are not widely used by the Ukrainian courts). In this connection, other ships (and any other property) owned by a debtor can be arrested.

304. The Ukrainian legislation does not contain an exact definition of arrest of property, but out of the general court practice the following definition can be given: arrest of property is a preliminary prohibition to dispose of property (or financial means) until the decision regarding the status of such property is taken (by court or other competent authority).

305. As can be seen from above, a claim regarding arrest of ships, depending on the jurisdiction ground can be filed either to a general court (typically – claims from natural persons, like injured seamen, etc.) or to a commercial court (typically – claims from legal entities). Different sets of procedural rules (CivPC or ComPC) will be applicable depending on in which court the arrest is sought.

306. Arrest of a ship (and any other property) can be decreed as a *measure of securing a claim* and as a pre-trial *measure of restraint*. Arrest as a *measure of securing a claim* can be decreed by general or commercial court. Procedural rules on its application are contained in the CivPC. The ComPC stipulates arrest as a *measure of securing a claim*, but does not contain specific procedural rules; therefore, the rules of CivPC are used basing on the principle of analogy. Arrest as a *measure of restraint* can be decreed only by a commercial court under the procedural rules of ComPC.

307. The main difference between these two measures is the following:

- Arrest as a measure of securing a claim is not a pre-trial measure and can be applied at any stage of the proceedings on the claim (Article 151, section 3 of CivPC, Article 67 of ComPC). It means that arrest application can be filed to general or commercial court *not earlier than together with the claim.* This creates several problems. The first problem is the time frames – general court is obliged to take a decision on acceptance of the claim within three days after receiving the application (Article 122, section 3 of CivPC); in the commercial court this period is five days (Article 64 of ComPC). The decision regarding application of a measure of securing a claim is taken at the same day, when the application is received, provided that the claim is accepted. The second problem is that the claim will not be accepted by the court if it has no jurisdiction or can be returned if the formal requirements are not met.

– Arrest as a pre-trial measure of restraint is much more favourable for arrest of ships. First, it can be decreed by a commercial court *before* the underlying claim is filed. Second, arrest must be decreed by the commercial court within *two days* from the date of application (Article 43-4, section 1 of ComPC). The underlying claim must be filed within *five days* after the arrest is decreed (Article 43-3 of ComPC), and if the claim is accepted, measure of restraint becomes a measure of securing a claim with all legal consequences. If the claim is not filed within this period or not accepted by the court on jurisdictional or formal grounds, the arrest can be stopped (Article 43-9 of ComPC). The above-mentioned rules of ComPC create a possibility for a potential claimant to arrest a ship, even if the commercial court does not have a jurisdiction with respect to the underlying claim. In such case the creditor (claimant) has at least five days, before the underlying claim must be filed, to convince the debtor to pay. But the claimant has to remember the strict liability for the damages caused to the defendant by arrest (see below).

308. CivPC and ComPC stipulate a number of legal requirements and conditions applicable both to measures of securing a claim and to measures of restraint:

(1) the most important is the requirement of cause of arrest that cannot be avoided under the Ukrainian legislation. The claimant has a burden of proof that if the arrest is not decreed, his rights will be violated or that the decision of the court on the underlying claim will be impossible/difficult to enforce. It is always in the discretion of the court whether to accept the cause of arrest or not;
(2) the court can require the claimant/potential claimant to post a security for potential damages to the defendant. The court defines the sum of security to be transferred to a deposit account of the court. It must be mentioned that in practice it does not happen often – the better evidences presented to the court, the better chances to avoid the payment of security;[137]
(3) it is in the discretion of the court to decide whether the arrest as a measure of restraint should be granted ex parte and the potential claimant has a burden to prove such necessity;
(4) the measure of securing a claim must be proportionate to the underlying claim (Article 152, section 3 of CivPC). It is in the discretion of the court to decide whether the measure sought is proportionate. Arrest of property can be rejected if the value of property, arrest of which is sought, is much bigger than the size of the underlying claim. Therefore, a ship can hardly be arrested if the size of

137. V. Mallayev, *Ship Arrest in Ukraine.*

claim is not significant. Moreover, the court, in its discretion, can decree a partial securing of a claim;

(5) claimant/potential claimant is strictly liable for the damages incurred by defendant in connection with arrest if the arrest is stopped, the underlying claim is not accepted or the decision on it is taken not in favour of the claimant.

309. Arrest is subject to immediate enforcement according to the general provisions of the Ukrainian law. According to the Law of Ukraine on Enforcement Proceedings dated 21 April 2009, No. 606-XIV, the property can be arrested if the property is found within the district of a specific law enforcement officer in Ukraine (Article 20). Therefore, the ship must be in the Ukrainian port in order to make any enforcement possible.

310. The basic effect of arrest of a ship is that the defendant loses his right to dispose of it or use it in any way during the time when the claim exists or until the decision on the said claim is taken.

§5. Problematic Issues and Ways to Solve Them

311. As can be seen from above, there are three sets of rules which can be applicable to arrest on ships in Ukraine, depending on the country of the ship's flag. Ratification of the Brussels Convention has clearly a positive effect on the transparency and predictability of Ukrainian legal environment related to arrest of ships. Nevertheless, there are still a number of practical problems since the named three sets of legal regimes do not coincide with each other and sometimes even contradict. These problems are states as follows:

(1) Non-application by the Ukrainian courts of the rules on arrest of ships in MSC even with respect to the Ukrainian ships to which the arrest rules in MSC clearly apply (Article 14(1) of MSC). This does not appear to be a diligent practice of the Ukrainian courts. The courts are obliged to use the special rules of MSC (as they constitute *lex specialis* with respect to the general procedural rules and have to prevail) and, thus, to arrest only the Ukrainian ships on the basis of a maritime claim as Article 42 of the MSC expressly provides that the ships can be arrested *only* to secure the maritime claims. But, unfortunately, the court practice shows that provisions of the MSC are simply ignored by the Ukrainian courts.

This can be illustrated by the SCCU Ruling dated 22 March 2007. In this case the SCCU in a cassation procedure has considered the Ruling of the Appeal Commercial Court that confirmed the Decision of the District Commercial Court regarding arrest of the ship *Vitaliy Bainov* flying the Ukrainian flag as a measure of securing a claim. The defendant argued that the court violated Article 42 of the MSC, as the claimant did not provide that he had a maritime claim against the defendant. Notably, it was stated in the application to the SCCU and was ignored by it. The SCCU in its Ruling stated that arrest was enforced in accordance with the general procedural rules of the ComPC and, accordingly, was lawful. Such position of the courts is not acceptable, but predictable as the norms of MSC do not contain provisions on the arrest procedure and ComPC and CivPC do not have any references to the MSC in the parts dealing with arrest. Thus, the existence of two parallel sets of legal rules, application of one of which does not explicitly exclude the application of another creates a possibility for their unpredictable application by the Ukrainian courts.

In order to solve this problem arrest of ships in Ukraine shall be considered as a specific case of arrest of property that shall be decreed according to the general procedural rules on arrest with special reservations regarding arrest of ships. Notably, specific references to the provisions of MSC regarding arrest of ships must be made in ComPC and CivPC in order to make provisions of MSC effective and to allow the arrest of Ukrainian ships based solely on maritime claims. Additionally, the amendments shall be made to other legislative Acts of Ukraine, namely the Law of Ukraine on Enforcement in order to provide a special status to ships.

(2) Another practical problem can be connected with the fact, that the Brussels Convention after its ratification in Ukraine was not incorporated into any of the existing Ukrainian laws or Codes. This creates a situation of three different legal regimes which can be applicable to ship arrests in Ukraine and thus creating a fruitful soil for potential ambiguity and incorrect application by the Ukrainian judges. This situation can be rectified by incorporating the provisions of the Brussels Convention into the Ukrainian legislation, namely in the MSC and CivPC and ComPC.

Chapter 5. Master and Seamen

§1. General Background

312. This chapter covers the legal status and employment conditions of seamen and the special position of a ship master in Ukraine. A short historical overview of seafaring tradition in Ukraine is given. Taking into account that these days the majority of the Ukrainian seafarers are working on board the ships flying a foreign flag or the so-called *flag of convenience*, international legal framework regulating the employment relationships of seafarers is discussed simultaneously with the national legislation applicable to seafarers working on ships flying the Ukrainian flag.

313. It is noted that 'seamen, throughout history, have been treated with respect, admiration and gratitude after the fact, but often harshly and unfairly at the moment. The various ancient sea codes attempted to provide seamen with rights against their employers'.[138] The world merchant fleet comprises 1.4 million seafarers of whom two-thirds work within multi-ethnic crews.[139] It is estimated to be in the order of 466,000 officers and 721,000 ratings.[140] Due to the international character of shipping, seafarer often works on aboard a ship that is registered in one country flying the flag of another country and managed from a company registered in the third country, etc. Eastern Europe has recently become an increasingly large supplier of seafarers with high numbers from countries including Ukraine, Croatia and Latvia.[141]

314. A general increasing shortage of seafarers is currently observed. Especially it concerns seafarers employed in the EU shipping industry.[142] The reasons can be named as follows. Seafaring becomes less attractive and more challenging in the twenty-first century. Modern ships are becoming larger and more sophisticated, allowing loading/discharge much faster than before and by that limiting the time ashore. Moreover, seafarers face many difficulties and challenges of a life, at sea such as harsh weather, a threat of piracy, long and frequent absence from home and families, etc. On the contrary seafaring is still attractive in developing countries, including Ukraine. The Ukrainian flagged ships cannot provide Ukrainian seafarers with permanent job; therefore, they are forced to search for employment opportunities abroad. Bearing in mind considerably low average salaries in Ukraine, seafaring is one of the opportunities to get a sufficient income to support the families. Therefore, unsurprisingly that Ukraine ranks 4 of 133 states supplying masters to the global fleet.[143]

---

138. W. Tetley, *Maritime Liens and Claims* 267 (2d ed., International Shipping Publications 1998).
139. O.C. Jensen et al., '*Working Conditions in International Seafaring*' 56 Occupational Med. 393–397 (2006).
140. Numbers and Nationality of World's Seafarers www.marisec.org/shippingfacts/worldtrade/world-seafarers.php, 1 May 2011.
141. *Ibid.*
142. V. Power, *EC Shipping Law* 241 (2d ed., London, Hong Kong: LLP 1998).
143. J.A.C. Cartner, R.P. Fiske & T.L. Leiter, *Law of Ship Master* 674 (Informa 2009).

315. In a campaign to attract entrants to the shipping industry under the name 'Go to sea!' it was observed that 'seafarers provide a vital service to an industry that contributes significantly to global and sustainable development and prosperity by carrying the world's commerce safely, securely, efficiently and at a fraction of the environmental impact and cost of other modes of transport'. The Periodic Baltic and International Maritime Council (BIMCO)/International Shipping Federation (ISF) studies have highlighted an anticipated shortage of some 27,000 officers worldwide by the year 2015, while a recent study predicts a shortage of up to 83,900 even sooner.[144]

316. An already mentioned threat of piracy became an evident danger in a number of regions and it is also one of the restrictive factors for young people to study marine science and work at sea. The piracy attacks in the Gulf of Aden and territorial waters of Somalia concern Ukrainian seafarers directly. In the majority of seized vessels the Ukrainian seafarers worked on board a ship. Among them, the seizure of m/v *Faina* flying the Ukrainian flag with some twenty crew members onboard should be mentioned. She was hijacked by more than fifty Somali pirates in 2008 and released after being held captive for five months for ransom. Another attack was made on m/v *Ariana* with the majority of Ukrainian seafarers that had been kept for almost eight months by the pirates.

§2. Historical Background

317. History of the Ukrainian fleet and seafaring traditions dates back to the old times. Before the rise of the Kievan Rus the southern part of great inland Dneiper-Volkhov waterway started to develop. Amid the deep forests and bogs the deep-water rivers such as Dnieper, Volga, Zapadnaya Dvina, Volkhov with its inflows formed a network of almost continuous merchant ways connecting the Baltic, the Black and the Caspian Seas. In the Kievan Rus sailing at rivers and lakes was a major means of movement. This apparently favoured the development of maritime features in population.[145]

318. Our ancestors were familiar with necessary knowledge of marine geography and seafaring; otherwise, it would not have been possible to accomplish maritime campaigns. The first mentions of the Byzantium historicists about the nautical art of eastern Slavs appeared in the seventh century. In 765 the Byzantium Emperor Konstantin V accomplished a campaign on Bulgarians on vessels of the Russian construction.[146] In 907, Grand Prince *(Knyaz)* Oleg, as the chronicle tells us, accomplished a big campaign against Byzantium on 2,000 ships that sailed down the Dnieper and on the Black Sea to Constantinople. The overseas boats, barks and canoes were mentioned in the *Russian Truth* in the first half of the eleventh century.

144. IMO in association with the ILO, BIMCO,ICS/ISF,INTERCARGO INTERTANKO, ITF, www.imo.org/includes/blastDataOnly.asp/data_id%3D23804/Gotosea!ampaigndocument.pdf.
145. See at www.nashflot.ru/page/way/0, 15 Nov. 2010.
146. See at www.nashflot.ru/page/way/0,15 Nov. 2010.

319. In the sixteenth century a large military force began to form in the southern Ukraine. These were the *Cossacks* who defended the borders of Ukraine from attacks of Turks and Tatars. At the beginning they did not have their own fleet that prevented them to influence events at sea, so they started the creation of the fleet. They used the wooden boats or the so-called *seagulls*. Marine service was very exhausting and only self-possessed *Cossacks* could bear the service. Every time a number of young *Cossacks* joined the fleet to be trained to maritime campaigns. It was strictly forbidden for *Cossacks* to drink alcohol during those campaigns. Therefore, if it was discovered that some *Cossack* had alcohol beverages he was thrown overboard.

320. In December 1917 the Ukrainian General Secretariat of Maritime Affairs was established and further renamed to the Ukrainian Maritime Ministry under the Decree of the Maritime Agency dated 3 March 1918. The temporary Law on Fleet was enacted on 14 January 1918. However, one of the part of that Law abolished mandatory enrolment to the fleet and introduced a voluntarily one that weakened the fleet's forces.

§3. Ukrainian Shipping Today

321. Ukrainian seafarers are also demanded these days. Following the dissolution of the USSR, a great number of Ukrainian ships were either sold for debts or still remained arrested in foreign ports. The state-owned Black Sea Shipping Company has only seven ships with a displacement tonnage of about 50,000 tonnes out of its formerly operated 260 cargo ships with a displacement tonnage of 3 million tonnes and over thirty passenger ships.[147] A similar situation is observed in the Danube Shipping Company and the Azov Sea Shipping Company. Accordingly, thousands of skilled seafarers lost their jobs in the beginning of the nineties. However, that opened a border to the western world which did not exist for almost seventy years and allowed Ukrainian seafarers to look for a job onboard foreign ships. First crewing agencies started to operate in then independent Ukraine mostly in port cities; however, at that time very few seafarers were ready to start working on foreign ships within multi-ethnic crews. Those who did benefited from finding a job despite the massive unemployment and economic crisis in Ukraine. That also brought millions of dollars in the country in a form of seafarers' wages.

322. Ukraine is one of the largest crew supply states to the world maritime fleet: the estimated number of Ukrainian seafarers is 45,000.[148] By a crew supply State is

147. Speech of the Ukrainian Parliament Commissioner for Human Rights at the Presentation to the Ukrainian Parliament of the Special Report on the Status of Observance and Protection of the Rights of Ukrainian Citizens Abroad (2 Apr. 2003), see at www.ombudsman.kiev.ua/ om_00.htm.
148. 'Safer and Cleaner Shipping in the European Union', EMSA. www.ecoports.com/ContentFiles/ emsa_brochure_en.pdf, 2006.

meant a State that through the agencies situated in that state regularly recruits seafarers and supplies them as crews for ships, usually foreign ships. Crew supply States are typically developing States.[149]

323. By the estimates of the Ministry of Social Policy, the Trade Union of Maritime Transport Workers and the Council of the Federation of Maritime Trade Unions, the number of permanently unemployed seafarers is over 70,000.[150] Despite this number, every year hundreds of young people graduate from maritime universities and colleges in Ukraine. A monitoring conducted by the Commissioner for Human Rights proved that a large number of crewing companies are set up for a short period of time and none of them is interested in their activities being governed by any laws.[151] The gaps in the legislation and absence of State control of crewing agencies favour such practice.

§4. Legal Regulation

324. At the international level, International Maritime Organization (IMO) has adopted more than forty Conventions and Protocols several of which implement standards that guarantee protection to seafarers in their working conditions. The most important among them are the Convention for the Unification of Certain Rules of Law Relating to Assistance and Salvage at Sea, 1974 (SOLAS) as amended by Protocols thereto, The International Convention on Standards of Training, Certification and Watch keeping for Seafarers 1978, amended in 1995 (the STCW Convention) and the International Management Code for the Safe Operation of Ships and for Pollution Prevention 1993 (ISM Code) adopted under Chapter 9 of the SOLAS Convention.

325. All the mentioned conventions do not impose obligations on crew supply States. In the case of the International Labour Organization (ILO) seafarers' Conventions, no Convention refers explicitly to its provisions being implemented by crew supply States.[152] Ukraine acceded to the STCW Convention through the enactment of the Ukrainian Law dated 1 November 1996, No. 464/96-BP.

326. Ukraine is also a party to the ILO Convention C147 Merchant Shipping (Minimum Standards) Convention, 1976. The provisions of the MSC apply to seafarers working onboard Ukrainian ships. The legal status of ship's crew is defined in Article 48 of the MSC. It is stated in particular that the legal status of the crew of a ship that is flying the Ukrainian flag, as well as the relationships among crew members and a ship owner are regulated by the Ukrainian legislation. The ship's crew is composed of a master, other officers and ratings. The officers in its turn

149. D. Fitzepatrick & M. Anderson, *Seafarer's rights* 165 (Oxford U. Press 2005).
150. Speech of the Ukrainian Parliament Commissioner for Human Rights at the Presentation to the Ukrainian Parliament of the Special Report on the Status of Observance and Protection of the Rights of Ukrainian Citizens Abroad (2 Apr. 2003), see at www.ombudsman.kiev.ua/ om_00.htm.
151. *Ibid.*
152. See D. Fitzepatrick & M. Anderson, *Seafarer's rights* 160, 165 (Oxford U. Press, 2005).

include a master, mates, ship's engineers, electric engineers, radio specialists, ship's doctor and boatswain. The owner may add other ship's specialists to the officers. The ratings consist of the persons performing official duties on a ship and not belonging to the officers.[153] A minimum number of crew members that permits a vessel to be put to sea are established by the Ministry of Infrastructure depending on type, region of sailing, designation of a ship and in accordance with the Ukrainian legislation.[154]

327. The legislation in many countries determines the nationality requirement to the crew members or separate crew members holding a particular post. For example, in the former USSR, *all* the crew members should be the citizens of the USSR in accordance with the MSC of USSR, Article 41. The MSC of the Russian Federation provides that the officers shall be the citizens of the Russian Federation as stipulated by Article 56.According to the MSC, crew members of the ship registered in the SRU and SBU can be the citizens of any state. However, a master shall be the citizen of Ukraine.[155] For instance, in the EU a state may protect the jobs of its own seafarers by prohibiting the employment of non-nationals to perform certain tasks (e.g., masters) or even all tasks. Such restrictions formed the basis of a European Court of Justice (ECJ) decision in *Commission v. France.*[156] This refers to the concept of non-discrimination on the basis of nationality and free movements of workers in the EU. Based on this, in Sweden for instance, a requirement for certain shipmasters to be Swedish nationals has been replaced by being citizens of a European Economic Area (EEA) country.[157]

§5. Employment

I. Qualifications

328. Pursuant to the UNCLOS, Article 91, ships have the nationality of the State whose flag they are entitled to fly. Additionally, every State has an obligation to effectively exercise its jurisdiction and control in administrative, technical and social matters over ships flying its flag. The flag States shall ensure safety at sea with regard, among others, the manning of ships, labour conditions and the training of crews taking into account the applicable international instruments (Article 94(3)(b)). These measures include that each ship is in charge of a master and officers who possess appropriate qualifications, in particular in seamanship, navigation, communications and marine engineering, and that the crew is appropriate in qualification and numbers for the type, size, machinery and equipment of the ship.[158]

153. MSC, Art. 50.
154. MSC, Art. 50.
155. MSC, Art. 53.
156. Case 167/73 [1974] ECR 359.
157. Vessel Safety Ordinance, Ch. 4, s. 2, see at Tiberg & Schelin on *Maritime and Transport Law* 76.
158. UNCLOS, Art. 94, s. 4(6).

329. The 1974 SOLAS Convention requires that all ships shall be sufficiently and efficiently manned (Chapter 5, Safety of Navigation, Regulation 14). Under the ILO Convention No. 147 of 1976 concerning the Minimum Standards in Merchant Ships each contracting State shall ensure that seafarers employed on ships registered in its territory are properly qualified or trained for the duties for which they are engaged (Article 2(e)).

330. At the international level STCW Convention was first to prescribe the minimum standards relating to training, certification and watch keeping for seafarers. One especially important feature of the STCW Convention is that it applies to ships of non-States parties when visiting ports of States that are parties to the Convention.[159] Ukraine joined the Convention on 1 November 1996.[160] The scope of application is provided in Article III and covers seafarers serving on board seagoing ships entitled to fly the flag of a Party except for those serving on board warships, fishing vessels, pleasure yachts and wooden ships.

331. Under the Maritime Labour Convention 2006, Regulation 1.3, seafarers shall not work on a ship unless they are trained or certified as competent or otherwise qualified to perform their duties. They also shall not be permitted to work on a ship unless they have successfully completed training for personal safety on board ship.

332. The requirements as to qualifications of crew members and their state of health are provided by Articles 51–52 of the MSC. The crew members shall be fit for working onboard a ship. The certificate of fitness for working onboard a ship is issued by an institution of the Ministry of Health of Ukraine pursuant to the regulations set by this Ministry.[161] In the Ukrainian legislation,[162] the necessary ranks are required in order to hold the post of a master and other officers. Those ranks are set by the Regulation on Ranks of Officers of Seagoing Vessels and the Order of Their Awarding established by the Ministry of Infrastructure. Such an award evidences by issuing diplomas or quality certificates after a successful passing of exams in the state qualification commission. The deprivation of ranks and withdrawal of diplomas or qualification certificates is permitted only upon the court's judgment.

333. The Unified State Register of Documents of Seafarers in Ukraine was created in 2003.[163] This Register is a database of all issued certificates, diplomas, qualification certificates and other documents on the territory of Ukraine that certify seafarers' qualification in line with requirements of the STCW 1978 and stored in

159. D. Fitzepatrick & M.Anderson, *Seafarer's rights* 160, 52 (Oxford U. Press 2005).
160. Law of Ukraine on Accession to the Convention on Standards of Training, Certification and Watch keeping for Seafarers dated 1 Nov. 1996, No. 464/96-BP.
161. MSC, Art. 52.
162. MSC, Art. 51.
163. Regulation on Keeping the Unified State Register of Documents of Seafarers, approved by the Order of the MTC dated 8 Jan. 2003, No. 3, registered at the Ministry of Justice on 4 Feb. 2003, No. 86/7407.

paper and electronic version. It covers the documents of seafarers working on sea-going vessels and have the right to work on board a vessel under the flag of State Member of the IMO.

II. Maritime Labour Convention

334. More than thirty conventions and recommendations with regard to working conditions of crews have been adopted by the ILO making up the International Seafarers' Code.[164] The Maritime Labour Convention was adopted in 2006 and ratified by forty-nine States. It enters into force on August 20, 2013. It consolidates and updates more than sixty-five international labour standards related to seafarers adopted over the last eighty years. Article II(2) lays down that except as expressly provided otherwise, this Convention applies to all seafarers. Article IV.2 enshrines that every seafarer has a right to fair employment. Further, this Article also states that each member shall ensure, within the limits of its jurisdiction, that the seafarers' employment and social rights set out in the preceding paragraphs of this Article are fully implemented in accordance with the requirements of this Convention. In particular, each member shall implement and enforce laws or regulations or other measures that it has adopted to fulfil its commitments under this Convention with respect to ships and seafarers under its jurisdiction.

335. An active discussion of possible accession of Ukraine to the Maritime Labour Convention (MLC) 2006 and its political, economic and social consequences is going on within various maritime quarters in Ukraine. The major alert is raised by the fact that Ukraine is not a party to a number of the ILO Conventions. Thus, upon accession to the MLC 2006 Ukraine will take the obligations to comply with more than thirty ILO Conventions. Ukraine is not ready to undertake such obligations. Moreover, the scope of application will not cover the seafarers working on ships under the flag of convenience. That means that accession to the Convention will not influence the protection of social-labour interests of the seafarers. The MLC prohibits charging the fee for the intermediary services. However, the Commercial Code of Ukraine sets in Article 3 that rendering the services of a price character has a price expression. Only few crewing agencies out of some 200 registered in Odessa can state that the ship owner covers their expenses on intermediary activity, since the state budget cannot cover those expenses.

III. Crewing in Ukraine

336. The Recruitment and Placement of Seafarers Convention, 1996 (No. 179), Article 4(1)(a), provides *inter alia* that no fees or other charges for recruitment or for providing employment to seafarers are borne directly or indirectly, in whole or in part, by the seafarer; for this purpose, costs of the national statutory medical examination, certificates, a personal travel document and the national seafarer's

164. Churchill, *The Law of the Sea*, 270.

book shall not be deemed to be 'fees or other charges for recruitment'. Ukraine is neither a party to the above-mentioned Convention nor there is legislation in force which regulates the legal status and protection of seafarers working on foreign flagged vessels. The term 'crewing' is not defined in the Ukrainian legislation. The Law of Ukraine on Enterprises Acting as Intermediaries for the Employment of Citizens Abroad is not yet adopted in Ukraine despite the recommendation of the Ukrainian Commissioner of the Human Rights.[165] The Draft on Enterprises Acting as Intermediaries for the Employment of Citizens Abroad was registered with *the Verkhovna Rada* on 10 December 2002. However, there is an Order of the Ministry of Social Policy on Approval of Licensing Conditions of Conducting the Intermediary Activity in Employment Abroad dated 6 September 2010 No. 272.

337. The terms of hiring a vessel's crew, their rights and obligations, the employment's conditions on a vessel, wages, social and living conditions at sea and in port and the terms of dismissal are determined by the Ukrainian legislation, the MSC, the Labour Code of Ukraine,[166] the Statutes of Service on Vessels of the Ministry of Maritime Fleet of the USSR which is still in force in Ukraine,[167] general and branch tariff agreements, collective and labour agreements (contracts).[168]

338. Taking into account that Article 43 of the Constitution of Ukraine grants everyone the right to labour, including the possibility to earn one's living by labour that he/she freely chooses or to which he/she freely agrees, the majority of seafarers choose to work abroad.

339. The regulation of the labour relations of Ukrainian citizens working abroad is contained in the Labour Code of Ukraine. Article 8 states in the broad terms that the labour relations of the citizens of Ukraine working abroad and the labour relations of foreign citizens working for entities in Ukraine are conducted in accordance with the Law of Ukraine on International Private Law, Part VIII. Article 52 maintains that the law applicable to the labour relations is the law of a country where the work in undertaken (performed), unless otherwise provided by other laws or international treaties ratified by Ukraine. Further, Article 53 reads that labour relations of Ukrainian citizens working abroad are subject to the Ukrainian law in case when:

– the Ukrainian citizens working in the diplomatic services abroad;

165. See Speech of The Ukrainian Parliament Commissioner for Human Rights (2 Apr. 2003), see at www.ombudsman.kiev.ua/om_00.htm.
166. The Labour Code of Ukraine dated 10 Dec. 1971, No. 322-VIII. Despite being adopted in USSR, it has been amended a number of times by the *Verkhovna Rada* of Ukraine.
167. Resolution of *Verkhovna Rada* on Temporary Application of Acts of the USSR Legislation on the Territory of Ukraine in Part, where they are not in Conflict with the Ukrainian Legislation dated September 1991, No. 1545-XII, the Statute of Service on Vessels of the Ministry of Maritime Fleet of the USSR approved by the Order dated 9 Jan. 1976, No. 6.
168. MSC, Art. 54.

- when they entered into with employers – natural persons or legal entities of Ukraine labour contracts on performing work abroad, provided that it is in compliance with the legislation of a country where the work is performed; and
- in cases provided by the international treaties.

340. Seafarers intended to work for the foreign ship owners conclude labour contracts in Ukraine through a crewing agency, which serves only as an intermediary in relations between a seafarer and a ship owner, and does not act as an employer. This implies that they are not considered as being employed in terms of the Ukrainian legislation. Considering that one employment contract might last longer than five months the seafarers do not fall under the definition of a *resident* for the purpose of taxation, since they stay in a country less than 183 days a year. Therefore, the length of their service is not counted for the retired pay in contrast to the Ukrainian citizens working in Ukraine. However, they are still entitled to the minimum pension benefits provided by the legislation. A similar situation exists regarding medical care. Earlier in the Ukrainian SSR a system of health institutions and health resorts was established where seafarers and their families could receive the necessary medical examination and treatment. All the seafarers were granted an access to the mentioned institutions.

IV. Working Hours

341. The norms on duration of working hours and hours of rest are stipulated in the Labour Code of Ukraine (Article 50). Chapters 4 and 5 contain more detailed provisions on that matter. However, these norms have a general character and concern the working hours for any profession. The specific norms are enshrined in the Statute on Service on Vessels of the Ministry of Maritime Fleet of the USSR and the Statute on Service on Fishing Vessels. Despite the mentioned number of Ukrainian seafarers, Ukraine is not a party to the ILO Convention (No. 180) concerning Seafarers' Hours of Work and the Manning of Ships (Geneva, 22 October 1996).

V. Repatriation of Crew Members

342. International framework on repatriation consists of the ILO Convention No. 23 1926 (entered into force in 1928). Ukraine is a party to the Convention since 1970.[169] It should be observed that the provisions of the Convention do not apply to a master of the ship and the trainees. The ILO Convention No. 166 on Repatriation of Seafarers 1987 provides a right of crew members to be repatriated. Ukraine is not a party to this Convention; however, the main principles of the Convention found its expression in Article 55 of the MSC. The repatriation of crew members for the owner's account is performed in the cases of dismissal at the owner's or authorized body's initiative; sickness and injury; ship's loss and if a ship owner cannot fulfil its obligations, according to the legislation of Ukraine and a contract.

169. See at www.ilo.org/ilolex/cgi-lex/ratifce.pl?C023.

343. Comparing provisions of the Ukrainian legislation with the named two conventions, it can be pointed out that the wording of provisions in the MSC differs to some extent from the international provisions. In particular, MSC makes an emphasis on *ship owner* who is covering the expenses, while the Convention simply states that the expenses on repatriation should not be conferred on a seafarer. The next important provision set in Article 5(2) of the Convention No. 23 says that 'when a seafarer is repatriated as a member of a crew, he is entitled to compensation for wages during all the time he worked onboard a ship'. In Ukrainian legislation is it stated that ship owner is responsible for ' ... paying the wages and benefits'; however, nothing is specified as to the period of time for which a seafarer is entitled to receive wages and benefits. This implies that a seafarer has to turn to the court in order to force a ship owner to fulfil his obligations. That leads to a situation when Ukrainian seafarers on board Ukrainian ships are compelled to wait for months for their full salaries and repatriation.

344. The ship owner repatriates the seafarer to the port specified in the contract or collective agreement, and in case of their absence – to the port of employment. The ship owner is responsible for the arrangements and the costs on repatriation, payments for the accommodation and food, salary and allowance, carriage of luggage and treatment (until the seafarer becomes transportable). If a ship owner cannot organize repatriation and pay the expenses, the Cabinet of Ministers shall authorize a body to carry out repatriation and pay the expenses. Afterwards that body shall recover all such expenses directly from the owner.[170]

345. Repatriation is also mentioned in Article 42 (maritime liens) in Chapter 4 of the MSC 'On Arrest of Ships'. According to it, a ship can be arrested based on the maritime lien regarding the 'wages and other means that are due to a master, officers and other crew members arising out their performance of service onboard a ship, including the expenses on repatriation'.[171] Article 358 continues with the priority of claims that are subject to be first of all liens, arising out of labour relations.

VI. Wages

346. According to the statistical data of the International Transport Federation (ITF), unpaid wages are the most common complaint that the ITF receives from seafarers. The ILO has adopted a number of Conventions concerning wages for seafarers, none of which has yet entered into force.[172] The ILO Protection of Wages Convention 1949 (ILO C95) is also relevant as it is one of the most ratified non-maritime ILO Conventions of general application. It prescribes that workers have the right to have wages paid directly to them and to have wages paid regularly.[173] In the event of the bankruptcy or judicial liquidation of employers, the ILO C 95

170. MSC, Art. 55.
171. MSC, Art. 42, s. 16.
172. D. Fitzepatrick & M.Anderson, *Seafarer's rights* 160, 71 (Oxford U. Press 2005).
173. ILO C95, Art. 12.

states that workers have the right to be treated as a privileged creditor in respect of certain wages. Thus, the responsibility may fall to the ship manager or manning agency or ship owner itself according to different national laws.[174]

347. The general conditions on wages are contained in Chapter VII of the Labour Code. In particular, Article 94 of the Labour Code stipulates that the issues of wages, right of workers to receive wages and their protection are determined by the Labour Code, the Law of Ukraine on Wages 1995[175] and other legal Acts.

§6. Master's Special Position

348. The legal status and regime of ship master enshrined in the MSC concerns only masters serving on the Ukrainian flagged ships. The two principal legal instruments comprise the MSC and the Statute of Service on Vessels of the Ministry of Maritime Fleet of the USSR defines organization of service and main obligations of crew members and a master of the ship.

349. Christopher Hills describes the Master of the ship:

> as a man of many parts. He needs to be part disciplinarian, part accountant, part lawyer and more than part seaman/navigator and also he needs to command the respect of his fellow men. He is servant at law, an agent both for his principal, the ship owner, and to some extent the owner of the goods he is carrying … He is absolutely responsible for the safety of his ship and remains in command regardless of whether or not his ship is in charge of a pilot at any given time.

350. The MSC contains separate provisions regarding the ship master in Part III, Chapter 2 of the MSC that relates to the status, rights and obligations of the ship master. According to it, the prime duty of a master is to administer the ship, including the navigation of it, undertaking of all measures necessary for securing the ship's safety, prevention of marine pollution, maintenance of discipline on a ship, prevention of causing of any damage to the ship, cargo and people onboard.

351. Master is recognized as a representative of the ship owner and cargo owner concerning the acts invoked by needs of a vessel, cargo or sailing, as well as actions concerning the entrusted property, provided that there are no other representatives of a ship owner or a cargo owner.[176] Articles 59–62 of the MSC particularly enshrines the master's obligations to render assistance to the persons in distress at sea, rendering assistance after the ships' collisions, assistance on providing the medical assistance to those who are in need of it and finally, the master's obligations in case of military threat, piracy, danger of ship's seizure. The master possesses a

174. ILO C95, Art. 15.
175. Law of Ukraine on Wages dated 24 Mar. No. 108/95-BP.
176. MSC, Art. 58.

right to own the fire arms and use it to protect himself and for the safety of persons and cargo onboard a ship.

352. In a situation when a vessel encounters an unavoidable loss, after having undertaken all the measures for saving the passengers, the master allows the crew to leave the vessel. The master shall leave the vessel in the last moment having undertaken all possible measure to save the log, radio and engine books, charts of the voyage, documents and valuables.[177] The master is also entitled to encourage and impose a disciplinary punishment on crew members, up to dismissal from a fulfilment of service.[178] A crew member cannot be appointed without the master's approval.[179] The master of a ship also serves as an agency of investigation in cases specified by the Ukrainian legislation. Additionally, a master certifies the fact of a child's birth and marriage; certifies testament and the fact of death.[180]

177. MSC, Art. 64.
178. MSC, Art. 65.
179. MSC, Art. 66.
180. MSC, Arts 70–71.

Chapter 6. Carriage by Sea

§1. General

353. This chapter deals with contracts for a vessel disposal (charter parties), contracts for the carriage of goods by sea (carriage under the bills of lading) and sea passenger contracts. The chapter includes legal provisions of the current Ukrainian legislation and the international treaties.

354. The majority of world trade is transported by sea nowadays. According to some estimation, around 90% of all trade is seaborne. Carriage of goods by sea is not solely limited to the actual carriage, but presents a highly complex system of relationships pertaining to the trade and transportation. Contract of sale of goods that is a basic agreement in export transactions, precedes the carriage. It defines the object of the contract, the price and method of payment, delivery terms and transportation. Depending on the delivery terms a seller or a buyer may appear as a shipper, charterer or consignee. This also defines the rights and obligations of the contracting parties and also their responsibility for late delivery, non-delivery, damage in goods, late payment, etc.[181]

355. When the contract of sale is concluded a seller or a buyer will enter into the contract of carriage with a carrier. Subject to the nature of goods there are two main categories of cargo, that is, bulk and general cargo. Usually the bulk cargo can take up the full cargo capacity of a vessel. Types of bulk cargo are dry bulk, bulk liquid and specialist bulk.[182] Such cargo requires special ships known as bulk carriers. In contrast to bulk cargo, general cargo requires some space on a ship, but not necessarily an entire ship. It includes containers, loose cargo, palletized cargo, refrigerated cargo, wheeled cargo.[183]

356. Ocean traffic usually distinguishes between liner transportation and tramp (free) shipping. In the liner shipping the ship owner (carrier) runs a regular service between more of less fixed ports and usually on a fixed time schedule, whereas in tramp shipping the vessels calls to different ports, where the owner can find a suitable cargo.

357. General norms on carriage by sea are contained in Part V of the MSC. The norms of law of obligation on transportation are dealt with in Chapter 64 of the Civil Code. Article 908 of the Civil Code envisages that the carriage of goods, passengers, their luggage, mail is carried out according to the contract of carriage.

181. The general regime of carriage in Ukraine will be discussed in more detail in Part III.
182. See further M.J. Rowbotham, *Introduction to Marine Cargo Management* 21 (Informa 2008); J.C.T. Chuah, *Law of International Trade: Cross-Border Commercial Transactions* 207 (4th ed., Sweet and Maxwell 2009).
183. J.C.T. Chuah, 208.

358. The activity pertaining to the carriage by sea is subject to license (see Part III). The transportation between Ukrainian ports (cabotage transportation) shall be performed by the ships flying the State flag of Ukraine, as well as by the ships flying a foreign flag, if there is a respective permit by the Ministry of Infrastructure. Transportation between Ukrainian and foreign (international transportation) ports may be performed by the ships flying the State flag of Ukraine, as well as by the ships flying a foreign flag upon respective agreement. It should be observed that in the Soviet times the carriers of goods by sea were the state shipping companies such as Black Sea Shipping Company, Azov Sea Shipping Company and others.

§2. Definition and Varieties of Charter Parties

359. The contract regarding the carriage of bulk cargo is known as a 'charter party'. This term originates from the Latin word *charta partita*, literally translated as 'a letter divided'.[184] Charter parties normally exist in tramp (free) shipping. Christopher Hills defines a charter party as 'the contract, a private contract between two principal parties, individual or corporate ... Like any other contract only those who entered into it can sue or be sued upon'.[185] It is a contract of hire of a ship in whole or in part for a long or short period of time or for a particular voyage. The owner places a vessel at the disposal of the charterer, against payment of agreed freight or hire by the charterer. Charter parties are not subject to the mandatory application of the Hague, the Hague-Visby Rules and the Hamburg Rules.

360. The most common forms for the time charters are New York Produce Exchange (NYPE)'93, BIMCO Uniform Time-Charter (BALTIME 39) (revised in 2001), Gencon, Polcoalvoy for the voyage charters and Barecon 2001 for bareboat charters, etc. However, there are a number of standard forms used in practice. BIMCO plays an important role in drafting of standard forms that have code names. In practice the parties usually make amendments in those forms. There is no international mandatory legal regime with regard to charter parties.

361. The Civil Code gives the definition of a charter party or contract of affreightment (*dogovor frakhtovania*) in Article 912. According to it one party (a freighter or an owner) shall dispose to all or part in one or several transport means to the other party (a charterer) for one or several trips to carry the goods, passengers, luggage and mail for payment.

362. Charter parties are also treated in Part VI of the MSC that is divided in two chapters: contracts for chartering a ship for a particular period of time and contracts for a ship lease. The definition of a charter party is envisaged in Article 203, pursuant to which a ship owner disposes its ship for a period of time to the charterer to carry passengers, goods and for other purposes of merchant shipping for payment (remuneration). The disposed vessel can be manned with a crew (time charter) or

184. M.J. Rowbotham, *Introduction to Marine Cargo Management*, 45.
185. C. Hill, *Maritime Law*, 177.

without it (bareboat chapter). The Ukrainian legislation does not define trip charters or charters for consecutive voyages.

363. A charter party shall be concluded in a written form. The following requisites must be indicated in the charter party: the parties, name of the vessel, its technical and exploitation details (cargo handling, cargo capacity and speed), region of sailing, aim of chartering, amount of freight, duration of charter party, place of delivery and redelivery of the vessel.

364. It is noteworthy that the MSC does not contain a separate chapter on voyage chartering; neither such a chapter exists in the MSC of the Russian Federation. The provisions of voyage charter are found in the chapter on the contract for the carriage of goods and not in the chapter devoted to the charter parties. On the contrary, there is a special chapter on the voyage chartering in the Maritime Codes of Norway and Sweden and extensive case law in common law countries. It can be surmised from the aforesaid that the provisions on the relations between the owner of the ship and the voyage charterer are not sufficiently regulated in the Ukrainian legislation. Moreover, the provisions regarding the bill of lading and voyage charter are contained in the same chapter on the contract for the carriage of goods. Voyage charter is considered as a document that evidences presence and content of the contract of carriage of goods with placing the whole vessel or her parts at the disposal.[186]

365. Voyage charter shall include the names of the parties, the ship and the goods, port of departure and port of destination. Other conditions and reservations might be included in the voyage charter upon agreement of the parties. It shall be signed by the freighter (carrier) and charterer or their representatives.[187]

366. The ship shall be delivered by a ship owner to a charterer in a seaworthy condition for the purposes determined in the charter party. With respect to a time charter an owner is also responsible to man and equip the ship and to keep her in a seaworthy condition during the whole period of a time charter party, to bear insurance costs and cost on manning.[188] A charterer is allowed, within the limits of his rights, to enter into a separate charter party for a period of time with a third party.[189]

§3. Contract of Ship Lease

367. Ukrainian legislation treats *ship lease* in Part VI, Chapter 2 of the MSC and in Chapter 58, §6 of the Civil Code that deals with contract of lease in Articles 806–809. Under the ship lease contract the ship owner (lessor) undertakes to transfer to the affreighter (lessee) a ship without crew to use it for the merchant shipping within a fixed period, after expiry of which the lessee becomes the owner of the

186. MSC, Art. 134.
187. MSC, Art. 136.
188. MSC, Art. 207.
189. MSC, Art. 206.

ship.[190] A lessee shall pay a lease fee that includes a fee for using the ship and her value under the contract of lease.

368. The contract of lease shall be concluded in a written form. Existence and content of the ship lease contract may be proved exclusively by written proofs.[191] A lessor should hand over a ship to a lessee in a condition fit for use with a purpose set by the contract of leasing.[192] A lessee in its turn shall maintain her in working order and bear all costs connected to her maintenance and repair. The risk of a sudden loss or sudden damage to a ship passes to the lessee after taking over of a ship.[193] In the event a lessee does not make the payment during three months after the due date of payment, a lessor has a right to renounce a contract and demand return of a ship.[194]

369. Upon returning of a vessel, a lessor is entitled to the lease payment due to the use of ship. Accordingly, a lessee shall return a ship to a lessor in the condition in which he received her, considering the normal tear and wear. In case of deterioration of a ship a lessee compensate a lessor the damaged caused.[195]

§4. Contract of Chartering for a Definite Time

I. General

370. Chapter 1, Part IV of the MSC deals with contracts of chartering for a definite time, namely *time charters* and *bareboat charters.*

371. The Dictionary of Shipping Terms states that:

> the owner places his ship, with crew and equipment, at the disposal of the charterer for which the charterer pays hire money. Subject to any restrictions in the contract, the charterer decides the type and quantity of cargo to be carried and the ports of loading and discharging. He is responsible for supplying the ship with bunkers and for the payment of cargo handling operation, port charges, pilotage, towage and ship's agency. The technical operation and navigation of the ship remain the responsibility of the ship owner.[196]

372. The bareboat charter is described as 'the fully-operational ship is delivered to the charterer in its 'bare' state (i.e., it has no crew, no stores, little or no fuel and no navigational charts)'.[197]

190. MSC, Art. 215, s. 1.
191. MSC, Art. 216.
192. MSC, Art. 218.
193. MSC, Art. 219.
194. MSC, Art. 220, s. 2.
195. MSC, Art. 221.
196. Dictionary of Shipping Terms.
197. M.J. Rowbotham, *Introduction to Marine Cargo Management*, 49.

373. In case a ship is chartered for carriage of goods, a charterer is entitled to conclude contracts of carriage on its behalf, to sign the charters, to issue bills of ladings and other transport documents.[198] Upon chartering a ship under time charter conditions the master and other crew members shall obey the charterer's orders concerning the exploitation of a ship, excluding the orders on navigation, internal order on a ship and crew composition.[199] With respect to liability of a charterer, he becomes liable for the damages resulting from salvage or loss of ship, if the damages occurred due to his fault.[200]

II. Payment of Freight

374. It should be mentioned that the Ukrainian legislator uses the notion 'freight' (*frakht*) in respect to the payment for the use of a ship in contrast to *hire* used in the common law countries, where hire is described as 'the price paid for the use of vessel and usually calculated on the basis of a fixed sum per tonne of a vessel deadweight for a specific period of time, such as thirty days or a calendar month'.[201] The same terminology is used in BALTIME 1939, section 6 'Hire' and NYPE'93, section 11 'Hire Payment'.

375. The payment of freight is treated in Article 212 of the MSC. The same Article refers to the conditions according to which the charterer shall be released from payment of freight during the period of time when a ship was unusable due to a number of reasons (so-called off-hire clause). However, the charterer is not released from payment in case the ship became unseaworthy due to his fault.

376. In case of loss of a ship, freight is to be paid until the day of loss or till the day it was mentioned the last time, pursuant to Article 213 of the MSC.

§5. Contracts for the Carriage of Goods by Sea

I. General

377. The most important international conventions on carriage of goods by sea are the Hague Rules, the Hague-Visby Rules, the Hamburg Rules and possibly the Rotterdam Rules in future. Over seventy nations, including almost all of the world's major shipping nations (with the exception of the United States), are party to or have the Hague-Visby in their national laws or have ratified it.[202] It should be noted that the above-mentioned conventions do not extend their application to the charter parties.

198. MSC, Art. 209.
199. MSC, Art. 210.
200. MSC, Art. 211.
201. J. Wilson, *Carriage of Goods by Sea*, 84.
202. W. Tetley, '*Reform of Carriage of Goods – the UNCITRAL Draft and Senate COGSA'99*', Tulane Maritime L. J. 28, 4 (Winter 2003).

378. Although Ukraine has not signed the above-mentioned conventions, some important provisions were reflected in the MSC. In the national legislation the contracts of carriage of goods are treated in Part V, Chapter 2 of the MSC. Article 133 defines the contract of carriage of goods by sea. Under the contract of carriage of goods by sea a carrier or freighter are under an obligation to transport the goods entrusted to them from a port of departure to a port of destination and hand it to the person entitled to receive the goods (consignee).[203] A shipper or a charterer shall pay the agreed price (*frakht*). The charterer and the freighter (owner) are parties to the charter party.

379. The contract of carriage shall be concluded in a written form. The documents that evidence existence and content of the contract of carriage of goods by sea are:

- voyage charter – whereas the contract provides a condition to dispose of the whole vessel, its part or separate premises for the carriage;
- bill of lading (*konosament*) – whereas a contract does not provide the abovementioned conditions;
- other written evidences.[204]

II. Definitions and Functions of the Bill of Lading

380. After receiving the goods for carriage, a master or an agent of the carrier shall issue the bill of lading to the shipper that serves as an evidence of receipt of the goods by the carrier specified in the bill of lading. It is also provided that a carrier may issue other document supporting the acceptance of the goods for carriage.

381. The bill of lading is defined as:

> a document issued by or on behalf of a carrier of goods by sea to the person (usually known as a shipper) with whom he has contracted for the carriage of the goods. Its basic features are that it contains promises by the carrier to carry the goods to the agreed destination subject to the terms of the document, and to deliver them there, in accordance with those terms; and a promise by the shipper to pay the agreed remuneration, known as freight.[205]

382. It should be pointed out that the bill of lading as a receipt for goods shipped on board a ship is not an actual contract.[206] The origin of the bill of lading as a non-negotiable receipt issued by a ship owner for cargo received to a merchant who did not intend to travel with his goods goes back to the fourteenth century.[207] The

203. MSC, Art. 133.
204. MSC, Art. 134.
205. *Carver on Bills of Lading*, 1–2.
206. M.J. Rowbotham, *Introduction to Marine Cargo Management*, 100.
207. J.F. Wilson, *Carriage of Goods by Sea*, 113.

historical evidence of the use of bills of lading goes back to the sixteenth century, and legal disputes relating to the use of these documents are found in the eighteenth century, with an important principle that of 'negotiability' being established in law as far back as 1794. These disputes resulted in the Bill of Lading Act of the UK (1855) that was further embodied in the Hague-Visby Rules.[208]

383. The shipper is liable to the carrier for the consequences resulting from inaccuracies or incompleteness of data declared in the mentioned document.[209] The shipper shall hand in to the carrier the documents concerning the goods in due time as it is required by the port, customs, sanitary and other administrative rules pursuant to Article 144 of the MSC. He shall be liable for any inaccuracies in these documents.

384. The provisions on lay time (*staliya*) and demurrage are dealt with in Part V of the MSC. Lay time is defined as a period of time during which goods are to be loaded (discharged) on/from a ship. The terms are agreed by the parties to the contract or in the absence of it – by the norms adopted in the port of loading/ discharging.[210] The parties may agree on the additional term after loading/ discharging the goods (*kontrstaliya*) and the fee for that term known as demurrage, as well as a reward for the completion of loading/discharging before the agreed term.[211] The rule with respect to demurrage is 'once on demurrage – always on demurrage'. The extensive case law on the calculation of lay time, the notion of the 'arrived ship', etc. is developed by the English courts. As it has been seen the provisions on voyage charter, lay time and demurrage found in the MSC are rather scarce and not fully developed.

III. Payment of Freight

385. All the necessary charges are to be paid by a shipper to the carrier according to Article 170 of the MSC. Other provisions on the payment of freight are found in Articles 171–175 of the MSC. A consignee upon receipt of the goods shall pay the carrier a due freight and demurrage to reimburse the mentioned expenses suffered by a carrier pertaining to the goods, and in case of general average – to fulfil the contribution or present an appropriate security.

386. In case of delayed payment for carriage, a shipper or a consignee shall pay a fine subject to the provisions of the contract or according to the rates set by the central executive body in the field of transport.[212]

208. M.J. Rowbotham, *Introduction to Marine Cargo Management*, 100.
209. MSC, Art. 137.
210. MSC, Art. 148.
211. MSC, Arts 148–149.
212. MSC, Art. 175.

§6. Cargo Documentation

387. According to Article 135 the legal relations between carrier and consignee are also determined by the bill of lading. Although the bill of lading is mentioned in the MSC, its definition has not been given.

388. The bill of lading fulfils three main functions. It serves as:

- receipt for goods shipped;
- evidence of the contract of carriage;
- document of title.

389. There are different types of bill of lading: the shipped on board bill of lading, the received bill of lading, through bill of lading, combined transport bill of lading and Federation of Freight Forwarders Associations (FIATA) multimodal bill of lading. It is notably that Association of International Freight Forwarders of Ukraine (AIFF) as a Member of FIATA is entitled to print FIATA multimodal bill of lading documents in Ukraine.

§7. Duties of the Carrier

390. According to Article 143 of the MSC a carrier bears the responsibility to make a ship seaworthy. Namely, it is provided that the carrier is under obligation to make a ship seaworthy *in advance before commencement of the voyage:* to provide the technical fit of a ship for the voyage, to supply and equip with all the required, to man the ship, to make the holds and other parts of the ship in which goods are carried in a condition suitable for their reception, carriage and preservation. This rule was literally transferred from the MSC USSR and enshrined in Article 124 of the MSCRF. These conditions correspond to the provisions on seaworthiness enshrined in the Hague-Visby Rules, Article III(1) where the condition to make a ship seaworthy is a separate duty and does not include the obligations to man, equip and supply the ship, etc. In the Ukrainian legislation the notion of 'seaworthiness' includes all the conditions mentioned above. Another distinctive feature is that MSC uses the wording *in advance before commencement of the voyage* (as envisaged in Article 143 of MSC), while the Hague-Visby Rules, 1968 (HVR) mention *before and at the beginning of the voyage* (HVR, Article III).

391. Another duty of the carrier is the reception and placement of the goods onboard a ship. Namely, the goods cannot be placed on a deck without the written permission of a shipper.[213] A carrier bears responsibility for correct placement, holding and separation of the goods on a ship.

392. In accordance with Article 160 of the MSC a carrier shall deliver the goods received for carriage in agreed terms and when the terms are not specified – in

213. MSC, Art. 146.

reasonable time. A deviation of a ship from a planned route shall not be deemed as a breach of the contract of carriage provided that it is for saving life at sea, ships and cargo, and any reasonable deviation if it is not done by wrong acts from the carrier's side. This is provided by Article 161 and also found in Article IV(4) of HVR.

§8. Carrier's Liability for Cargo

393. Since Ukraine is not a party to any international conventions on carriage of goods by sea, the legal regulation of carriage of goods by sea is the subject to the Civil Code, Commercial Code, MSC and other legal provisions.

394. A carrier is liable for loss, shortage and damage to the goods received for carriage unless proved that the loss, shortage and damage occurred beyond its fault. Its liability starts from the moment of receiving the goods for carriage and ends in the moment of handing over the goods.[214] Further, it is stated that the damages that became a result of loss of or damage to the goods shall be bearable by the carrier in the following cases:

- for loss and shortage in goods – in amount of actual value of the lost and missing goods;
- for damage and spoiling the goods – in amount in which the value of the goods lessened.[215]

395. For container's loss or damage or other means a carrier shall be liable in the following amounts:

- for loss of a container or device – in the amount of actual value considering the real tear and wear of a container or other device at the moment of its loss;
- for damage to a container or device – in the amount of actual value of its repair in the port of destination, unless repair is performed by a carrier himself or for his own account by the moment of handing in a container to a consignee.[216]

396. By virtue of Article 5 of the Hamburg Rules the carrier is liable for loss resulting from loss or damage to the goods, as well as from delay in delivery, if the occurrence that caused the loss, damage or delay took place while the goods were in his charge as defined in Article 4, unless the carrier proves that he, his servants or agents took all measures that could reasonably be required to avoid the occurrence and its consequences. Article 10 of the Hamburg Rules also bears the provisions on liability of the carrier and actual carrier. Here it is stated in section 4 that where and to the extent that both the carrier and the actual carrier are liable, their liability is joint and several.

214. MSC, Art. 176.
215. MSC, Art. 179.
216. MSC, Art. 182.

397. It should also be mentioned that the Ukrainian legislator uses the notion of a 'carrier' and does not make a distinction between a *carrier* and *actual carrier*, as in terminology used in the Hamburg Rules. On the other hand, this distinction is made in the MSCRF in Articles 166 and 173.

398. The Rotterdam Rules also define and distinct the carrier, performing party and maritime performing party. The Rotterdam Rules contain provisions on carrier's liability in Chapter 5 'Liability of the carrier for loss, damage or delay' that also includes the liability of maritime performing parties.

§9. Limitation of Liability and Immunities

399. Article 176 of MSC defines the conditions when the carrier is released from loss, damage and shortage of cargo. These provisions were imported from Article IV(2) of the HVR.

400. A carrier is not liable for loss, shortage and damage to the goods if proven that it happened due to actions or omissions of a master or other crew members and a pilot in navigation or in the management of the ship. This refers to the so-called navigational fault which is also reflected in Article IV(2)(a) of the HVR.

401. A carrier is relieved from liability for shortage of cargo delivered to the port of destination in:

- correct ship's premises, lighters, containers with correct seals by a shipper;
- in a whole and correct package without the traces of its opening;
- accompanied by a shipper's or consignee's guide unless proves that shortage occurred due to the carrier's fault.[217]

402. Unless the value of the goods has been declared and inserted in the bill of lading, the compensation for the damaged place or missing unit of cargo cannot be higher than 666.67 of Special Drawing Rights (SDR) or 2.0 of SDR for 1 kg brutto of damaged, missed cargo[218] as it is stated in the Hague-Visby Rules, Article IV 5(a). The unit of account is the Special Drawing Right as defined by the International Monetary Fund (IMF).

403. In the Hamburg Rules, Article 6(1)(a), the limit was increased to 835 units of account per package or other shipping unit, or 2.5 units of account per kilogram. Further, Article 59 of the Rotterdam Rules limits the carrier liability for breach of its obligation to 875 units of account per package or other shipping unit, or 3 units of account per kilogram.

217. MSC, Art. 178.
218. MSC, Art. 181.

§10. PASSENGER CARRIAGE

I. General

404. The Athens Convention Relating to the Carriage of Passengers and their Luggage by Sea 1974 (further – the Athens Convention) entered into force on 28 April 1987 and was supplemented by the Protocol 2002 that will become effective on 23April 2014. Ukraine acceded to the Convention in 1994.[219]

405. The legal regulation on contract of carriage of passengers by sea is stipulated in the above-mentioned Convention, Part V Chapter 3 of the MSC and the Civil Code of Ukraine. The MSC makes a distinction between the sea passenger transportation agreement and the sea cruise.

406. Additionally, the Conditions and Rules on Carrying out the Domestic and International Carriage of Passengers and Goods by Sea and Inland Water Transport and Control over its compliance were enacted as the Instruction of the Ministry of Transport of Ukraine (MTU) dated 5 August 1994, No. 424.

II. Contracts for the Carriage of Passengers by Sea

407. The contract for the carriage of passengers and their luggage is defined in Article 910 of the Civil Code, whereas the contract of sea transportation of passengers is treated in Article 184 of the MSC. The definition of contract given below summarizes the provisions of the Civil Code and MSC:

> Pursuant to the contract for the carriage of passengers by sea, the carrier undertakes to carry the passenger and his/her cabin baggage to the destination point, and in case of registry of luggage – also to carry it to the destination point and deliver it to the person authorized thereof; the passenger shall pay the set fare, and in case of registry of luggage – to pay for carriage of luggage. Transportation includes the whole time of staying of a passenger and his/her cabin baggage aboard, boarding and disembarkation time, as well as delivery of passenger on water route from the coast to the ship and back, if payment for delivery is included in the fare, or, if the ship used for this additional carriage was provided by the carrier.

408. The aforementioned definition given in the MSC basically restates the one envisaged in the Civil Code. The contracting parties are the carrier and the passenger. Chapter 3, Part V of the MSC applies to the carriage of passengers and their luggage if:

219. Law of Ukraine on Ukraine's Accession to Athens Convention relating to the Carriage of Passengers and their Luggage by Sea and Protocol 1976 dated 15 Jul. 1994, No. 115/94-BP.

– the ship is flying the Ukrainian flag;
– the contract is concluded in Ukraine;
– the place of departure or arrival is in Ukraine pursuant to the contract.

409. The evidence of the contract's conclusion and payment of fare shall be a ticket given by a carrier. The check-in of luggage is evidenced by a luggage receipt.[220] Article 188 of the MSC provides the right to resign the trip and get a refund under the terms and conditions defined by the Ministry of Infrastructure in its subordinate Acts. Passengers are subject to the obligatory insurance from the accident on transport pursuant to the Ukrainian legislation. The insurance premium is paid as a part of the ticket.[221]

410. The liability of the parties and limitation of liability are considered in Articles 193 and 194 of the MSC. The carrier's liability is limited to 175,000 SDR per passenger for death or injury. The liability for the loss or damage of cabin's luggage is limited to 1,800 SDR per passenger.

III. Contract of Sea Cruise

411. Part V, Chapter 4 of the MSC defines the sea cruise contract. Pursuant to it, one party – the organizer of a cruise – undertakes to perform collective sea travel (cruise) according to a fixed programme and provides the participants of cruise with all services related thereof (sea transportation, catering, everyday and excursion services, etc.), and the other party – participant of cruise – undertakes to pay for it the set payment. The document confirming the presence of a sea cruise contract is a nominal ticket or other similar document issued by the cruise organizer.

412. The liability of the cruise's organizer is subject to the provisions of Articles 193 and 194 of the MSC. The general grounds of liability for any damage and moral harm are provided in the Civil Code of Ukraine (Articles 1166, 1167). It also states the compensation of damage has to be in a full amount regardless of the fault.

§11. Claims and Actions

413. If, upon receipt of the goods that were carried under the bill of lading, a consignee did not inform the carrier in writing on shortage or damage to the goods, it is considered, unless proved otherwise, that the consignee received the goods in conformity with the conditions under the bill of lading. When loss, shortage or damage could not have been detected in a conventional manner of receiving the goods, a statement to the carrier can be made by a consignee within three days after receiving the goods.[222]

220. MSC, Art. 187.
221. MSC, Art. 191.
222. MSC, Art. 166.

414. The MSC regulates the claims and actions in Part XI. The claims are brought to the carrier who performed the carriage of goods by sea and in case the carriage was not performed – to a carrier who according to the contract was supposed to perform it.[223]

415. As a result of legal regulation of claims and actions in the contract of carriage by sea by the MSC and Civil Code of Ukraine, there is a legal confusion related to the procedure of bringing a claim and its terms.

416. The general three-year time limit (Article 257 of the Civil Code) is not applicable to carriage of goods. The special one-year time limit is dealt with in Article 258 of the Civil Code, and applies to *inter alia* carriage of goods. Article 388 of the MSC provides one-year time limit in respect to the claims arising out of the contracts of carriage of goods. Additionally, Article 389 of the MSC constitutes the two-year time limit regarding the claims with respect to the contracts of carriage of passengers and luggage, charter parties and lease of ships.

417. It is possible to make a pre-trial claim in a manner prescribed by the law and transport codes. The shipper or consignee can bring a claim to the carrier and in case of complete or partial failure to satisfy this claim or in case of absence of a reply in the monthly term the claimants put a lawsuit. In accordance with Article 387 of the MSC a carrier shall consider a claim during the three months and inform a claimant about satisfying or declining the claim.

418. The general rule in civil law is that any person can rely on the legal provision which grants higher level of protection. Thus, it is often encountered that the claims can be brought to the court in three-year term and without the pre-trial settlement.

223. MSC, Art. 383.

Chapter 7. Limitation of Ship Owner's Liability

§1. General Limitation of Liability

419. The general rules on limitation of ship owner's liability are contained in Chapter 1 of Part X of the MSC (Articles 348–357).

420. The key international legal instruments regulating the general limitation of liability for maritime claims, such as the International Convention relating to the Limitation of the Liability of Owners of Seagoing Ships (Brussels, 10 October 1957) and the IMO Convention on Limitation of Liability for Maritime Claims (London, 19 November 1976) (hereinafter – the LLMC) and the Protocol to it of 1996 are not ratified by Ukraine. Nevertheless, the majority of the provisions of the LLMC (but not the Protocol of 1996) are in fact incorporated into Part X of the MSC and generally resemble the key standards of the general limitation of liability existing in other countries.

421. Article 20 of the MSC defines the ship owner as a legal entity or natural person, who uses the vessel on its own behalf, notwithstanding the fact whether such person is an actual owner of the vessel. Such definition complies with general understanding of the notion 'ship owner' that exists in the maritime legislation of most of the maritime jurisdictions. Moreover, the mentioned definition corresponds with the definition of the ship owner provided in Article 1 of the LLMC and stipulates that the term 'ship owner' shall mean the owner, charterer, manager and operator of a seagoing ship. In contrast to the LLMC that regulates limitation of liability not only of ship owners, but also of salvors, the provisions of MSC relate to ship owners only.

422. In accordance with the MSC the ship owner is liable for its obligations with all property belonging to him and which in accordance with the current legislation of Ukraine may be subject to foreclosure (almost all property with minor exceptions like clothes, personal hygiene items and similar things to secure minimum standard of living).

423. Article 349 of the MSC provides that liability of ship owner is limited in accordance with Article 352 with respect to the claims that regardless of their legal ground arise out of:

(1) loss of life or personal injury to a person on board the vessel or loss of or damage to property on board the vessel;
(2) damage caused in connection with sailing or exploitation of the vessel, to persons or property not situated on board the vessel.

424. If damage stipulated in the latter case is caused by a person not situated on board the vessel, the ship owner responsible for actions of such person can limit his liability if the action that caused the damage arose in connection with the operation of the vessel, loading or discharging of the cargo, baggage or hand luggage or with embarkation/debarkation of passengers.

425. The list of claims subject to limitation in the MSC is at the first glance much narrower than the list of such claims in the LLMC, though it is not as straightforward as it seems. Article 2 of the LLMC, except of the claims indicated above, also includes other claims resulting from infringement of rights other than contractual rights arising out of removal of sunken ship in respect of removal or rendering harmless of the cargo of the ship, etc., as well as the claims in respect of the loss resulting from delay. In principle, the named claims, except of claims resulting from delay and claims arising in connection with removal of sunken property (expressly excluded from the scope of limitation by Article 351 of the MSC), can fall within the scope of section 2 of Article 349 of the MSC.

426. The MSC contains the same provision as the LLMC on conduct barring limitation, providing that a person liable shall not be entitled to limit his liability if it is proved that the loss resulted from his personal act or omission committed with the intent to cause such loss or recklessly and with knowledge that such loss would probably result.

427. The claims excepted from the limitation are listed in Article 351 of the MSC. The list of exception is very similar to the list of exceptions contained in Article 3 of the LLMC and is the following:

(1) claims for salvage or contribution in general average;
(2) claims by servants of the ship owner or salvor whose duties are connected with the ship or the salvage operations, including claims of their heirs, dependants or other persons entitled to make such claims, if under the law governing the contract of service between the ship owner or salvor and such servants, the ship owner or salvor is not entitled to limit his liability in respect of such claims, or if he is permitted only by such law to limit his liability to an amount greater than that provided for in Article 352 of the MSC;
(3) claims connected with lifting the sunken property;
(4) claims for oil pollution damage, as well as for pollution by other substances that are harmful for life and health of humans or sea life to which the rules of Chapter 4 of Part IX of this Code are applied;
(5) claims regarding nuclear damage, if to the liability for such damage the rules of Chapter 5 of Part IX of this Code are applied.

428. The limits of liability provided in Article 352 of the MSC are the following:

(1) in respect of claims for loss of life or personal injury:
    (a) 333,000 Units of Account for a ship with a tonnage not exceeding 500 tonnes;
    (b) for a ship with a tonnage in excess thereof, the following amount is added to that mentioned in (a):

– for each tonne from 501 to 3,000 tonnes, 500 Units of Account;
– for each tonne from 3,001 to 30,000 tonnes, 333 Units of Account;
– for each tonne from 30,001 to 70,000 tonnes, 250 Units of Account; and
– for each tonne in excess of 70,000 tonnes, 167 Units of Account;

(2) in respect of any other claims:
   (a) 167,000 Units of Account for a ship with a tonnage not exceeding 500 tonnes;
   (b) for a ship with a tonnage in excess thereof the following amount is added to that mentioned in (a):
   – for each tonne from 501 to 30,000 tonnes, 167 Units of Account;
   – for each tonne from 30,001 to 70,000 tonnes, 125 Units of Account; and
   – for each tonne in excess of 70,000 tonnes, 83 Units of Account.

429. Moreover, the named Article stipulates that where the amount calculated in accordance with paragraph 1 is insufficient to pay the claims mentioned therein in full, the amount calculated in accordance with paragraph 2 shall be available for payment of the unpaid balance of claims under paragraph 1 and such unpaid balance shall rank rateably with claims mentioned under paragraph 2.

430. For the purposes of limitation of liability:

(1) the ship's tonnage for the ships with mechanic engines shall be the net tonnage plus the volume of the engine room, and for all other ships – their net tonnage;
(2) the limits of liability for any salvor not operating from any ship or for any salvor operating solely on the ship to, or in respect of which he is rendering salvage services, shall be calculated according to a tonnage of 1,500 tonnes.

431. The provision regarding limitation of liability of the salvor is not clear in MSC, as it constitutes a resemblance of the similar provision of section 4, Article 6 of the LLMC that follows the provisions on limits of liability. This provision was introduced into the MSC despite that salvors are not included within the scope of Chapter 1 of Part X of the MSC. Such controversial provisions may lead to a conclusion that the named chapter of the MSC was written basing partly on the provisions of the LLMC which were not properly incorporated into the MSC.

432. The limits of liability provided by Article 352 of the MSC are applied to the aggregate of all claims arising from one occurrence and filed against one ship owner or other relevant person.

433. If a ship owner whose liability is subject to limitation in accordance with Article 349 of the MSC has a right on a counter-claim arising out of the same accident, limitation of liability is applied to the difference that remains after offsetting the claims.

434. If any of the claims with respect to which liability of the ship owner can be limited is filed directly against a person for the actions of which the ship owner is liable, this person has a right to make use of all the provisions regarding limitation of liability applied for the ship owner, if it is not proven that the harm was done by this person intentionally.

435. Agreements regarding limitation of the ship owner's liability to the extent lesser than provided by Chapter 1 of Part X of the MSC are invalid.

436. The Unit of Account is defined by Article 9 of the MSC and corresponds to the notion of the Unit of Account defined in Article 8 of the LLMC and constitutes the Special Drawing Right as defined by the IMF.

§2. Limitation of Liability for Pollution

437. Liability for pollution of the sea by oil and by other harmful substances is regulated by Chapter 4 of Part IX of the MSC.

438. The key international act in the sphere of pollution by oil is the International Convention on Civil Liability for Oil Pollution Damage (CLC), 1969, as well as 1992 Protocol that amends it. The CLC Convention, with 1992 Protocol was ratified by Ukraine on 4 July 2002 by the Law No. 44IV and the key provisions of the CLC are incorporated into the MSC.

439. Other important international Acts regulating pollution by oil, such as the International Convention on Civil Liability for Bunker Oil Pollution Damage of 2001 or the International Convention on the Establishment of an International Fund for Compensation for Oil Pollution Damage (1971) and 1992 Protocol to it are not ratified by Ukraine.

440. The International Convention on Liability and Compensation for Damage in Connection with the Carriage of Hazardous and Noxious Substances by Sea (HNS), 1996, and its 2010 Protocol are not ratified by Ukraine as well.

441. In contrast to the general limitation of liability that applies for the ship owner, liability for oil and other harmful substances pollution lies with the owner of the ship defined in Article 20 of the MSC as a person who has the right of ownership to the ship or who realizes with respect of the ship the rights to which the rules on the right of ownership apply.

442. In accordance with Article 304 of MSC, the owner of the ship is liable for the pollution damage caused by discharge or leakage from the ship of oil or other substances that are harmful for human health or sea life (hereinafter – contaminative substances), except of the cases stipulated by Article 305 of the MSC regarded below.

443. As it can be seen from the provision above, MSC does not distinguish between pollution caused by oil and pollution caused by other contaminative substances – all pollution is subject to the same norms regarding liability and the same provisions regarding limitation of liability for damage. Moreover, the liability of the owner is strict and it is up to him to prove whether or not one or another exemption from liability actually applies.

444. MSC defines pollution damage as damage caused outside the ship by contaminative substances to the sea environment, sea shore or to any other objects (ships, fishing appurtenances, etc.). The damage also includes the costs of preventive measures taken by any person after the accident that could cause or caused leakage or discharge of contaminative substances in order to prevent or minimize the harm from the pollution, as well as damages caused in the course of such measures.

445. The owner of the ship is exempted from the liability for pollution in case one of the following circumstances takes place (Article 305 of MSC):

- acts of God;
- acts of war, hostilities or riots;
- actions of the third parties done with intent to cause harm;
- faulty in lights or other navigational aids happened due to negligence or other unlawful actions on the part of state bodies, who are responsible for maintaining the named aids in due order;
- emergency discharge of household-faecal waters or waste caused by non-acceptance of them by the port in the due period after proper filing of the necessary application by the ship;
- providing of untrue information by the sender.

446. Article 306 of MSC restates the provisions of Article III(3) of the CLC and provides that if the owner proves that the pollution damage resulted wholly or partially either from an act or omission done with intent to cause damage by the person who suffered the damage or from the negligence of that person, the owner may be exonerated wholly or partially from his liability to such person.

447. In line with Article IV of the CLC, Article 307 of the MSC provides that if the damage is caused by discharge of contaminative substances from two or more ships, the owners of all the ships concerned shall be jointly and severally liable for all such damage that is not reasonably separable.

448. The limits of liability in MSC, Article 308, resemble the limits provided by the CLC and are set as follows:

- for a ship not exceeding 5,000 units of gross tonnage, liability is limited to 3 million Units of Account;
- for a ship exceeding 5,000 units of gross tonnage the liability is limited to 3 million Units of Account plus 420 Units of account for each additional unit of tonnage.

449. The ship's tonnage for the purpose of Article 308 is the net tonnage plus the volume of the engine room. If the ship's tonnage is impossible to define in accordance with usual measuring rules, the ship's tonnage shall constitute 40% of weight of oil or other substances that the ship can carry, in tonnes.

450. The MSC also contains provisions on compulsory insurance. Thus, according to Article 309, the owner of a ship carrying more than 2,000 tonnes of oil in bulk as cargo must maintain insurance or other financial security, such as the guarantee of a bank, to cover its liability for pollution damage.

451. A claim for compensation of damage caused by pollution can be filed directly against the insurer or other person, who provided security to cover the liability of the ship owner. The person against whom such claim is filed can limit its liability in accordance with the provisions of the chapter even if the ship owner is deprived of the possibility to limit its liability under Article 350 of the MSC. He may further avail himself of the defence (other than the bankruptcy or winding up of the owner) that the owner himself would have been entitled to invoke. Furthermore, the defendant may avail himself of the defence that the pollution damage resulted from the wilful misconduct of the owner himself, but the defendant has a burden of proof in this respect. The defendant shall in any accident have the right to require the owner to join the proceedings.

452. It must be noted that the provisions of Chapter 1 of Part X of the MSC regarding the exceptions from the general rule of limitation of liability also apply to the limitation of liability for pollution.

§3. Limitation of Liability for Nuclear Damage

453. Liability for nuclear damage caused by a nuclear vessel on the territory of Ukraine, including its territorial sea, as well as by a nuclear vessel flying the Ukrainian flag in the EEZ, is regulated by Chapter 5, Part IX, MSC. According to the provisions of Chapter 5, liability for nuclear damage caused by a nuclear accident with a nuclear vessel lies with the operator of the nuclear vessel. The term nuclear vessel is defined in Article 15 of the MSC as a vessel equipped with the nuclear installation.

454. Nuclear damage means damage caused to persons or property by radioactive characteristics or by combination of radioactive characteristics with toxic, explosive and other dangerous characteristics of nuclear fuel, radioactive products of the nuclear vessel or nuclear waste, as well as expenses connected with attempts to avoid or minimize the damage. Nuclear accident means accident or several accidents caused by one or several casualties that caused nuclear damage.

455. Operator of the nuclear vessel is a legal entity or a natural person empowered by the state which flag the vessel flies, to use the nuclear vessel or the state that uses such vessel. Operator of the nuclear vessel is obliged to compensate the nuclear damage unless he proves that the damage arose as a result of war actions, hostilities, riots or acts of God.

456. If the operator can prove that the nuclear damage wholly or partly arose as a result of intent of the suffering party, the operator is wholly or partly free from liability before such party. Operator can also in certain cases file a regress claim against a person who caused the damage by intent, against a person, who lifted up the sunken nuclear vessel without proper consent from operator or a country of the flag, as well as against a person who took an obligation to compensate a nuclear damage.

457. According to Article 318 of the MSC, liability of the operator of the nuclear vessel for nuclear damage caused by one nuclear accident with this vessel is limited by the sum of 99,75 million Units of Account including legal expenses. If the claims for personal as well as property damage are filed as a result of nuclear accident, 69,825 million Units of Account shall be accrued to compensation of personal damage and 29,925 million Units of Account shall be accrued to compensation of property damage from the total limitation amount. If the first part of the sum is not enough for reimbursement of personal damage, unpaid amount shall be proportionally paid from the other part of the sum on equal terms with other claims for proprietary damage. The sums intended for payment of claims are divided between the claimants proportionally to the proved sizes of their claims.

458. Several operators of nuclear vessels that caused nuclear damage are jointly and severally liable, though liability of an operator against whom the claim is filed cannot be over the settled limitation amount for one nuclear accident.

459. If nuclear damage is caused by the nuclear vessel that on the moment of nuclear accident did not receive a permit on sailing from a country of the vessel's flag, liability lies with the owner of the nuclear vessel. In such case the limitation of liability of an operator of the nuclear vessel is not applicable.

460. According to the provisions of MSC, the nuclear vessel is obliged to have a valid certificate attesting that insurance or other financial security regarding liability of an operator of the nuclear vessel is maintained.

461. The claim for compensation of nuclear damage can be filed directly against the insurer or other person that provided financial security to the operator of the nuclear vessel.

462. In case when the size of caused damage exceeds the limits of liability of operator of the nuclear vessel under Article 318 of the MSC, a fund for securing the limitation of liability in the amount of such limitation is created during the hearing of the case. This fund is created at the request of the operator of the nuclear vessel, claimant or authority that issued a permit for usage of the nuclear vessel by means of the operator's payment of necessary amount as a deposit to the court or by providing other security considered by the court as sufficient (Article 324 of the MSC).

Chapter 8. Collisions

§1. Introduction

463. The main provisions on collisions of vessels are stipulated by Chapter 3 'Compensation for Damages Caused by Collision of Ships' of Part IX 'Extraordinary Perils at Sea' of the MSC. It should be noted that the provisions of the chapter were mainly transferred from the MSC USSR that had been based on the provisions of the International Convention for the Unification of Certain Rules of Law with respect to Collisions between Vessels dated 23 September 1910. This Convention had been recognized as being valid for the Soviet Union by the Decree of the SOVNARKOM (SNK) of the USSR on 2 February 1926 and the Soviet Union had officially acceded to this Convention on 27 August 1936.

§2. Collision Avoidance Rules

I. History

464. Regardless of the level of navigational aids and safety devices, computerization and automatization, the human fault will always exist and will remain the prime cause of collisions in navigable waters.[224]

465. The word 'collision' is translated from Latin as a contact and/or impact between vessels. It is also important to note that the contact does not always imply a contact between hulls, it could easily be a contact with an anchor chain for instance or no contact at all, but it still can cause damage to another vessel.[225] As it was observed there were hardly any provisions on collisions in the ancient law.[226] The international regulation on prevention of collisions at sea goes back to the nineteenth century, when the International Rules for Preventing Collisions at Sea were adopted in 1897 and even today serve as the foundation of the new Rules.[227] The important amendments to the Rules were made in 1948, 1960 and finally in the Rules 1972.[228]

466. In 1992 Ukraine acceded to the Convention on the International Regulations for Preventing Collisions at Sea 1972 (hereinafter – COLREG), by means of adopting the Resolution by the *Verkhovna Rada* of Ukraine on 17 November 1992, No. 2785-XII.[229]

---

224. C. Hill, 245.
225. C. Hill, 246.
226. D.R. Owen, '*The Origins and Development of Marine Collision Law*', 51 Tul. L. Rev. 759 (June 1976–1977).
227. See further at W.W. Barrow, '*Consideration of the New International Rules for Preventing Collisions at Sea*' 51 Tul. L. Rev. 1182 (1976–1977).
228. *Ibid.*
229. Although the Convention has not been not ratified by means of a law on ratification but by a Resolution, its legal force is equal to the law.

467. Collision avoidance rules can be found in MSC and in the Convention. It is necessary to note that COLREG consists of five Parts and four Annexes. Part A contains rules on applicability of the Rules, responsibility and definitions. Here Rule 1(a) states that the Rules apply to all vessels on the high seas and in all waters connected therewith navigable by seagoing vessels. Part B concerns steering and sailing Rules, Part C is devoted to the lights and shapes. Part D is on sound and light signals and Part E contains a list of exemptions.

468. The latest amendments were adopted on 29 November 2007 and entered into force on 1 December 2009. They concern Annex IV on Distress Signals.[230]

II. Liability for Collision

A. *Applicability of the Rules*

469. Article 296 of the MSC stipulates that relations related to compensation of damages due to vessels' collisions in internal waters or territorial sea are regulated by the legislation of the state, where the collision has occurred. And if all collided ships fly the same flag and does not concern third parties, the law of flag state shall apply in spite of the place where collision has occurred.

470. Taking into account the provisions of the MSC it is necessary to outline that these provisions shall be applied in the following situations:

- if the collision is occurred in the high seas and the dispute concerning this collision is adjudicated in Ukraine;
- if the collision has occurred between the ships flying the Ukrainian flag and interests of the third party, especially foreign entity, has not been concerned;
- if the collision has occurred at sea and other waters between seagoing ships, as well as between seagoing ships and inland water ships. It is important that one of the participants of the collision is a seagoing ship for applicability of the provisions of the MSC.

471. According to Article 297 of the MSC, the damages caused by one ship to another ship, or persons, cargo or other property on board thereof, either by manoeuvre or by the non-observance of navigation rules, even if no collisions between ships had actually taken place, shall be treated as collision of ships.

472. Facilities of fisheries is an integral part of a fishing ship and therefore, in cases of sea perils related to the damage to such facilities of fisheries of the fishing ship by other ships, shall be classified as collision at sea according to Article 15 of the MSC.

230. See at www.imo.org/conventions/contents.asp?doc_id=649&topic_id=257.

B. Liability Rules

473. It is to be noted that the origin of legal rules on liability for collision stipulated by the MSC can be found in the International Convention for the Unification of Certain Rules of Law with respect to Collisions between Vessels dated 23 September 1910, namely:

(a) if the collision occurred accidentally or is caused by force majeure, or it is impossible to determine the causes of the collision, the damages are borne by those who have suffered them (Article 298 of the MSC). This rule shall apply even in the case when ships or one of them had been anchored or fixed by other method at the moment of collision;
(b) if the collision is caused by the fault of one of the ships, the damages shall be borne by which fault the collision occurred (Article 299 of the MSC). The origin of this legal provision can be found in the common law countries, and thus contradicts the legal system of Ukraine;
(c) if the collision has happened through the fault of all ships, each of them shall be liable proportionally to the degree of their fault for the damage. And if the degree of the fault cannot be established, the ships shall be liable equally (Article 300 of the MSC).

474. In the last case the owners of the ships shall be jointly liable for damages resulting of death or personal injury; and the owner which on the basis of the joint liability has paid a part larger than his duty, shall be entitled to regress a claim against the rest of the ships for the overpaid sum.

475. All other damages shall be compensated by the owners of the ship proportionally to the degree of their fault for the damage.

476. The above-mentioned rules shall also apply to the cases where the collision has happened through the fault of the pilot or ship traffic management service. In spite of that, no ship involved in the collision shall be deemed guilty unless the contrary is proved.

Chapter 9. General and Particular Average

§1. General Average

477. Definition of general average is stipulated by Article 277 of the MSC according to which *general average* shall be deemed as the damages resulted from extraordinary expenditures or sacrifices that have been made intentionally and reasonably for saving the ship, the freight and the cargo carried on board the ship from common peril.

478. The general average under the conditions of Article 277 of the MSC shall be according to Article 279 of the MSC as follows:

(1) the damages arising of jettison of cargo or ship's equipment off board and also any damage caused to the ship or the cargo when measures for their saving as a whole are taken, especially as a result of penetration of water in the holds through the hatches opened for jettison of the cargo or through other openings made therefore;
(2) the damages caused to the ship or the cargo when extinguishing fire on board the ship, including the damages of sinking of the burning ship;
(3) the damages caused by intentional stranding of the ship or getting afloat of this ship;
(4) the damages related to the breakdown of engines and other machinery or boilers of the ship caused during the attempts to release the ship of being stranded;
(5) extraordinary expenses made when the ship is stranded, related to the overloading of the ship, the fuel or the objects of the ship's supply from the ship to lighter, for rental of the latter and for reloading on the ship;
(6) the losses of damaging and destruction of cargoes, fuel or stores caused by their moving, discharging and reloading and stowage on the ship, as well as for their storage in the cases when the expenses for performing these activities are recognized as a general average;
(7) the expenses made with the purpose to receive assistance as according to the salvage agreement so without this agreement, inasmuch as these salvage operations are carried out with the purpose to prevent peril for the ship, the freight and the cargo;
(8) the damages of pollution of the environment caused due to the general average;
(9) the loss of the freight resulting from the loss of the cargo, in cases when the loss of cargo shall be compensated due to distribution of general average by excluding from its freight the expenses which would be made by the carrier for the realization of the freight, but which were not made because of the sacrifices.

479. According to Article 280 of the MSC the following expenses shall be recognized as general average:

(1) the expenses caused by compulsory call of the ship to the place of refuge or her returning to the place of loading in consequence of accident or any other

extraordinary circumstance rendering the necessity of deviation or returning for the common safety;

(2) the expenses related to leaving the place of refuge or the place of loading in case of compulsory returning by the ship with the cargo or a part of it;

(3) the expenses on moving cargo, fuel or stores at the place of loading, call or refuge, when it was necessary for the common safety or to enable damages to the ship caused by accident or other extraordinary circumstances to be repaired, if the repairs were necessary for the safe prosecution of the voyage;

(4) the expenses for safe custody of cargo, including reasonable insurance, reloading and stowage of the cargo, fuel and stores, discharged or moved under the circumstances noted in the preceding item; however, if the ship is considered unfit for navigation, if the ship does not continue its original voyage, the expenses for safe custody shall be admitted as general average up to the date when the ship is considered unfit for navigation or the date of refusal of voyage, or the date of completion of unloading of the cargo, if the vessel shall be recognized as unfitted for navigation or refuses the voyage before this date;

(5) the expenses for wages and maintenance of crew of the ship, stores and fuel consumed during the prolongation of the voyage resulting from the deviation of the ship to the place of refuge or returning to her place of loading in the cases referred to items above; however, if the ship is considered unfit for navigation, or if the ship does not continue her original voyage, such expenses shall be admitted as general average up to the date when the ship is considered unfit for navigation or the date of refusal of voyage, or the date of completion of unloading of the cargo, if the ship is considered unfit for navigation or refuses the voyage before this date;

(6) the expenses for wages and maintenance of crew of the ship arising from detention of the ship in the interests of common safety in any place in consequence of accident or other extraordinary circumstances or to repair damages caused by this circumstance, if the repairs were necessary for the safe prosecution of the voyage. The expenses for fuel, stores and port charges incurred during the detention shall likewise be admitted as general average except such expenses as are incurred solely by reason of repairs not allowable in general average;

(7) the expenses specified from items above, if arising from the transfer of the ship from the place of refuge to another place, because of impossibility to make the repair at the place of refuge, as well as expenses for such transfer, including temporary repair and towage;

(8) the value of the temporary repairs of the ship for the purpose of common safety at the place of loading, call or refuge, for common safety, as well as the temporary repairs of damage admitted as general average; however, the value of the temporary repair of the accidental damage necessary only to complete the voyage, shall be allowed only up to the amount of these preliminary expenses that would be admitted as general average if such repairs had not been effected there;

(9) all extraordinary expenses done instead of other expenses are admitted as general average; however, they shall be allowed only up to the amount of these preliminary expenses regardless of saving received from any participant of general average due to such replaced expenses.

480. According to Article 277 of the MSC, the general average shall be adjusted between the ship, the cargo and the freight proportionally to their value and even if the peril causing the extraordinary sacrifices or expenses has occurred through the fault of the person who has a property interest in the ship, the cargo or the freight. The adjustment of the damages shall not deprive the participants in the general average of their right of regress claim against the person through the fault of whom the damages are caused, as well as shall not deprive this person of means of protection.

481. In time of general average calculation and compensation the following shall be taken into account:

As regards to the cargo:

(1) *not declared or declared wrongfully:* such cargo shall not be adjusted according to Article 277 of the MSC, however, if this cargo is saved, it shall remain liable to contribute to the general average according to the general rules. Moreover, if the value of the cargo was declared upon acceptance to be less than the actual value, the damages shall be calculated in the general average according to the declared value, but obligations weighing on this cargo shall be apportioned according to the actual value of the cargo;
(2) *sacrificed cargo*: the damages shall be determined according to the price at the moment of discharge under the invoice issued to the consignee, and if such invoice is absent, according to the shipping value. The value at the moment of discharge includes insurance and freight, except for the cases when the freight is located at the risk of other interests than cargo.

In case of sale of damaged cargo, the allowance shall be determined by the difference between its value and the sum received of its sale.

As regards to the ship:

(1) in cases of damage to the ship, her machinery and equipment shall be determined as follows:
    (a) in case of repair or substitution of parts of the ship – by means of actual value of the repair or substitution. In cases, where old materials or parts are substituted with new on the ship, the age of which exceeds fifteen years, 'new for old' deductions shall be made from the value of repair in the amount of one-third;
    (b) in other cases – by decrease of the value of the ship not exceeding the normal repair value;
(2) in cases of actual or total constructive loss of the ship, the sum intended for a general average allowance of a damage of the ship shall be calculated on the basis of the assessment of the ship in undamaged condition by deducting from it the usual value of the repairs that are not deemed a general average, and the value of the ship in damaged condition that can be identified by the amount of sale of the ship, if she was sold.

482. The total value of the properties involved in the contribution to the general average (contributory value) shall be determined according to the actual net value of the properties at the termination of the voyage, except contribution for the cargo that shall be determined according to the value at the moment of discharge under the invoice issued to the consignee, and if such invoice is absent, according to the shipping value.

483. The cargo and personal property of the passengers shall not be included in the contributory value, if the bill of lading has not been issued.

§2. Particular Average

484. The particular (non-substantive) average is regulated by Articles 294 and 295 of the MSC. According to Article 294 of the MSC, the damages that do not come within the definition of Articles 277, 279 and 280 of the MSC shall be considered as *particular (non-substantive) average*. Such damages shall not be adjusted between the ship, the cargo and the freight. These damages shall be borne by person who has suffered these damages or the person who is liable for their causing.

485. Article 295 of the MSC supplements the meaning of the particular average and provides that even under the presence of the circumstances specified in Article 277 of the MSC, the general average shall not be deemed:

(1) the value of the jettisoned self-inflammable cargo and the cargo transported on the ship which is non-compliant with the rules and customs recognized in the marine trade;
(2) the damages caused to the vessel or cargo in the course of the ship board fire-fighting, including the damages caused by sinking the vessel on fire;
(3) the damages resulting of cutting away wrecks or parts of the ship carried away or lost due to casualty before sacrifice with the purpose to save from the common peril;
(4) the expenses on moving cargo, fuel or stores at the port of loading, call or refuge, when damage to the ship is identified at the port of loading or port of call provided that there is no other accident or other extraordinary circumstances related to this damage during the voyage, and also when such expenses have been done only with the purpose to transposition of the cargo due to its displacement during the voyage if such displacement is not necessary for the common safety;
(5) the expenses for wages and maintenance of the crew, fuel and stores consumed during the period of repair of the damaged ship, even if it is necessary for the safety continuation of the voyage in cases when damage to the ship is identified at the port of loading or port of call, provided that there is no other accident related to the damage during the voyage;
(6) any damages or expenses incurred by the ship or the cargo resulting from the prolongation of the voyage (such as stays, change in price and other).

Chapter 10. Salvage

§1. Introduction

486. The definition of 'salvage'[231] provides that:

> The right to salvage … is a presumption of law arising out the fact that property has been saved that the owner of the property who has had the benefit of it should make remuneration to those who have conferred the benefit upon him, notwithstanding that he has not entered into any contract on the subject.

487. At the time of the Soviet Union the salvage law had a great development through the arbitration practice of the Maritime Arbitration Commission at the Soviet Union Chamber of Commerce and Industry, the legal research and practice of lawyers.

488. However, the current Ukrainian salvage law is not subject to any obvious development due to the economic and political circumstances in Ukraine from the time of its independence. As a general rule the parties try to agree signing the Lloyd's open forms and bring their legal relations under the English law. And this is a reason why the Ukrainian courts do not have disputes arisen from salvage. In spite of that there are a lot of questions which have practical relevance.

§2. History of Salvage

489. The law of maritime salvage is an ancient and important part of the wider law governing marine perils and safety at sea but modern law is primarily governed by the International Convention on Salvage 1989.[232] The Convention came into force on 14 July 1996 and replaced the Brussels Salvage Convention 1910. Article 1 of the Convention defines salvage operation as act or activity undertaken to assist a vessel or any other property in danger in navigable waters or in any other waters.

490. The law of salvage applies where there is a recognized subject of salvage which has come into a position of danger necessitating a salvage service to preserve it from loss or damage and a person falling within the classification of salvors is successful or meritoriously contributes to success in preserving the subject from danger.[233]

231. Kennedy & Rose, *Law of Salvage*, 5, The definition given by Hannen J. in the case of Five Steel Barges (1980), 15 PD 142, 146.
232. Kennedy and Rose, *Law of Salvage*, 1.
233. Kennedy and Rose, *Law of Salvage*, 1.

§3. LEGAL REGULATION OF SALVAGE

I. Private Law Relations

491. The private law relations are mainly regulated by the MSC and by the SIWT where the main aim of the MSC is salvage at sea, and SIWT – salvage at inland waters.

492. The International Convention on Salvage, 1989 is not ratified by Ukraine, but the main provisions of the Convention are incorporated in the MSC in Chapter 6 Part IX and have been transferred from the MSC USSR with immaterial amendments.

493. According to Article 326 of the MSC, the regulations of the chapter shall apply in case of salvage of seagoing vessels which are in distress, as well as in case of salvage by means of seagoing vessels of inland water vessels or any other floating objects or such as taken in tow, irrespective of waters where salvage has taken place in case when adjudication concerning salvage proceeds in Ukraine. The regulations of the chapter shall not apply to fixed or floating platforms, offshore drilling units when such platforms or units are on location engaged in the exploration, exploitation or production of sea-bed mineral resources.

494. It is clear from Article 326 that the MSC is applicable if at least one of the participants of salvage operation is seagoing vessel and *adjudication concerning salvage proceeds in Ukraine.*

495. The MSC relates to inland water vessels provided that seagoing vessel participates in salvage operations. Otherwise such relations are regulated by the SIWT. According to Article 4 of the SIWT it covers all navigable and floatable rivers, navigable lakes, the Aral Sea and man-made waterways within the territory of the USSR. Taking into account that the SIWT has been adopted in the times of the Soviet Union, its provisions shall be applied if they do not contradict the Ukrainian legislation in force.

496. At first sight there is a gap in legislation concerning salvage in the territorial sea or inland waters of Ukraine where salvor and salved vessel are inland water vessels. In this situation Article 13 of the MSC shall apply stipulating that provisions of this Code shall apply to inland water vessels in time of passage by sea routes, as well as by rivers, lakes, water storage basins and others waterways during carrying out of transportation with calling at foreign sea port and in cases stipulated by Articles 297 and 327 of the MSC.

497. It is necessary to note that according to Article 327 of the MSC there are two provisions concerning what law shall be applied to relationships arising from salvage, namely:

(1) if the vessel which makes a rescue and salvaged vessel flies a flag of the same state, the law of this state shall apply; and
(2) in time of distribution of the reward between the owner and crew of the vessel that has made a rescue, as well as among the crew members the applicable law is the law of the state whose flag this vessel flies.

II. Public Law Relations

498. Ukraine has acceded to the International Convention on Maritime Search and Rescue (SAR) according to the Resolution of the *Verkhovna Rada* of Ukraine on 17 November 1992, No. 2786-XII and today it is one of the principal laws embracing public-law relations in the sphere of salvage. Despite that the Convention was not ratified in the form of law, its legal force is equal to the law.

499. With the purpose of implementation of the provisions of SAR, the executive authorities of Ukraine have issued several Acts, namely:

(1) The Rules on Safety Management System at Navigation of Seagoing and Inland Waterways Transport approved by the Order of the MTU dated 20 November 2003, No. 904, registered by the Ministry of Justice of Ukraine on 19 December 2003 under No. 1193/8514. These Rules set forth the order on organization of works to prevent emergency actions on maritime and inland water transport, tasks, functions, bodies, subjects and objects of management system on safety of navigation, establish forms of control over performance of measures concerning safety of navigation (subsection 1.2). These Rules shall apply to the Ministry of Infrastructure, the State Inspectorate of Ukraine for Maritime and Inland Water Transport Safety, legal entities of maritime and inland water transport, other legal entities irrespective of their form of ownership and natural persons whose activities are connected with shipping (except the Ministry of Defence of Ukraine, the State Border Guard Service of Ukraine, the Security Service of Ukraine and the Ministry of Internal Affairs of Ukraine) (subsection 1.3).
(2) The Resolution of the CMU on Improvement of the Effectiveness of Functioning of the Search and Rescue System at Sea dated 5 March 2009, No. 178. The Resolution imposes on the Ministry of Infrastructure the functions on general coordination of activity between the ministries, other executive authorities, legal entities related to search and rescue at sea; establishes the Coordinating Committee on Search and Rescue at Sea and its Statute.

§4. 'No Cure No Pay'

500. The principle 'no cure – no pay' stipulated by Article 2 of the SOLAS, is also incorporated in the Ukrainian salvage law and can be found in Article 327 of the MSC. According to it every act with useful result as regards the vessel in distress, cargo and other subject-matters situated on board and also concerning the freight and payment for carriage of passengers and luggage or other property, as well as environment, gives the right to certain remuneration.

501. At the same time, the services rendered in spite of express and reasonable prohibition of the owner or master concerning salvage of the vessel or any other property that is not situated and has not been situated on board the vessel and has met with disaster, do not give the right to any remuneration (see Article 329 of the MSC).

502. Remuneration shall be paid even if the vessel that has rendered salvage services, belongs to the owner of the salvaged vessel (see Article 331 of the MSC).

503. The SIWT provides the same principles. According to Article 37 the remuneration shall be paid for rendering assistance to the vessel or raft that had incurred danger provided that the full or partial safety of the vessel, raft, cargo or other valuable property was ensured.

504. It should be noted that the SIWT does not include the freight and payment for carriage of passengers and luggage, as well as environment as a basis for payment of reward.

§5. Life Rescue

505. Article 330 of the MSC stipulates that no reward is due from the persons whose lives are salved. Salvors of life who have taken part in the services rendered in the case of the accident causing a necessity of salvage are entitled to a fair share of the amount awarded to the salvor for salving the vessel or other property or preventing or minimizing damage to the environment.

506. The same principle is set forth in Article 38 of the SIWT, that is, *persons whose lives are saved shall not pay reward for their salvage.*

507. However, salvage of persons can lead to a higher reward according to Article 333 of the MSC, because *the skill and efforts of the salvors in salving the … life* is one of criteria for reward stipulation.

§6. Salvage Remuneration

508. According to Article 332 of the MSC, the amount of the reward shall be fixed by agreement of the parties, and in case of failure – by the court, commercial court or by the Maritime Arbitration Commission. Any salvage agreement concluded at the time of or under the influence of danger can be held invalid or changed judicially on demand of one of the parties, if it is adjudicated that the conditions of the agreement are unreasonable.

509. The amount of reward can be decreased or reward can be denied, if the salvor being at fault has caused the necessity to make a rescue or commit theft, embezzle or has caused other illegal actions.

510. According to Article 333 of the MSC, the reward shall be stipulated with the purpose of motivation of salvage operations taking into account the following criteria (in spite of order of their description):

(1) the salved value of the vessel and other property;
(2) the skills and efforts of the salvors in preventing or minimizing damage to the environment;
(3) the measure of success obtained by the salvor;
(4) the nature and degree of the danger;
(5) the skills and efforts of the salvors in salving the vessel, other property and life;
(6) the time used and expenses and losses incurred by the salvors;
(7) the risk of liability and other risks run by the salvors or other equipment;
(8) the promptness of the services rendered;
(9) the availability and use of vessels *or* other equipment intended for salvage operations;
(10) the state of readiness and efficiency of the salvor's equipment and the value thereof.

511. Payment of the reward shall be made by all persons interested in the vessel and other property in proportion to their respective salved values. If the reward is paid by one person, the person has a right of recourse against the other persons for their respective shares.

512. Article 334 of the MSC provides that the reward, exclusive of any interest and recoverable legal costs that may be payable thereon, shall not exceed the salved value of the vessel and other property.

513. The apportionment of a reward is regulated by Articles 335 and 336 of the MSC. The first one regulates apportionment of a reward between salvors to be made under the agreement, and failing such agreement – by the court using the criteria contained in Article 333 of the MSC. The second one, covers the apportionment between the owner, master and other persons, who have participated in salvage operation, to be made with account of individual contribution to achieve the positive result of salvage by mutual agreement of interested persons, and failing such agreement – by the court, commercial court or by the Maritime Arbitration Commission. However, this provision does not relate to the apportionment of a reward for salvage operation by the vessels for which such operations is professional activity.

514. Article 340 of the MSC deals with securities for the salvor's demand. This Article stipulates the right of the salvor to claim a person, who is responsible for payment of salvage award, to give satisfactory security for the claim, including interest and legal costs of the salvor. The owner of the salved vessel shall use its best endeavours to ensure that the cargo owners provide satisfactory security for the claim against them, including interest and legal costs of the salvor, up to the moment when cargo is delivered.

515. Without consent of the salvor, the salved vessel or other property shall not be removed from the port or other place whereto the property has been delivered at first after completion of the salvage operations until satisfactory security of the salvor's claim is provided against the relevant vessel or property.

516. The situation with the SIWT slightly differs. According to Article 37 of the SIWT the amount of reward shall:

- include payment of services and all expenses related to these services;
- be established by agreement of the parties, and failing such agreement – by the court;
- not exceed the value of salved property.

517. Article 39 of the SIWT provides the list of persons who do not have any right to a reward for rendering assistance, namely:

- crew of the vessel or raft that incurred danger, as well as its tug or the vessel being towed;
- persons, who have rendered services in spite of reasonable prohibition of the master of the vessel or foreman (agent, pilot) of the raft that is incurred danger.

518. The SIWT does not stipulate any criteria which can be considered in time of agreement of the amount of the award. In this case it is necessary to use analogy in law and general practice on these issues.

I. Contract Salvage

519. Article 332 of the MSC and Article 37 of the SIWT provide the possibility to conclude salvage agreement that are based on the principle of 'freedom of contract'. There are no imperative provisions to be included in the agreement; however, the Maritime Arbitration Commission at the Ukrainian Chamber of Commerce and Industry has developed a standard form of the salvage agreement, which is recommended for signing.[234]

II. Special Compensation

520. Following Article 14 of the International Convention on Salvage, 1989, Article 338 of the MSC provides the right of the salvor to a special compensation.

234. See at www.ucci.org.ua/arb/mac/en/contract.html.

The wording of Article 338 of the MSC is almost the same as in the Convention and provides that if the salvor has carried out salvage operations in respect of a vessel which by itself or its cargo threatened damage to the environment and has failed to earn a reward, he shall be entitled to special compensation from the owner of that vessel equivalent to his expenses that can be increased up to a maximum of 30% of the expenses incurred by the salvor.

521. However, the court, commercial court or the Maritime Arbitration Commission, if it deems fair taking into account the relevant criteria set out in Article 333 of the MSC, may increase such special compensation further, but in no event shall the total increase be more than 100% of the expenses incurred by the salvor.

522. The SIWT does not stipulate any provisions concerning 'special compensation'. Therefore, in this case it is necessary to apply the relevant provisions of the MSC by analogy.

III. State-Owned Cargoes

523. Article 339 of the MSC incorporates into the national law the legal rule stipulated by the International Convention on Salvage, 1989, Article 25. According to the Article 339 of the MSC unless the state owner consents, no provisions of the Chapter 6 of Part IX of the Code shall be used as a basis for the seizure, arrest or detention of non-commercial cargoes owned by a state and entitled at the time of the salvage operations to sovereign immunity under the generally recognized principles of international law. The SIWT does not have any provisions concerning state-owned cargoes.

§7. Conclusion

524. In conclusion it shall be mentioned that despite the fact that the Ukrainian salvage law does not have enough law enforcement in Ukraine, it keeps up vital international principles of salvage law that is important for development of the Ukrainian maritime law.

Chapter 11. Towage

§1. Introduction

525. The relevant provisions of the contract of towage can be found in Part VII of the MSC and in Part VI of the SIWT of the USSR.

§2. Definition of Towage Contract

526. Definition of the towage contract can be found in both MSC and SIWT and, therefore, towage in Ukraine can be divided into 'sea towage' regulated by the MSC, and 'inland water towage' regulated by the SIWT, where the first one consists of 'port towage' and 'inter-port towage'.

527. It is important to illustrate different kinds of towages because each of them has its own peculiar features and liability regimes.

528. Article 222 of the MSC stipulates that the contract of sea towage means a contract under which the owner of one vessel contracts in exchange of payment:

- to tow other vessel or waterborne object for certain distance;
- to tow it during the certain time; or
- for performance of manoeuvre.

529. According to section 126 of the SIWT, a shipping company is obliged to tow a raft or vessel for a fixed payment under the contract of towage:

- up to a certain point;
- during a certain time; or
- for performance of a certain manoeuvre.

530. Pursuant to Article 229 of the MSC the contract of port towage means a contract under which the owner of the tug in exchange for a payment carries out calling at or leaving the port by vessels or other waterborne objects, performance by towing vessel of manoeuvring, mooring and other operations in the harbour waters.

531. Under the contract of inter-port towage the owner of one vessel (of the tug) is obliged in exchange for a payment to tow other vessel or other waterborne object from one port (point) to another port (point) of the MSC.

532. Considering all these contracts in general, it shall be noted that the towage contract under the Ukrainian law is:

- *consensual*, except the cases when towage contract is concluded as a long-term ('navigational') contract as such type of towage contract can be considered as a

'framework contract' where each towage depends on the fact of delivery of the object to the tug that in its turn implies this contract is real unless otherwise agreed;
- *onerous*, because towage shall be carried out in consideration of any kind of remuneration;
- *bilateral,* as there are two parties.

§3. Entering into a Towage Contract

533. Taking into account distinctions of the above-mentioned contracts it is preferable to consider each of them separately.

534. Port Towage Contract. According to Article 229 of the MSC the contract of port towage can be concluded orally. However, it is recommended to conclude this contract in writing, especially if the owner or master of the vessel to be towed wishes to make the master of the tug responsible for port towage. According to Article 230 of the MSC the master of the vessel (object) which is in tow shall manage towage operations, unless otherwise stipulated by the contract. Agreement on imposing a duty to manage towage on the master of the tug can be proved by writing evidences only. According to Article 231 of the MSC, in order to ensure the safety of navigation in the harbour waters, the harbourmaster of the seaport is entitled to stipulate compulsory usage of tugs and terms and conditions of towage for calling, leaving or displacement of the vessel in the harbour waters, carrying out of manoeuvring, mooring and other operations.

535. Inter-Port Towage Contract. In contrast to the port towage contract, the inter-port towage contract (Article 233 of the MSC) shall be in writing and contain the following terms as regards to:

- ports (points) of departure and destination;
- time of towage;
- the rights and obligations of the parties;
- responsibility for breach of contract;
- particularities of objects being towed that can take effect on safety of towage; and
- other terms that the parties have decided to agree separately.

536. These terms are essential and if the parties fail to follow this rule, the contract can be declared as invalid.

537. Inland Water Towage Contract. The SIWT does not contain any particular requirements to the contract which shall be followed by the parties. Therefore, the general principles of the contract law of Ukraine shall apply to this contract, that is, the inland water towage contract shall be concluded in writing and shall contain such essential terms of the contract as:

– terms about subject of the contract; and
– terms in respect of which the agreement shall be reached on the application of one of the parties.

§4. Duties of Tug and Tow

538. The Chapter 1 of Part VII of the MSC stipulates the principal obligations of the maritime towage contract:

– First of all, it is an obligation concerning the seaworthiness of vessels. The MSC defines in Article 223 that each of the parties of the sea towage contract shall in good time provide the fitness of the vessel or other waterborne object for carrying out the services in accordance with the contract of sea towage. This obligation relates both to the owner of the tug and to the owner of the tow.
– The second obligation related to all sea towage contracts is assistance to the ship in distress (Article 228 of the MSC). The master of the tug is obliged to ensure the tow or other waterborne object in distress by the life-saving equipment and to carry out the assistance up to the moment when such ship or waterborne object is able to be without such assistance of the tug. The owner of the tug is entitled to claim compensation of actual expenses of the tug without payment of salvage remuneration.

539. The above-mentioned obligations are stipulated by the law and shall be fulfilled by the parties.

§5. Control and Liability in Towage

540. The issue of who is in control of towage is of importance since it influences on the capacity of the responsibility of the parties especially in case of collision.

541. Therefore, it is preferable to divide all objects that can be towed depending on whether the object is manned or not, and in each particular case consider the question of control.

542. If the object is not manned, for example, barge, it is quite reasonable to consider that the tug is in control of the towage and is responsible for safety. In case of port towage it is quite understandable that in most cases this towage is directed to provide calling in or leaving the vessels from the port and that such vessels are manned by the crew. Therefore, Article 230 of the MSC provides an obligation of the master of the tow to control the towage and to be responsible for towage and its consequences, unless otherwise agreed by the parties in writing. In respect to interport towage the master of the tug is in charge for towage operation. And one of the reasons of such obligation is that the towing object could be unmanned and therefore the master of the tug should provide safe towage.

543. If the owner of the towing object nominates a person as a head of towage operation who is not a master of the tug during the performance of the inter-port towage, the relationships of this person with the master of the tug are regulated by the inter-port towage contract (Article 236 of the MSC).

544. As regards to the question of liability in towage operation, it usually depends on the question of control, that is, the party who is in charge for towage is liable.

545. The party who is in control (the tug or the tow) can be discharged from liability if it proves its guiltlessness (the burden to prove is carried by this party). The appropriate provisions in this respect are laid down in Articles 225 and 226 of the MSC.

Chapter 12. Marine Insurance in Ukraine

§1. Legal Regulation of Marine Insurance Activity in Ukraine

546. Ukrainian marine insurance is regulated mainly by Chapter 1 Part VIII of the MSC. Article 241 of the MSC stipulates that the rules of this chapter shall be applied in circumstances unless otherwise agreed by the parties. However, the agreement that does not correspond to these rules shall be invalid in the cases expressly provided in this Chapter.

547. This chapter of the MSC along with Article 2 of the Law on Insurance,[235] Chapter 35 of the Commercial Code of Ukraine and Chapter 67 of the Civil Code of Ukraine contains the insurance provisions. These provisions shall be applied according to Article 4 of the MSC: in case the civil, administrative, commercial and other legal relations arising from the shipping activity are not regulated by the MSC, the appropriate provisions of the civil, administrative, commercial and other legislation of Ukraine shall be applied.

§2. Contract of Marine Insurance

548. Article 239 of the MSC provides that under the contract of marine insurance the insurer undertakes to indemnify the assured or other person for whose benefit the contract is concluded, against the incurred expenses for agreed amount of payment (insurance premium) and upon the occurrence of dangers or fortuities with an object of insurance (insured event) as agreed in the contract. The contract of marine insurance shall be concluded in writing (Article 240 of the MSC).

549. The objects of marine insurance stipulated by Article 242 of the MSC are any objects referred to shipping property interest, namely: the vessel, including that is under construction, cargo, freight, payment for passage, lease payment, profit expected from cargo and claims secured by the vessel, cargo and freight, salaries, other kinds of remuneration of the master, other crew members, civil liability of ship owner and carrier, as well as risk undertaken by the insurer (reinsurance).

550. The object of insurance shall be stipulated by the contract of marine insurance. Failure to comply with this rule leads to invalidity of the contract according to Article 241 of the MSC.

551. Section 3 of Article 242 of the MSC defines two types of contracts of marine insurance, namely *contracts of marine insurance with assured-residents* and *contracts of obligatory insurance of passengers against accident, arisen in time of sea carriage*. These contracts can be concluded by the insurers only that shall satisfy the following requirements:

---

235. Dated 7 Mar. 1996, No. 85/96-BP.

– recognized as such according to the legislation of Ukraine;
– have a license to carry out this type of insurance in the prescribed manner; and – members of the Marine Insurance Bureau.

552. Taking into account Article 241 of the MSC, failure to comply with this rule can also lead to invalidity of the contract, but nowadays it is impossible to fulfil all these requirements as it explained below.

553. According to section 4 of Article 242 of the MSC, the Marine Insurance Bureau shall carry out coordination of the insurers' activity in the field of insurance against marine risks and shall represent their interests in international associations of insurers. The incorporation and the state registration of the Marine Insurance Bureau shall be carried out under the procedure established by the CMU.

554. Basing on this provision of the MSC, the Cabinet of Ministers issued the Decree dated 27 April 1998, No. 561, according to which the Marine Insurance Bureau and the Aviation Insurance Bureau had been formed. However, in 2005 the Cabinet of Ministers issued Decree dated 20 August 2005, No. 788 by means of which the previous Decree of the CMU No. 561 dated 27 April 1998 become void. Hence, the Marine Insurance Bureau does not exist in present day and in compliance with section 3 of Article 242 of the MSC it is impossible to fulfil all the requirements in order to become the insurer.

555. The principal obligations under the contract of marine insurance are as follows:

(1) An assured shall:
  - make a payment of insurance premium (Article 245 of the MSC, subsection 1 of section 1, Article 21 of the Law of Ukraine on Insurance);
  - notify an insurer about conditions which are essential for determination of degree of risk and known or shall be known to the insurer, as well as about the information requested by insurer; and immediate notification concerning any essential changes that have happened to the object of insurance or in relation to this object (overloading, changing of the mode of carriage, port of delivery, course deviation, etc.) as this gives an insurer the right to review the contract of marine insurance (Articles 243 and 262 of the MSC, subsection 2 of section 1, Article 21 of the Law of Ukraine on Insurance). An assured is not obliged to notify on well-known facts. Failure to provide with information gives an insurer the right to withdraw from the contract of marine insurance;
  - notify an insurer about other contracts of insurance concerning an object of insurance and if an assured does not inform about that, the new contract of insurance shall be null and void (subsection 3, section 1, Article 21 of the Law of Ukraine on Insurance);
  - take measures on prevention of damages caused by occurrence of insured event, and their reduction (Article 263 of the MSC, subsection 4, section 1, Article 21 of the Law of Ukraine on Insurance);

- notify an insurer about the insured event (Article 263 of the MSC, subsection 5, section 1, Article 21 of the Law of Ukraine on Insurance).

(2) An insurer shall:

- familiarize an assured with the terms and conditions of the insurance (subsection 1, section 1, Article 20 of the Law of Ukraine on Insurance);
- fill in all necessary documents during two working days since he has known about insurance event to make a payment of insurance premium or insurance compensation in due time (subsection 2, section 1, Article 20 of the Law of Ukraine on Insurance);
- make a payment of insurance premium or insurance compensation according to the contract of insurance (subsection 3, section 1, Article 20 of the Law of Ukraine on Insurance);
- compensate all the costs incurred by an assured to avoid or minimize the losses covered by the contract of insurance, as well as the costs incurred due to the instructions of an insurer for the purpose of clarification and establishment of the losses to be compensated by an insurer and with the purpose of adjustment of the general average (Article 267 of the MSC, subsection 4, section 1, Article 20 of the Law of Ukraine on Insurance);
- renew the contract of insurance upon application of an assured in case of taking measures that led to minimization of losses, or increase of cost of the property (subsection 5, section 1, Article 20 of the Law of Ukraine on Insurance);
- not disseminate information about an assured (subsection 6, section 1, Article 20 of the Law of Ukraine on Insurance).

§3. Subrogation

556. Article 269 of the MSC stipulates that in case of payment of the insurance amount, except the case provided by Article 266 of the MSC, the following shall be transferred to an insurer upon its consent:

- all rights to the insured property – in case of insurance for the full value;
- the right to the part of the insured property proportionally to the insurance amount and insurance value – in case of insurance for part of value.

§4. Abandonment

557. According to Article 271 of the MSC an assured is able to notify an insurer about renunciation of its own rights concerning all insured property (abandonment) and to receive the full insurance amount in the following cases:

- the vessel is being missing;
- constructive total loss;
- capture of the vessel or cargo insured against such risk, if this capture is more than two months.

558. Moreover, any agreement of the parties that does not comply with the Article 271 shall be null and void.

559. The application concerning abandonment shall be submitted to an insurer during six months from the moment of expiry of the time limit (occurrence of circumstances) mentioned in Articles 270 and 271 of the MSC.

560. According to Article 270 of the MSC, the vessel shall be considered as missing when there is no information about this vessel during three months, or if receipt of this information could be delayed due to military operations – during six months. An insurer is responsible for the vessel which is missed under the contract of marine insurance for a particular period of time, if the last notification about the vessel is received before the date of termination of the contract and if an insurer does not prove that the vessel has been missed before expiry of this term.

§5. Policy

561. Upon request of an assured, an insurer shall issue under his own signature a document containing the terms of contract of marine insurance to an assured (policy, insurance certificate, etc.) (Article 244 of the MSC.)

562. In case of payment of insurance compensation an insurer is able to request to present the policy or other insurance document issued by an insurer (Article 247 of the MSC.).

563. Under the separate agreement (general policy) to the contract an insurer and assured can insure all cargoes that an assured receives or sends during the fixed period of time (Article 253 of the MSC). In this case as regards to each shipment of cargo covered by the general policy, an assured undertakes to provide an insurer with all necessary information immediately after its receipt, in particular, name of the vessel that carries the cargo, moving direction of cargo and insurance amount.

564. In spite of that an insurer is obliged to issue the policy or insurance certificate upon the request of an assured concerning particular shipments covered by the general policy. And if there is a discrepancy between the general policy and thc policy (insurance certificate), information contained in the policy (insurance certificate) shall prevail according to Article 255 of the MSC.

565. An assured cannot be released from this obligation even if he receives information about shipment after its delivery at the place of destination free of damage.

566. If an assured fails to inform or provides information untimely, an insurer will be entitled to refuse in reimbursement of damages as regards the appropriate cargoes. Nevertheless, an insurer reserves a right on insurance premium which he could have received, unless an assured proves that failure to give notice or provision of untimely information has occurred through no fault of an assured.

567. Moreover, an insurer is able to withdraw from insurance under the general policy, if an assured intentionally fails to provide the information or does not inform about it at all or intentionally and incorrectly has notified about the cargo and the insurance amount. Upon that an insurer reserves a right on insurance premium which he could have received, if the contract of marine insurance has been fully performed by an assured.

568. It follows from the Article 254 of the MSC that an insurer has a burden to prove that an assured fails to perform his own obligation properly according to the contract of marine insurance.

§6. Insurance of the State Seagoing Vessels

569. In order to regulate effectively the insurance activity in the field of maritime transport and to increase cash inflow to the State Budget of Ukraine, the MTC issued the Order dated 17 May 1999, No. 260 registered in the Ministry of Justice on 17 June 1999, No. 386/3679, by means of which the Procedure of the Conclusion of Contracts of Insurance of the Seagoing Vessels that are Sovereign-owned, Chartered out, Rented out, Leased out by the Ship Owner (hereinafter referred to in this chapter as 'Procedure') was approved.

570. The main features of this Procedure are as follows:

– the Procedure relates to the seagoing vessels of the state ownership subject to the Ministry of Infrastructure that are freighted out, rented out or leased out;
– contract of insurance of the vessel shall contain the following conditions:
  (1) all policies of insurance shall bear the name of ship owner;
  (2) insurance shall cover at least the full destruction of the vessel;
  (3) if there is a creditor-pledgee, policies shall stipulate the possibility to pay him an insurance indemnity in case of loosing of the pledge item (destruction of the vessel);
  (4) amount of insurance shall not be less than the balance value of the vessel.

571. In time of renting out of the vessel, the bailor shall stipulate in the rental contract the requirement to insure the vessel by the tenant for the good of the bailor according to this Procedure. In time of chartering out, renting out or leasing out the vessel to the non-resident, the insurance costs of the ship owner can be taken into account in time of calculation of the freight rate, rent and lease payments.

572. Moreover, according to section 5 of the Procedure, an insurer shall, by means of incorporation of the insurance terms into the contract of affreightment (rent or lease agreements) of the vessel, familiarize charterer (tenant, lessee) with essential terms and conditions of the insurance that can lead to default of payment of the insurance indemnity.

Chapter 13. Pilotage

§1. Introduction

573. The legal provisions regulating pilotage in Ukraine can be found in the MSC. It is also necessary to note that these provisions regulate only pilotage at sea and do not relate to the pilotage at inland waterways. The most of these provisions have 'migrated' from the MSC USSR and at present require the follow-up revision. Therefore, pilotage in Ukraine is also regulated by the subordinate regulatory Acts that will be mentioned in this Chapter.

§2. Legal Regulation

574. Before June 2013, the MSC provided that pilotage in Ukraine should be carried out exclusively by the state sea pilots. However, in 2012 the *Verchovna Rada* has passed the Law of Ukraine on Sea Ports of Ukraine dated 17 May 2012 No. 4709-VI amending the rules on pilotage. The Law of Ukraine on Sea Ports of Ukraine is aimed at reforming the seaport sector. Since pilotage relates to this sector of economic activity, it has been decided to abolish the state monopoly. Therefore, according to these amendments to the MSC, which are in force from June 2013, a sea pilot, regardless of being an employee of private or state legal entity, is entitled to carry out pilotage in Ukraine. Thus, the MSC stipulates in Article 92 that with the purpose of ensuring the safety of navigation on approaches to sea ports within the limits of these ports, as well as between sea ports irrespective of the state flag under which the vessel sails, and form of ownership thereof, pilotage of the vessels shall be carried out exclusively by the sea pilots.

575. The MIU shall prescribe the requirements for sea pilots and legal entities, whose employees are sea pilots, as well as the order of exercising their activity. For this reason, Regulation on Sea Pilots has been approved by the Order of the MIU dated 08 May 2013, No. 292, registered by the Ministry of Justice of Ukraine on 10 June 2013, No. 920/23452. The requirements of the Regulation on Sea Pilots are compulsory for sea pilots and legal entities, whose employees are sea pilots and who pilot the vessels on the way to seaports, within the harbour of these ports, as well as between seaports which is within the stipulated areas of pilotage regardless to flag and type of ownership of the vessel. Moreover, provisions of this Regulation are compulsory for ship owners, charterers, marine agents, masters of the vessels and other persons authorized by the ship owner, who ordered the pilot service.

576. The following kinds of pilotage services are stipulated by section 1.5 of the Regulation on Sea Pilots:

- linear pilot services (provided in shipping lanes in territorial waters, the fairways and channels)
- harbour pilot services (provided within port areas)

577. Moreover, there are compulsory and non-compulsory pilotages. In the area of compulsory pilotage the vessel shall not carry out navigation without the state sea pilot, unless the vessel belongs to the types of the vessels that dispense with compulsory pilotage. As regards non-compulsory pilotage, the master of the vessel is entitled to take a pilot aboard, if it is necessary.

578. According to Article 94 of the MSC the MIU with the concurrence of other interested ministries and authorities is entitled to establish areas of compulsory pilotage, types of vessels which dispense with compulsory pilotage, and publish this information in sailing directions and Notices to mariners. The harbourmaster of the seaport shall control passage of vessels without a pilot in the relevant area of compulsory pilotage and shall inform the pilot legal entity about the detected happenings.

579. In the area of non-compulsory pilotage the master of the vessel is entitled to request the pilot service and to take a pilot aboard when necessary.

Additionally, in the area of non-compulsory pilotage the harbourmaster of the seaport is entitled to establish compulsory pilotage for the following types of vessels:

- vessels which in itself (nuclear and other vessels) or its cargo constitutes a menace to the environment (types of these vessels shall be published in the port's regulations);
- vessels which have a serious hull damage, damage to the mechanisms or equipment, that can assert essential influence on the safety navigation in the area (in this case the master of the vessel shall be served with a notice that his vessel is subject to compulsory pilotage).

580. The pilot shall be ordered on board the vessel according to the request of the shipmaster and/or marine agent, authorized by the ship owner. In case of a pilot call, the pilot legal entity shall order the pilot on board the vessel immediately. If it is impossible to do, the pilot legal entity shall inform the shipmaster about the time of pilot's arrival on board the vessel.

581. Moreover, additional remuneration shall be paid in the following cases:

- if the sea pilot stays on the vessel longer than two hours due to necessity of additional loading or discharging, defect of vessel's mechanisms, locating of the vessel in quarantine and other circumstances, unless they are occurred due to force majeure circumstances, the shipmaster shall sign the pilot's bill, state the reason of pilot's delayed stay on the vessel on the back of the pilot's bill and pay to the pilot legal entity additional remuneration, stipulated by the state authorities according to Article 106 of the MSC (Article 107 of the MSC; section 4.13 of the Regulation on Sea Pilots);
- if the sea pilot and a trainee have been taken by the vessel, which has been piloted, beyond the area of pilot service, the shipmaster shall compensate the costs of their return to the place of employment (travel expenses, daily allowances, accommodation), as well as he shall pay remuneration, stipulated by Article 107 of the MSC, for each day of stay beyond the area of pilot service (Article 108 of the MSC; section 4.15 of the Regulation on Sea Pilots).

§3. Duties of the Pilot

582. At the time of pilotage the pilot shall keep watch over conditions and correctness of marking the fairway, conditions of coastal navigation markers and immediately inform the harbourmaster about any changes in the fairway and incidents with the vessels piloted by him.

583. The pilot shall point out the master of the vessel piloted by him, on violations of the navigational rules, port's regulations and other rules, as well as to demand rectification of such violations and in case of master's non-fulfilment of these legitimate demands of the state pilot – immediately notify the harbourmaster about it.

584. Moreover, the pilot is not allowed to leave the vessel without consent of the shipmaster before the vessel is anchored, berthed to the safe place, taken out to sea or changed by other pilot (Article 103 of the MSC).

585. At the same time the pilot is entitled to refuse to carry out pilotage in the presence of the third person if the master overrides the pilot's recommendations. Pilot is entitled to request to make an appropriate record on the pilot's bill and in the ship's log concerning his refusal. However, even in this case pilot is not entitled to leave the vessel and if the master requires any information for safety navigation of the vessel, the pilot shall provide it, or, if the master requires, shall continue pilotage.

586. If the master has any doubts concerning correctness of the pilot's recommendations, he is entitled to waive its services. And, if it happens in the area of compulsory pilotage, the master, if it is possible, shall block the traffic of the vessel before arrival of another pilot. In spite of that, the master shall pay pilot fee in full, if he calls pilot and after that waives its services. Moreover, if it is necessary to ensure the safety of navigation, to prevent accidental maritime events, to protect the environment and human life, the pilot is entitled to stop the pilotage of the vessel. In this case and immediately, if it is possible, the pilot shall inform the harbormaster and require to make a record in the pilot's bill concerning this stoppage.

§4. Liability of the Pilot

587. According to Article 97 of the MSC the presence of the pilot on board of vessel does not release the master from liability for navigation of the vessel. And in case of leaving the vessel bridge the master shall indicate for the pilot a person who is responsible for navigation of the vessel when he is absent.

588. The liability for incidents at sea occurred due to failure of the pilot to perform its own employment duties shall be borne by organization that employed a pilot. However, this liability is restricted by the amounts of emergency pilot's fund. Such fund is created by 10% of deductions from the amounts of pilot fees received in the calendar year passed before the incident (Article 98 of the MSC).

Chapter 14. Liability For Marine Pollution

§1. Introduction

589. Ukraine has been recently hit by the oil pollution from ships in the Black Sea region. In November 2007 due to the sea storm and poor weather conditions three ships with oil and sulphur cargo were wrecked (m/v *Volganeft* with oil cargo 4,077 tonnes, m/v *Volnogorsk* with sulphur cargo 2,100 tonnes and *Kovel* with sulphur cargo 1,923 tonnes), in the territorial waters of Ukraine, namely in the Strait of Kerch. This significantly damaged the vulnerable ecosystem in the Kerch Bay area.

590. The Strait of Kerch is a body of water of the highest fisheries category as it is the migration route for fish between the Sea of Azov and Black Sea, including many species that are included in the Red List of the International Union for Conservation of Nature (IUCN). Despite this, oil activities in the Black Sea region are quite extensive; therefore, the potential detriment to the environment in this area is self-evident. Other threats to the vulnerable Black Sea ecosystem can be listed as the following: overfishing, industrial pollutants, a recent invasion of alien jellyfish delivered via ballast waters from other parts of the world. A duly notion should be given to the impact of the Chernobyl nuclear accident in May 1986 when substantial quantities of reactor-produced nuclides were released into the environment.

§2. Legal Regulation

591. The main provision on the protection and preservation of the marine environment is enshrined in Part XII of the UNCLOS. Article 192 imposes general obligation on States *to protect and preserve marine environment.*[236] Ukraine is a party to the International Convention for the Prevention of Pollution from Ships, 1973 adopted by the IMO and subsequently modified by the Protocol of 1978 or in short form MARPOL 73/78.[237]

592. The national legislation on marine environment consists of the Law of Ukraine on Environmental Protection[238] (Articles 68–70) and the Water Code of Ukraine[239] (Articles 236–254). The liability issues are found in the Code on Administrative Offences[240] (Articles 59–62) and in the Criminal Code of Ukraine[241] (Part

236. UNCLOS, Art. 194(3)(b).
237. Resolution of the CMU dated 21 Sep. 1993, No. 771 on Accession of Ukraine to the International Convention for the Prevention of Pollution from Ships (MARPOL), 1973, amendments of 1984, 1985, 1987, 1990 and 1992 and the Protocol 1987 to it.
238. Dated 25 Jun. 1991, No. 1264-XII.
239. Dated 6 Jun. 1995, No. 213/95-BP.
240. Resolution of *Verkhovna Rada* of Ukrainian SSR, dated 07 Dec. 84, No. 8074-10.
241. Dated 5 Apr. 2001, No. 2341-III.

VIII). The Law of Ukraine on Environmental Protection[242] defines legal, economic and social basis of organization of environmental protection in the interests of current and future generations. Article 39 of the Law stipulates that territorial sea and internal waters and natural resources of continental shelf and EEZ belong to natural recourses of national importance.

593. The Water Code of Ukraine defines the circle of water users, as well as their rights and obligations. Pursuant to it the water users in Ukraine can be legal entities, citizens of Ukraine, foreign natural persons and legal entities and persons without nationality. The Code also defines the right of general and special water usage. The general usage is conducted by citizens for satisfying their needs free of charge and without any permission, while special usage is fulfilled on the basis of permission. The protection of waters is dealt with in Part IV of the Water Code of Ukraine. Besides, it regulates the water protection zones, coastal protected lines, the limitations of commercial activity in coastal zones along the sea, maritime bays and on islands in internal waters.

§3. Sources of Pollution

594. Article 102 of the Water Code concerns protection of internal waters and the territorial sea. In particular it provides that discharge of the chemicals, nuclear and other dangerous items, as well as nuclear and other waters, items and garbage that might cause pollutions of the sea is forbidden from ships and waterborne objects, platforms and other maritime installations and aircrafts in the internal waters and the territorial sea. In line with Article 102 protection of inland waters and territorial sea against pollution and contamination is held in accordance with the Rules on Protection of Inland Waters and the Territorial Sea against Pollution and Contamination[243] and other legal Acts.

595. The conditions of discharge of waters into the water objects are dealt with in Chapter 14 of the Water Code of Ukraine. Under Article 70 of the Water Code of Ukraine discharge of sewage into water objects is allowed only if the standards of maximum permissible concentration and the standards of maximum permissible discharge of pollutants are complied with. Article 71 further provides that in case of exceeding the standards of maximum allowable pollutant discharge of sewage into surface water bodies may be limited, temporary banned or suspended in the manner prescribed by law.

596. MARPOL, Annex I, bears the Regulation 10 concerning the prevention of oil pollution from ships while operating in special areas. Here, the Black Sea is given the status of a 'special area' which means that discharge into the sea of oil or

---

242. Dated 25 Jun. 1991, No. 1264-XII.

243. Rules on Protection of Inland Waters and the Territorial Sea against Pollution and Contamination approved by Resolution of CMU dated 29 Feb. 1996, No. 269.

oily mixture is having a special regime. Ukraine is a party to the International Convention on Civil Liability for Oil Pollution Damage (CLC Protocol 1992).[244]

597. The Rules on Pollution Prevention from Vessels on Inland Waterways of Ukraine[245] (further – Rules on Prevention) determine the main requirements for civil vessels of all types and purposes with regard to pollution prevention of inland waterways by oil, hazardous substances, the residue of dangerous chemicals carried in bulk and package, oily and sewage waters and waste. The Rules cover all vessels regardless of ownership that are in inland waterways of Ukraine in exploitation, repair, in the process of modernization or construction.

598. The requirements of the Rules on Prevention are compulsory for masters, crew members and passengers of all vessels, including small vessels, management and staff of shipping companies, ports, industrial enterprises, technical stations of inland waterways, shipping hydrotechnical installations, objects of river transport whose activity is connected with exploitation and service of river fleet vessels on inland waterways, their repair, modernization, as well as development of projects and construction of new vessels (section 2.1).

599. Ship master, commander, captain are responsible for performing the organizational and technical measures concerning the pollution prevention from a vessel. Part IV of the Rules on Prevention is dealing with technology and registration of ship operation with oil, hazardous substances, water ballast, sewage and waste. It is provided that dumping of the mentioned above substances into inland waterways is prohibited. An exception from this list is isolated water ballast. The procedure for receiving and dumping is defined further in the Rules. The mentioned substances accumulated on a vessel during her voyage, stay or repair must be handed over to special vessels, purification stations and piers of all-inclusive fleet service (section 2.2).

600. With regard to the procedure of isolated water ballast dumping mentioned above, the Rules on Prevention give reference to the Instruction of Receiving and Dumping of Isolated Water Ballast within the Harbour of River Inland Waterways of Ukraine[246] and apply to the vessels of inland water transport and mixed river-sea ships used for navigation on inland waterways. Part IX of the Rules on Prevention gives special attention to pollution prevention of inland waterways from tankers carrying the oil in bulk and from bunker oil from vessels other than tankers. Part XI considers pollution prevention of discharge of sewage and wastes from vessels in inland waterways.

---

244. Law of Ukraine on Accession to the International Convention on Civil Liability dated 4 Jul. 2002, No. 44-IV.
245. Order of the MTC dated 13 Aug. 2007, No. 694, registered at the Ministry of Justice of Ukraine on 11 Oct. 2007, No. 1167/14434.
246. Order of the MTC dated 13 Jun. 2007, No. 491, registered at the Ministry of Justice on 27 Jun. 2007, No. 740/14007.

601. The Rules on Protection of Inland Waters and Territorial Sea against Pollution and Contamination[247] (further – Rules on Protection) establish requirements regarding prevention of pollution and contamination of internal waters and territorial sea of Ukraine by legal entities regardless of ownership, by citizens of Ukraine, foreign natural and legal entities and persons without nationality, Ukrainian and foreign vessels which stay in these waters. The scope of application of the Rules also extends to protection of waters in mouths of the rivers flowing into the sea, coastal strips of sea and islands in inland sea waters.

602. It is forbidden to dump into internal waters and territorial sea the cargo that is carried in bulk or is in liquefied condition, waste and garbage and waters containing contaminants in concentration that exceeds maximum allowable concentration of main pollutants, according to Annex to the Rules on Protection.

603. All contaminating substances including waters containing them and garbage shall be accumulated in special storage capacities. While staying in internal waters and territorial sea, the vessels may release contaminants including waters containing them and garbage only to the vessels-gatherers floating reception facilities, and while staying in port – to shore reception facilities.

604. In case of discharge and a threat arising from such discharge or loss, the ship master shall immediately inform administration of the nearest port of Ukraine to undertake measures to minimize dumping or loss and to liquidate the pollution.

§4. Liability Regime

605. Violation of environmental legislation entails disciplinary, administrative, civil and criminal liability. In particular, Articles 69–70 of the Law of Ukraine on Environmental Protection envisage the objects of legal protection of environment which also include waters. This Law establishes the basis of liability on violation of environmental protection. Article 69 contains the application of civil liability and Article 70 deals with administrative and criminal liability. Administrative liability arises basing on the provisions of Articles 59–62 of the Code on Administrative Offences of Ukraine. The Criminal Code of Ukraine contains Part VIII devoted to the crimes against environment. In particular Article 242 deals with the violation of water protection and Article 243 deals with the pollution of the sea in internal waters, territorial sea and within the EEZ that creates a threat to life and health of people or natural resources of the sea. Article 244 provides the punishment for the violation of the legislation on continental shelf of Ukraine. The Civil Code enshrines a right to environment that is safe for life and health and stipulates that activity of natural and legal persons that cause harm to environment is illegal. This activity can be stopped by virtue of a court's decision. (Civil Code, Article 293.)

247. Resolution of CMU dated 29 Feb. 1996, No. 269.

§5. MARINE POLLUTION CONTROL AND COOPERATION

606. The Convention on the Protection of the Black Sea against Pollution and the Protocol was signed in Bucharest in April 1992 and was ratified by all six legislative assemblies of the Black Sea countries in 1994 known as Bucharest Convention. The main objectives of the Convention are the control of land-based sources of pollution, dumping of waste and joint action in the case of accidents (such as oil spills).

607. Ukraine acceded to the Agreement on the Conservation of Cetaceans of the Black Sea, the Mediterranean Sea and the Contiguous Atlantic Area in 2003.[248] Ukraine ratified the Agreement for the Implementation of the Provisions of the UNCLOS 1982 Relating to the Conservation and Management of Straddling Fish Stock and Highly Migratory Fish Stocks in 2003.[249]

608. Regarding the protection, cooperation and trans-boundary water management of the Danube River, the Convention on Cooperation for the Protection and Sustainable Use of the River Danube was signed on 29 June 1994 in Sofia, Bulgaria, by eleven of the Danube Riparian States, including Ukraine and duly became effective as from October 1998 (in Ukraine in 2003).

248. Law of Ukraine dated 9 Jul. 2003, No. 1067IV.
249. Law of Ukraine dated 28 Nov. 2002, No. 319IV.

Part III. Other Transport

Chapter 1. General Introduction to Transport Law

§1. Introduction

609. The level of social and economic development of Ukraine is provided by continuous traffic in goods from internal and international transportations by all types of transport. This Part is divided into nine chapters. Both the Civil and Commercial Codes set the general provisions on contract of carriage and liability of the parties. They are illustrated in Chapter 1 and the following chapters encompass specific legal instruments regarding motor, rail, air, inland water, multimodal, pipeline transport, transit of goods and forwarding activity.

610. The general provisions on carriage are provided by the Civil Code[250] in Chapter 64, Articles 908–928 and in the Commercial Code (Chapter 32, Articles 306–316). Contract of carriage of passengers, baggage and mail is performed in accordance with the Civil Code's provisions; however, it also defines the contract of the carriage of goods. The Commercial Code applies only to the contract of carriage of goods. It should be observed that the provisions of the Commercial Code are *lex specialis* in the sphere of carriage of goods. The specific legal provisions concerning liability of the carrier, consignee, consignor, and the grounds for liability, amounts and types are also contained in subordinate regulatory Acts, statutes, etc.

§2. Licensing of Transport Activity in Ukraine

611. Pursuant to Article 9 of the Law of Ukraine on Licensing of Certain Types of Economic Activity[251] rendering the services on carriage of passengers and their luggage, dangerous goods, carriage by inland waterways, sea, motor, and railway transport are governed by this Law. With respect to sea and inland waterway transport, there is also an Order of the Ministry of Infrastructure dated 26 July 2013, No.

250. Civil Code dated 16 Jan. 2003, No. 435-IV.
251. Law of Ukraine on Licensing of Certain Type of Economical Activity dated 1 Jun. 2000, No. 1775-III.

524 that governs licensing of the carriage of goods and passengers and their luggage by sea and inland waterway transport, carriage of goods and carriage of dangerous goods. There are some of the types of commercial activity that are subject to licensing according to special laws, namely:

- foreign economic activity; and
- carriage of passengers and goods by air transport according to the Air Code of Ukraine.

612. Basing on a license issued by a licensing body,

which is the central body of executive power, commercial activity is performed within the entire territory of Ukraine. Correspondingly, the economic activity based on the license issued by a licensing body,
which is a local body of the executive power or a specially authorized executive body of the local government,
is performed within the territory of a relevant administrative-territorial unit.

§3. Insurance

I. General

613. Determination of liability of a carrier is closely related to the insurance of its liability. Some important provisions of the insurance law in Ukraine are underlined in this chapter and where relevant in other chapters.

614. The limit of liability (sum covered) is generally set in the contract of carriage. The sum covered can be determined by the capacity of transportations and value of goods from the maximum possible sums of claims that the carrier shall pay and by the current legal practice in countries where the carrier Acts. There is a strong opinion in the Ukrainian legal practice that if the carrier performs a carriage in one particular country, its liability is less than in case of international carriage.

615. In the contract of carriage the parties shall foresee the following issues: geographical limits of action of insurance coverage (e.g., only on the territory of Ukraine, the CIS); limits of liability of insurance company for single carriage or by one transport vehicle; requirements of safety and also information about alarm and protective devices used in the process of loading, unloading, transportation and temporal storage; terms of acceptance of claims by a carrier and conditions of terms and procedure for drawing of an insurer's act, types of cargoes, liability for which will not be covered.

616. Chapter 67 of the Civil Code of Ukraine defines the contract of insurance, its main conditions and the parties to it. The special provisions regarding the insurance in Ukraine are dealt with in the Law of Ukraine on Insurance that can be referred to as the *code of insurance*[252]. Notably, Articles 353–355 of the Commercial Code also defines insurance, main conditions of the contract and refers to *lex specialis*.

617. Insurers are financial institutions established in the form of the joint stock company, limited liability company, full liability company or differentiated liability company. Insurance activity in Ukraine is performed exclusively by insurers – residents of Ukraine who obtained the corresponding license.

618. Article 7 of the Law on Insurance defines the types of compulsory insurance in Ukraine that include medical insurance (Article 7, section 1); personal accident insurance on transport (Article 7, section 6); civil aviation insurance (Article 7, section 7); insurance of liability of a sea carrier and a contractor related to the maritime transport services for compensation to passengers, baggage, mail, cargo, marine transport to other users and third parties (Article 7, section 8); insurance of liability of vehicles' owners (Article 7, section 9); insurance of inland water transport (Article 7, section 10); liability insurance of entities for damages that may be caused by fires and accidents at high risk, including fire and explosion of the facilities that could lead to environmental damage (Article 7, section 14); liability insurance of dangerous goods in the event of adverse consequences for the carriage of dangerous goods (Article 7, section 26); liability insurance of the commercial tourist activity for the damage caused to life or health of the tourist or his property (Article 7, section 31); liability insurance of a ship owner (Article 7, section 32).

II. Compulsory Personal Insurance from Accidents on Transport

619. According to the Regulation on the Compulsory Personal Insurance from Accidents on Transport in Ukraine (further – Regulation)[253] the insured persons are passengers (from the moment of boarding) on the sea or river vessel, train, bus or other vehicle until the completion of a trip; and drivers only during the actual trip. Insurance does not cover passengers using:

- rail, maritime and inland water transport on excursion routes;
- intercity inland water transport and crossings;
- motor and city electric transport on municipal routes.

620. A carrier is acting as an agent of an insurer and shall issue insurance policy to each insured printed on the back of the ticket or as a separate document to the ticket. The document that confirms insurance for passengers during the regular passenger transport is a ticket. Type of compulsory insurance, name, address, phone of the insurer, the size of insurance premium and sum insured are stated in the insurance policy. Insurance fee is included in the fare. Passengers that have right on free

252. Law of Ukraine on Insurance dated 7 Mar. 1996, No. 85/96-BP.
253. Regulation Concerning the Compulsory Personal Insurance from Accidents on Transport in Ukraine approved by the Decree of the CMU dated 14 Aug. 1996, No. 959.

of charge carriage according to the current legislation, are entitled for compulsory insurance without payment and policy. Pursuant to section 6 of the Regulation a size of insurance premium for each insured constitutes 3,000 untaxed minimum of income of citizens (UMIC).[254]

621. As stated in the Regulation the insured accidents are as follows (section 7):

- death of insured person as a result of transport accident;
- injury caused as a result of transport accident if disability is defined by the medical institution;
- temporal disability as a result of transport accident.

622. An insured premium is to be paid not later than ten days after receiving of all necessary documents, namely, the statements of passenger (or his heirs) about payment, act on the accident, medical certificate regarding temporal loss of capacity or certificate on disability or copies of death certificate and documents about the competence of heirs. If the accident has occurred due to the wrongful and wilful conduct of the insured person, it is not considered as an insurance accident and does not entail the insurance payment to the insured passenger.

III. Insurance Related to the Carriage of Dangerous Goods

623. The Law of Ukraine on Transportation of Dangerous Goods[255] defines the legal, organizational, social and economic principles of the activity related to the carriage of dangerous goods by sea, inland waterways, motor, rail and air transport. It envisages compulsory insurance of carrier's liability for transportation of dangerous goods providing the compensation for harm caused to life and health of natural persons to the environment and property during the transportation of dangerous goods. The Law of Ukraine on Insurance provides compulsory insurance of carriers' liability for transportation of dangerous goods in cases of detrimental accidents during the carriage. The carrier is under obligation to conclude the contract of insurance before the beginning of transportation of dangerous goods. A separate contract of insurance is given out to a sender and a consignee for each carriage, pointing out a transport vehicle and quantity of dangerous goods. In the case when the carrier appears as both a sender and a recipient he must insure his liability in full. The order of insurance payment is determined by the contract of insurance. An insurer has the right to get all necessary information about the quantity of transportation of dangerous goods for previous period of insurance.[256]

254. Untaxed minimum of income of citizens is defined in the Tax Code of Ukraine dated 2 Dec. 2010, No. 2755-VI, Part XX, subs. 5 of s. 1 and equal to UAH 17.
255. Law of Ukraine on Transportation of Dangerous Goods dated 13 May 2000, No. 1644-III.
256. *Ibid.* Arts 5, 7, 8, 9 and 22.

§4. General Provisions of the Civil Code of Ukraine on Carriage of Passengers and Goods

I. Carriage of Passengers

624. It is envisaged by the Civil Code that under the contract for the carriage of passengers a carrier shall undertake to transport a passenger to the place of destination, and in case of delivery of the luggage, to deliver it as well to the place of destination and to hand it over to the person entitled to receive it. In its turn the passenger shall pay a fixed fare and a fee for luggage in case of its registry.[257] The conclusion of a contract is confirmed by a ticket and by a luggage receipt in case of its registry by the passenger.[258]

625. Passenger has a right to receive all information about the time and place of departure and any other relevant information. The passenger can carry one child free of charge (under 6 years old) or at a reduced fare (for children under 14 years old), to carry (with himself) hand luggage free of charge within the limits of fixed norms, to register luggage for carriage, to waive from the journey, to return the ticket and receive full or partial fare. The passenger has also the right to make one stopover with the extension of travel documents for no more than ten days. In case of illness the stopover could be defined for the duration of illness (Article 911 of the Civil Code).

II. Carriage of Goods

626. The Commercial Code regulates the carriage of goods in Chapter 32, Articles 306–315. The definition of contract of carriage of goods contained in Article 307 of the Commercial Code is identical to the one in the Civil Code. The Civil Code defines that under the contract of carriage of goods the carrier shall undertake to deliver the goods entrusted to him by a consignor to the point of destination and to issue it for the consignee entitled to receive it while the consignor undertakes to pay a fixed charge for the carriage of goods.[259] The conclusion of a contract is confirmed by drawing up and issuing of a consignment note stipulated by the relevant transport statute or code serving as a receipt for goods and evidence of the contract of carriage.[260]

627. According to Article 917 of the Civil Code of Ukraine a carrier shall provide the consignor with serviceable transport vehicles in a condition fit for the carriage of cargo for loading the cargo in stipulated time, while the consignor shall have the right to waive the supplied transport vehicles that are not fit for the carriage of cargo. Further it is stated that the carrier may refuse from discharging the

257. Civil Code, Art. 910, s. 1.
258. Civil Code, Art. 910, s. 2.
259. Civil Code, Art. 909.
260. Civil Code, Art. 909, s. 3, Commercial Code, Art. 307, s. 3.

goods in case they are presented in package which does not satisfy the requirements and also in case of absence or improper marking of the goods.[261]

628. The carrier shall deliver the goods to the place of destination within the time-limits stipulated in the contract, as well as in transport statutes and codes and in the absence of such time-limits – within a reasonable time.[262] The goods are considered lost if they are not delivered to the consignee upon its request within thirty days after delivery deadline, unless a longer term is provided (section 2 of Article 919 of the Civil Code).

629. The loading (discharging) of the cargo performed by forces and means of the consignor (consignee) is effective in the periods of time stipulated by the contract, unless such periods have been fixed by the transport statutes, codes and rules.[263]

630. The carrier has the right to withhold cargo and baggage given to him for carriage as a security for payments for carriage being due to him unless otherwise stipulated by laws, subordinate regulatory Acts and the contract of carriage or unless the contrary follows from the substance of obligation.[264]

631. Payment for carriage of goods is estimated on the basis of the rates approved in the manner and established by the transport statutes and codes unless the parties envisaged otherwise.[265] The party of the contract shall agree to all additional services and rates that were made on its request.[266]

§5. Liability Provisions and Exoneration of Liability

632. The Article 920 of the Civil Code sets the main rule regarding the liability. It states that in case the parties fail to fulfil the obligations under the contract of carriage, they shall bear liability pursuant to this Code, transport statutes and laws. A carrier shall also be liable for maintenance of the goods, luggage and mail from the moment of taking over to transportation until its delivery or transfer for storage. Carrier shall bear liability for its own actions, as well as for actions of other persons whose services were rendered to the carrier. Carrier is liable for taking care of the cargo from the moment it has been taken over for carriage and before its delivery to the consignee unless he proves that the loss of or damage to cargo has taken place due to the circumstances which the carrier was unable to prevent and not dependent on him.[267] Further, the carrier's liability includes:

261. Civil Code, Art. 917, s. 3.
262. Civil Code, Art. 919, s. 1.
263. Civil Code, Art. 918.
264. Civil Code, Art. 916, s. 4.
265. Civil Code, Art. 916, s. 1.
266. Civil Code, Art. 916, s. 3.
267. Civil Code, Art. 924, s. 1, Commercial Code, Art. 315.

- not providing with a transport vehicle (Article 921 of the Civil Code);
- delay in departure of a passenger and breach of delivery term in getting the passenger to the place of destination (Article 921 of the Civil Code);
- loss of, shortage in and damage to the goods (Article 924 of the Civil Code).

633. The damage caused during the carriage of goods is recovered by the carrier in the following cases:

- in the case of loss or shortage of goods or baggage – in the amount of the failure of the lost or missing cargo;
- in the case of damage to goods in the amount of the sum by which its value fell and if it is impossible to restore the damaged goods – in the amount of its value;
- in the case of loss of goods delivered for carriage with the stated value – in the amount of the stated value of goods.

634. The carrier and the consignor are relieved from liability if a failure to provide a transport vehicle or non-use of a provided vehicle occurred under the force majeure circumstances that they were unable to prevent, particularly, in case of termination (limitation) in transportation of goods in certain directions in a manner prescribed by the transport codes (statutes).[268]

635. The liability of the carrier for harm inflicted to life and health of a passenger shall be determined according to the rules of Chapter 82 of the Civil Code of Ukraine, unless the law or the contract of carriage provides for the carrier's liability without fault.[269]

§6. Time-Limits for Claims and Actions

636. The Procedure for settlement of disputes arising from the carriage of goods is covered in Article 925 of the Civil Code and Article 315 of the Commercial Code. The ComPC[270] provides that before bringing a suit against the carrier that follows from the carriage of cargo it is not necessary to bring a claim in the manner stipulated by the respective transport statute or code.[271] The same provision is maintained in Article 315 of the Commercial Code. However, the subordinate regulatory Acts vest parties with an obligation to try solving a dispute on a pre-trial stage. Following the practice in the Ukrainian courts, the court will normally request party/parties to exchange with claims before starting the process.

637. In line with the ComPC the legal entity that violated property rights and interests of other legal entity must restore them without waiting for a claim. The legal entity whose rights and legal interests are violated shall send the violator a

268. Civil Code, Art. 921, s. 2.
269. Civil Code, Art. 928.
270. ComPC dated 6 Nov. 1991, No. 1798-XII.
271. ComPC, Art. 5.

claim in order to resolve the dispute directly with the violator of these rights and interests (Article 6 of the Code). A claim is considered within a month calculated from the date of receipt of the claim. The legal entity that received a claim must satisfy the reasonable requirements of the applicant. The applicant shall be notified in writing on the results of examination of a claim (Article 7 of the Code).

638. According to Article 8 of the ComPC a reply to the claim shall include:

(1) full name and postal details of the legal entity that provide a reply and legal entity to whom the reply is addressed;
(2) whether the claim is recognized in whole or in part – acknowledged amount, name, number and date of the calculation document for the transfer of that amount or term and means of satisfying a claim, unless it is not subject to monetary evaluation;
(3) whether the claim is denied in whole or in part – the reasoning of dismissal with reference to the relevant regulations and documents that justify the dismissal of the claim;
(4) list of the documents annexed to the reply and other evidences.

639. When a claim is dismissed in whole or in part, the original documents obtained with a claim should be returned to the applicant and along with them the documents reasoning the dismissal of the claim. Claims concerning transportation of goods may be presented within six months, and claims for penalties and bonuses within forty-five days under Article 315, section 2 of the Commercial Code.

640. Claims arising from the contract of carriage of goods and mail are time barred in one year from the moment determined by transport statutes and codes.[272] For the claims following from the carriage of cargo delivered to the foreign destinations, the time-limits on claims are provided by the international instruments ratified by Ukraine.[273]

272. Civil Code, Art. 925, s. 3.
273. Civil Code, Art. 926.

Chapter 2. Carriage by Road

§1. Introduction

641. This chapter illustrates the legal provisions related to the carriage of passengers and goods by motor transport, liability of the carrier, including the national legislation and the international treaties, ratified by the *Verkhovna Rada*.

§2. Legal Regulation

I. International Treaties

642.

The Convention on the International Carriage of Passengers and Luggage by Road (CVR) (1973)	The USSR joined this Convention on 1 August 1983	The Law of Ukraine on Ukraine's Accession to the Convention on the Contract for the International Carriage of Passengers and Luggage by Road (CVR) dated 16 January 2005, No. 2239-IV
The Convention on the Contract for the International Carriage of Goods by Road (CMR) (1956)	The USSR joined this Convention on 1 August 1983	The Law of Ukraine on Ukraine's Accession to the Convention on the Contract for the International Carriage of goods by Road dated 1 August 2006, No. 57-V
The Vienna Convention on Road Traffic and the Vienna Convention on the Road Signs and Signals (1968)	Is in force for Ukraine as the successor of the USSR	
The Custom Convention on the International Transport of Goods under Cover of TIR Carnets (1959)		The Law of Ukraine on Ukraine's Accession to the Customs Convention on the International Transport of Goods under Cover of TIR Carnets dated 15 July 1994, No. 117/94-BP

The Convention on the ATA (Admission Temporaire – Temporary Admission) Carnet for the Temporary Admission of Goods (1961)	Is in force for Ukraine as the successor of the USSR	
The European Agreement Concerning the International Carriage of Dangerous Goods (ADR) (1957)		The Law of Ukraine on Ukraine's Accession to the European Agreement on International Carriage of Dangerous Goods (ADR) dated 2 March 2000, No. 1511-III
The European Agreement on Main International Traffic Arteries (1975)		The Decree on the Accession of the Ukrainian Soviet Socialist Republic to the European Agreement on Main International Traffic Arteries of 15 November 1975 dated 9 November 1982, No. 537
The Agreement on Special Equipment for the Transport of Perishable Foodstuffs and on the Use of Such Equipment for the International Transport of Some Foodstuffs (1962)		Presidential Decree on Ukraine's Accession to the Agreement on Special Equipment for the Transport of Perishable Foodstuffs and on the Use of Such Equipment for the International Transport of Some Foodstuffs dated 2 April 2007, No. 262/2007
The Agreement on international transport of perishable foodstuffs, and the special vehicles used for such carriage (Agreement on Special Equipment for the Transport of Perishable Foodstuffs and on the Use of Such Equipment for the International Transport of Some Foodstuffs) (1962)		Presidential Decree on Accession of Ukraine to the Agreement on International Carriage of Perishable Foodstuffs and on Special Vehicles dated 2 April 2007, No. 262/2007

The Agreement Concerning the Work of Crews of Vehicle Engaged in International Road Transport (1970)	The Law of Ukraine on Ukraine's Accession to the Agreement Concerning the Work of Crews of Vehicle Engaged in International Road Transport dated 9 September 2005, No. 2819-IV
The Agreement Concerning the Adoption of Uniform Technical Prescriptions for Wheeled Vehicles, Equipment and Parts which can be Installed and/or Used on Wheeled Vehicles and the Conditions for Reciprocal Recognition of Approvals Issued on the Basis of These Prescriptions (1958)	The Law of Ukraine on Ukraine's Accession to the Agreement Concerning the Adoption of Uniform Technical Prescriptions for Wheeled Vehicles, Equipment and Parts which can be Installed and/or Used on Wheeled Vehicles and the Conditions for Reciprocal Recognition of Approvals Issued on the Basis of These Prescriptions dated 10 February 2000, No. 1448-III

643. There are also a number of bilateral governmental agreements on international motor communication. Ukraine joined to some of them during the USSR (e.g., Agreement between the Government of the Ukrainian SSR and the Government of Italy, Spain, Norway, etc.). A number of agreements have been concluded and/or entered into force in the period of independence (e.g., Agreements between the governments of Ukraine and Latvia, Estonia, Belarus, Lithuania, Moldova, Azerbaijan, Armenia, Uzbekistan, Russia, Hungary, Belgium, etc.). In accordance with such arrangements, the regular and irregular passenger buses, carriage of goods and mail exist between the two countries and transit through the territories of the third countries.

II. National Legislation

644. The national legislation on carriage by motor transport could be divided in three main groups: the legal Acts on carriage of passengers and goods by motor transport; standards of rendering services on motor transport and technical standards for transport involved in carriage of passengers and goods. The legislation on motor transport has its own *code of transport* consisting of the Law of Ukraine on

Transport,[274] the Law of Ukraine on Traffic,[275] the Law of Ukraine on Motor Transport,[276] the Statute of Motor Transport (1969),[277] the Law of Ukraine on Functioning of the Unified Transport System of Ukraine in a Special Period,[278] the Law of Ukraine on Roads,[279] Rules on Carriage of Goods by Motor Transport in Ukraine,[280] Rules on Carriage of Mail by Motor Transport,[281] Rules on Rendering the Services on Motor Transport for Passengers[282] and legislation on insurance. Most of the listed laws were amended by the Law dated 20 November 2012 based on the ongoing Administrative Reform; these amendments mainly concern public administration and regulation in the field of transportation.

645. The Statute of Motor Transport defines the rights and obligations of motor carrier on the territory of Ukraine. On the base of this Statute the Ministry of Transport approved the Rules on Carriage of Goods by Motor Transport in Ukraine. These Rules include the conditions of transportation of certain types of goods. The Rules of Carriage of Goods by Motor Transport in Ukraine do not regulate the carriage of dangerous cargo, mail and cargo in international traffic.

646. The state control on motor transport is performed by the central executive body in the field of transport, its territorial bodies, including international motor transportation services and the State Motor Transport Service and others. In case of finding of violations related to the legislation on motor transport the territorial bodies of the central executive power in the field of transport are entitled to order removal of violation, to impose financial sanctions, etc. not later than ten working days starting from the day of finding of such a violation.

647. The Law of Ukraine on Motor Transport divides the motor transport by its use into passenger, cargo and passenger motor vehicles and trailers. There are provisions on the basic rights and duties of a bus and a taxi driver during the carriage of passengers (Articles 39–43), procedure for the tender for carriage of passengers on bus routes of common use (Articles 44–47), internal transportation of cargoes by motor transport (Articles 48–51), international carriage of passengers and cargoes by motor transport (Articles 53–58), liability of the carrier (Article 60), etc., in this Law.

---

274. Law of Ukraine on Transport dated 10 Nov. 1994, No. 232/94.
275. Law of Ukraine on Traffic dated 30 Jun. 1993, No. 3353-XII.
276. Law of Ukraine on Motor Transport dated 5 Apr. 2001, No. 2344-III.
277. Decree of the Government No. 401 dated 27 Jun. 1969.
278. Law of Ukraine on Functioning of the Unified Transport System of Ukraine in a Special Period dated 26 Nov. 1998, No. 194-XIV.
279. Law of Ukraine on Roads dated 8 Sep. 2005, No. 2862-IV.
280. Rules of Carriage of Goods by Motor Transport in Ukraine approved by the Ministry of Transport's Order dated 14 Oct. 1997, No. 363, registered at the Ministry of Justice on 20 Feb. 1998, No. 128/2568.
281. Rules on Carriage of Mail by Motor Transport in Ukraine approved by the Ministry of Transport's Order dated 12 Mar. 1997, No. 32/76, registered at the Ministry of Justice on 28 May 1997, No. 195/1999.
282. Rules on Rendering the Services on Motor Transport for Passengers approved by the Decree of the CMU dated 18 Feb. 1997, No. 176.

648. The Law of Ukraine on Roads[283] defines the legal, economic, organizational and social principles on operation of roads, their construction, reconstruction, repair and maintenance. According to this Law, the roads are divided into the roads of common use; streets and roads in cities and other settlements, departmental (technological) roads and roads at private territories (Article 5). Roads of common use are a part of the single transport system of Ukraine and meet the needs of the society in carriage of the passengers and goods by motor transport. Roads of common use belong to the State and are not subject to privatization. Roads of common use consist of roads of state and local importance (Article 7). In its turn, the roads of state importance can be international, national and regional (Article 8).

§3. Insurance Provisions

649. The Law of Ukraine on Compulsory Civil and Legal Liability Insurance for Vehicles Owners[284] regulates the compulsory insurance of the civil liability of the vehicles' owners and aims to provide the compensation for harm caused to life, health and property of persons during the exploitation of transport vehicles on the territory of Ukraine. Article 6 of the Law defines that an insured accident is an event due to which harm is caused to the third persons during a transport accident. Had this accident happened with participation of the insured vehicle, it entails civil liability of a person whose liability is insured.

650. Part II of the Law regulates the conclusion of the contract on insurance. The contract on insurance can provide on the individual terms certain limits which are higher than the limits specified in this Law. The obligatory limit of insurer's liability for the harm caused to the property of the insured constitutes Ukrainian Hryvnia (UAH) 50,000 per person. In the case when the general size of the harm after one insured accident exceeds the fivefold limit of the insurer's liability, the compensation to every victim diminishes proportionally. The obligatory limit of the insurer's liability for the harm caused to life and health of victims constitutes UAH 100,000 per person. The mentioned insurance compensations are paid on every insured accident occurred during the period of action of the contract on compulsory insurance within the limits of the insurer's liability.

651. The Law in Article 10 defines the types of contracts on compulsory insurance and the territory of action of the contract. Thus, two types of contracts are determined:

- internal contract on compulsory insurance of civil liability (further – an internal contract on insurance) operating exclusively on the territory of Ukraine;

283. Dated 8 Sep. 2005, No. 2862-IV.
284. Law of Ukraine on Compulsory Civil and Legal Liability Insurance for Vehicles Owners dated 1 Jul. 2004, No. 1961-IV.

- contract on international compulsory insurance of civil liability (further – a contract on international insurance) operating on the territory of the countries specified in such contracts. The contracts on international insurance operating on the territories of the countries being members of the international system of motor insurance the 'Green Card', are certified by the corresponding unified certificate the 'Green Card' which is recognized and operates in these countries.

652. Upon entrance into the territory of Ukraine a vehicle's owner registered in another country is under an obligation to have the certificate on international motor-car insurance the 'Green Card' or internal contract on insurance of civil liability during the stay of such transport vehicle on the territory of Ukraine.

653. It is important to mention that in accordance with this Law (Article 21.1) it is forbidden to exploit vehicles (except for vehicles in relation to which a correcting coefficient is not set depending on a vehicle) without a policy on compulsory insurance of civil liability operating on the territory of Ukraine, or policy (certificate) on compulsory insurance of civil liability concluded on the territory of another country with the authorized organization with which the Motor Transport Insurance Bureau of Ukraine has an agreement on mutual recognition of contracts on insurance. In case of violation of the above obligation, a liability is set under the law (Article 21.4).[285]

654. The harm caused to life and health of a victim due to the traffic accident is a harm connected with medical treatment of the victim, temporal disability, permanent disability and death of the victim (Article 23). It should be also noted that a moral damage is recoverable and it is established by the court (Article 22.3).

§4. Carriage of Passengers

655. The general terms of carriage of passengers by motor transport are contained in Part II of the Law on Motor Transport. According to it the documents for regular passenger carriage are as follows:

- for a passenger carrier – license, agreement with the bodies of executive power or local executive bodies on carriage of passengers, route passport, document that certifies legal use of bus, other documents of a certain category;
- for a bus driver – driving license, vehicle registration documents, ticket registration form, route scheme, route timetable, table of fare and/or their permission on a transport vehicle;
- for a passenger – a ticket for a bus trip and for carriage of luggage.

656. The basic rights and obligations of a carrier are enshrined in Articles 40 and 41 of the Law on Motor Transport. The main rights of passengers are defined in

---

285. See the text of the Law at http://rada.gov.ua.

Article 911 of the Civil Code. As to the obligations, passenger shall have the ticket with himself and observe the rules on transport.

657. Additionally, legal provisions on carriage of passenger by motor transport are stipulated in the Statute of Motor Transport. Part IV of the Statute contains rights and obligations of passengers, conditions of carriage of luggage without the passenger. The Statute also contains provisions on storage of hand luggage. The main document for carriage or storage luggage is a baggage check. The baggage check is a document issued by a carrier on confirmation of baggage for transportation or storage, indicating its value, the cost of transportation and storage. A passenger has the right to treat luggage as lost and demand compensation of its value if it does not arrive to the point of destination ten days after due time of its delivery.[286]

658. Organization of international transportations of passengers and goods by motor transport is carried out in accordance with the international treaties of Ukraine regarding the international carriage of passengers by motor transport (Law on Motor Transport Article 53).

659. The Rules on Rendering the Services on Motor Transport for Passengers (further – the Rules) are compulsory for carriers, bus stations of all ownership forms, passengers and drivers.[287].

660. Under these Rules, the carrier shall:

(1) ensure compliance with current legislation and according to the provisions on protection of consumers;
(2) take (appropriate) measures to ensure a safe, convenient journey for passengers and storage and/or delivery of baggage under the ticket, baggage check and schedule;
(3) check the technical and sanitary condition of buses or cars before operation;
(4) have documents for transportation in accordance with the law;
(5) keep vehicles in good technical and sanitary condition, to ensure their timely submission for boarding and departure of passengers;
(6) organize transportation of passengers to their destination on the route without any additional financial costs of passengers, especially people with disabilities, elderly, pregnant women, passengers with children under school age;
(7) provide passengers with the information about the names of stops, possible transfers, fees for travel, etc.;
(8) compensate for damage caused to health and property of passengers;
(9) provide current and preliminary ticket sales;
(10) take out compulsory private insurance for passengers of transport accidents;
(11) check (during international transport) the passenger's visa and immigration documents.[288]

286. Statute on Motor Transport, s. 140.
287. Rules on Rendering Services on Motor Transport for Passengers approved by the Decree of the CMU dated 18 Feb. 1997, No. 176.
288. Rules on Rendering Services on Motor Transport for Passengers, s. 145.

§5. Carriage of Goods

661. The special legal provisions on carriage of goods by motor transport are contained in the Rules on Carriage of Cargo by Motor Transport[289] and the Statute. Moreover, the CMR is dealing with the contract for the international carriage of goods by road. The CMR stipulates the provisions of conclusion and performance of the contract. It provides that the contract of carriage shall be confirmed by the issuing of a consignment note. Under Article 9 of the CMR the consignment note shall be prima facie evidence of making the contract of carriage, the conditions of the contract and the receipt of the goods by the carrier.

662. The Law on Motor Transport maintains in Part III, Chapter 8, the general provisions on domestic carriage of goods, documents, rights and obligations of the carrier, contract for the carriage of goods (Article 50). A contract shall be concluded in conformity with the legislation between the sender and the carrier in writing (a contract, invoice, receipt). Both senders and carriers are vested with the rights and obligations. The most important is that the sender is entitled to compensate in case of damage or deterioration of goods, partial or full loss and delay in delivery. Whereas a carrier shall take care of goods until their delivery to the place of destination. He shall be under an obligation to compensate the sender against losses for damage or deterioration of the goods, partial of full loss and delay in delivery.

663. The Law on Motor Transport in Article 50 defines the obligatory conditions of contract of carriage, namely: names of the parties, their place of commercial activity, name of the cargo, its quantity, type of packing, conditions and date of delivery, date, time and place of loading and discharging, value of the cargo. Naturally, in case of carriage of the dangerous cargo the contract also contains the sections related to it. A sender and a recipient are responsible for all consequences due to inaccuracy, incompleteness and wrongfulness of data stated in the consignment notes pursuant to Article 47.

664. The Statute of Motor Transport provides *inter alia* that consignment notes and measurement Acts are the main transport documents that define relations among consignors, consignees and carriers.[290]

665. The Rules on Carriage of Goods by Motor Transport in Ukraine along with the Statute define the contract of carriage and its conclusion. It is provided that the contractor can insure its property pursuant to the Law on Insurance to be compensated due to the caused losses in case of full or partial loss, damage or deterioration of the goods during the carriage and due to the natural disasters.[291] Among others, the Rules contain the provisions on packaging and marking of the goods, on loading and discharging of the goods and on issuing the transport documents (section 4).

---

289. Rules on Carriage of Goods by Motor Transport approved by the Decree of the MTU dated 14 Oct. 1997, No. 363, registered in the Ministry of Justice on 20 Feb. 1998, No. 128/2568.
290. Statute of Motor Transport, s. 47.
291. Rules on Carriage of Goods by Motor Transport in Ukraine, s. 4.

The main documents on carriage are consignment notes and road waybill of a cargo vehicle. Depending on the type of cargo and its specific features, other documents could be added, such as veterinary, sanitary and quality certificates, other certificates, passport, etc. (section 11.1). It is to be noted that the road waybill is considered as a document without which the carriage of goods is not allowed (section 11.3).

§6. Liability of the Carrier

666. According to Articles 5(3) and 8(3) of the CVR the carrier shall be liable for any damage that may be caused to the passengers for any damage to the luggage of passenger by a breach of the obligations. The CVR defines that the carrier shall be liable for loss or damage resulting from the death or injury of or from any other body or mental injury caused to a passenger as a result of accident connected with the carriage and occurring while the passenger is inside the vehicle or is entering or alighting from the vehicle or occurring in connection with the loading or discharging of the luggage (Article 11(1)).

667. The CVR establishes the liability of the carrier for personal injuries. Namely, it provides that the total damages payable by the carrier in respect of the same occurrence shall not exceed 83,333 units of account[292] for each victim. The State Parties are allowed to set higher limits or no limits at all (Article 13(1)). With respect to the luggage, the CVR stipulates that the amount of compensation in case of partial or total loss of the luggage, the total amount shall not exceed 166.67 units of accounts for each piece of luggage and 666.67 units of account for each passenger (Article 16).

668. The Convention clearly defines the grounds of the liability of the carrier that performs international motor transportations by means of Article 13, which are:

- death, corporal or any other injury caused to the passenger during the transportation irrespective of the place and time of the accident (during transportation, boarding, landing or loading, reloading of luggage);
- full or partial loss of luggage or its damage.

669. The liability provisions of the CMR Convention are built on the presumption that the carrier has got the liability insurance and that the goods transported are covered by the cargo insurance. Under Article 17(1) of the CMR the carrier shall be liable for the total or partial loss of the goods and for damage thereto occurring between the time when he takes over the goods and the time of delivery, as well as for any delay in delivery. However, the carrier shall be relieved of liability if the loss, damage or delay was caused by the wrongful act or neglect of the claimant, by the instructions of the claimant given otherwise than as the result of a wrongful act

292. Protocol to the CVR dated 5 Jul. 1978.

or neglect on the part of the carrier, by inherent vice of the goods or through circumstances which the carrier could not avoid and the consequences of which he was unable to prevent (Article 17(2)).

670. Pursuant to Article 920 of the Civil Code in case the parties fail to fulfil the obligations under the contract of carriage they shall bear liability pursuant to this Code, transport statutes and codes. This implies that the Ukrainian legislator did not include the provisions of the CMR or other Convention on carriage of goods into the Civil or Commercial Codes and other laws. Article 1166 of the Civil Code sets a common rule on liability for pecuniary harm to person and Article 1167 of the Civil Code provides liability for moral harm to person. Considering these provisions the party of contract of carriage has the right for indemnification in case of failure to fulfil the obligations by the carrier. According to Article 362 of the Civil Code and section 133 of the Statute of Motor Transport, a motor carrier bears liability for the loss, defect, spoilage or damage to the goods accepted to transportation, etc. The Law on Motor Transport, also in Article 60, contains the general provisions on liability of the carrier.

671. Part IX of the Statute is dealing with the liability of motor carriers, consignors and consignees, passengers, as well as claims and actions. Motor carriers shall be liable for taking care of the goods from the moment of their acceptance and until their delivery to the consignee, unless they prove that loss, shortage, damage or deterioration to the goods could not be prevented by them.[293]

672. For delay in delivery in intercity transportations the motor carriers pay the cargo recipients a fine in the amount of 12% of fare for each day of delay unless they prove that the delay occurred due to the circumstances beyond their fault. The total sum of fine for delay in delivery shall not be higher than 60% of fare. Payment of fine for delay does not release the motor carriers from liability for loss, damage, shortage and deterioration due to this delay (section 138 of the Statute).

673. A consignor and consignee are entitled to treat the goods as lost and demand compensation for the lost in case of failure to hand the goods over to the consignee on its request: for urban and suburban transportation – within ten days from the date of the goods acceptance; for intercity transportation – within thirty days after expiry of the delivery period; and for through intermodal transportation – after expiry of four months from the date of the goods acceptance for carriage (section 140 of the Statute).

674. Claims arising from carriage of goods are brought to the motor carrier that handed over the goods or in case of its total loss – to the motor carrier that took over the goods for carriage. Claims arising from the carriage of passengers and luggage can be brought to the motor carrier of the place of departure or arrival at the discretion of the applicant (section 161 of the Statute). Along with the Statute, the Rules contain the provisions on claims and actions in section 16.

---

293. Statute of Motor Transport, s. 133.

675. During intercity carriage the goods are considered lost, unless delivered within thirty days after the term of delivery. In case the goods arrive in a defective package or with the damaged seals a carrier is obligated to give out the goods with the relevant documents. The goods are also presented with verification when loading is carried out by the carrier from warehouse of the station or in case of delivery from warehouse of the station (section 66 of the Statute). In all cases packing-case and artificial goods are given out with verification of weight and condition of goods. Circumstances of the liability of the carrier are proven in transport documents.

676. The terms of limitation of actions have a substantial value for the insurer. During six months the consignee has a right to bring a claim to the carrier which gave out the goods, and in case of loss of goods.[294] This claim must be accompanied by the documents supporting the harm and calculation of losses. If a claim is declined by the carrier, it can be brought to the court within one month. The carrier can be released from liability, if he proves the absence of guilt.

677. Although the transport sector of Ukraine meets the needs of national economy and residents in transportation, the level of safety, standards of quality, efficiency of passenger and freight services and pressure on the environment do not comply with modern requirements. Nowadays, the transport sector faces crucial challenges, such as significant wear and tear of plants and equipment, fleet, insufficient investment required for renewing and developing this sector. It is urgent to implement the newest achievements of management in transport sphere, to put in an operation new transport highways being in conformity with the world standards of quality of transportations and to update the legal framework in the field of motor transport to make it more efficient, safe and environmentally friendly.

294. Statute of Motor Transport of Ukraine, s. 165.

Chapter 3. Carriage by Rail

§1. Introduction

678. The chapter is dealing with the legal regulation on carriage by rail including international conventions ratified by the *Verkhovna Rada*, issues regarding the carriage of goods and passengers by railways and the liability regime.

679. Railway transport is one of the most important basic industries of the Ukrainian economy that ensures its internal and external transport economic relations and transportation needs of the population. Ukraine exceeds the index of the European countries in traffic railway concentration by 3 to 5 times.

680. The subordinate legislation of Ukraine determines the conditions and procedure for organization of activity of railway transport of general use, assists to its priority development, renders support in satisfaction of necessities of railways in rolling stock (material and technical, fuel and energy resources). The Ministry of Infrastructure refuses to let tariffs evolve in the market economy on the ground that the Ukrainian manufacturers would not be in position to handle the resulting transport cost increases.

§2. Legal Regulation

I. International Treaties

681.

The Convention Concerning International Carriage by Rail (COTIF) (1980)	Law of Ukraine on Ukraine's Accession to the Convention on International Carriage by Rail (COTIF) of 5 June 2003, No. 943-IV with reservations
The Uniform Rules Concerning the Contract of International Carriage of Goods by Rail (CIM)	
The Uniform Rules Concerning the Contract of International Carriage of Passengers and Luggage by Rail (CIV)	
The Agreement on International Railway Cargo Transportation by Rail (SMGS) (1951)	

The European Agreement on Main International Railway Lines (1985)	Ukraine joined it on 5 July 1992 is in force for Ukraine as the successor of the USSR

682. It should be observed here that The Agreement on International Railway Cargo Transportation (the Russian abbreviation – SMGS) applies to all types of carriage of goods in through international railway cargo transportation between SMGS Member States[295] on the basis of an SMGS waybill and only within the network of SMGS Member Countries (Article 2, §1). The Agreement has an obligatory force for railways, consignors and consignees regardless of state belonging of the parties to the contract of carriage.

II. National Legislation

683. The legislation on rail transport and carriage of goods by railways has not been reformed or essentially changed since 1999, except for an accession to the COTIF in 2003.[296]

684. The Law of Ukraine on Rail Transport[297] contains the general principles of activity of rail transport of general use, its role in economic and social sphere of Ukraine, and also regulates its relationships with the bodies of executive power and of local self-government, passengers, senders and recipients of cargoes, luggage and mail.

685. In accordance with Article 9 of the Law on Rail Transport the establishment of tariffs on cargo, passenger and luggage transportation by the rail transport (except for suburban passenger transportations) within Ukraine is performed on the basis of the state budget, price and tariff policy according to the procedure determined by the Cabinet of Ministers. Tariffs on passenger and luggage transportation in suburban communication are set by the respective railways upon approval with the local bodies of the executive power. If the level of tariffs does not provide profitability of these transportations, losses of railways are covered from the local budgets. Tariffs on goods, passenger and luggage transportation by the rail transport in international communication are set in accordance with the international treaties and the current legislation of Ukraine.[298]

295. Member States are mainly the former USSR countries.
296. Law of Ukraine on Ukraine's Accession to the Convention Concerning International Carriage by Rail (COTIF), dated. 5 Jun. 2003, No. 943-IV.
297. Law of Ukraine on Rail Transport dated 4 Jul. 1996, No. 273/96-BP.
298. Law of Ukraine on Rail Transport, Art. 9, s. 2.

686. Heads of the railways – subjects of the former USSR – decided to extend the application of the Statute of the Railways of the USSR[299] to the interstate transport of goods on 20 October 1992. Additionally the new Statute of the Railways of Ukraine was approved by the Cabinet of Ministers in 1998.[300] It defines the conditions and procedure for the organization of transportations, including direct mixed communication with participation of railways and other types of transport, quality standards of cargo transportations and servicing of passengers. It follows from the above that two Rail Statutes in Ukraine exist simultaneously and can possibly contradict to each other as they were focused on planned/market economy respectively.

687. The relations of rail transport enterprises with the owners of railway spur tracks, the procedure for and conditions of operation of these tracks, circulation of rolling stock that does not belong to the railway transport of general use, are determined by the Statute of the Railways and contracts concluded on its basis. The Statute of the Railways relates to transportation of passengers, goods, mail by rail in accordance with Article 1(3).

688. The Statute defines that railways have the right:

- to set the boundaries of areas of increased danger;
- to impose fine on the shippers in the amount and according to the procedure set by the Statute of the Railways in case of untimely payment for transportation;
- to require from shippers and consignees unconditional observation of requirements and norms in relation to the use of mechanization facilities of loading/unloading works, package, specialized containers that eliminate damage of rolling stock, buildings and devices of track economy and provide safety of cargoes.

689. There are also d Rules on Carriage of Passengers, Luggage, Cargo and Mail by Rail Transport in Ukraine.[301]

690. All the possible accounts between the carrier and other parties to the contract are based on the Trade Catalogues. These Trade Catalogues are approved by *UkrZaliznytsya* including all the aspects of transportation by rail. Settlements for works and services related to cargo, passenger, luggage, mail transportation are made by free tariffs which are determined upon the agreement between the parties according to the procedure that does not contradict the legislation on protection of economic competition. However, tariffs on cargo, passenger and luggage transportation by the rail transport in international communication are set in accordance with the international treaties and the current legislation of Ukraine.

---

299. Statute of the Railways of the USSR approved by the USSR Council of Ministers in 6 Apr. 1964, No. 270.
300. Statute of the Railways of Ukraine approved by the CMU dated 6 Apr. 1998, No. 457. In the monograph, the authors will refer to the Statute of the Railways of Ukraine, 1998.
301. Order of the MTU, No. 1196 dated 27 Dec. 2006, registered at the Ministry of Justice on 4 Apr. 2007, No. 310/13577.

§3. CARRIAGE OF PASSENGERS

691. Under the contract of carriage of passengers one party (the carrier) is obliged to carry the other party (passenger) to the destination (and if check-in baggage – to deliver it to the destination) and the passenger agrees to pay a set fare. The contract of carriage of passenger and baggage is concluded in the form of a fare and a baggage check.[302] The passenger is entitled to receive at the railway station full and immediate information about the time and place of departure, fares, rules, passengers, baggage, schedule banks, chambers storage space station location, the services provided at the railway station, as well as addresses and phone numbers of authorities to carry out consumer protection.

692. Each coach must have visible information about train schedules, the cost of paid services, statements regarding the rules of the train. All disputes and conflicts arising between the passenger and railway workers shall be solved by the head of the station and during the voyage by the head of the train.

693. The Rules on Carriage of Passengers, Luggage, Goods and Mail by Rail Transport of Ukraine[303] provide that all passengers must be insured by the carrier. Insurance fee is included in the ticket.[304] The insurance premium and insurance amounts are determined by the Regulation on Compulsory Personal Accident Insurance on Transport approved by the CMU dated 14 August 1996, No. 959.[305] A representative of the *UkrZaliznytsya* shall draw up a statement related to any accidents to passengers, as well as trauma, injury occurred with passengers at the station or in a train.[306]

694. With regard to luggage, the Rules stipulate that if there are (during transportation, loading, discharging, delivery by railway) any signs of shortage, damage or loss of luggage, a railway employee shall check the luggage and draw a commercial act on its results.[307] Further, in case of damage or loss in baggage, the railway of arrival shall pay a passenger the value of lost or damaged luggage according to its declared value.[308]

695. The Rules on Carriage of Passengers, Luggage, Goods and Mail by Rail Transport define the categories of compartments:

---

302. Civil Code, Art. 910, s. 2.
303. Rules on Carriage of Passengers, Luggage, Goods and Mail by Rail Transport of Ukraine were approved by the Order of the MTC dated 27 Dec. 2006, No. 1196, registered by the Ministry of Justice on 4 Apr. 2007, No. 310/13577.
304. *Ibid.* s. 11.1.
305. *Ibid.* s. 11.5.
306. *Ibid.* s. 9.1.
307. Rules on Carriage of Passengers, Luggage, Goods and Mail by Rail Transport of Ukraine were approved by the Order of the MTC dated 27 Dec. 2006, No. 1196, registered at the Ministry of Justice on 4 Apr. 2007, No. 310/13577 s. 27.1.
308. Rules on Carriage of Passengers, Luggage, Goods and Mail by Rail Transport of Ukraine were approved by the Order of the MTC dated 27 Dec. 2006, No. 1196, registered at the Ministry of Justice on 4 Apr. 2007, No. 310/13577 s. 27.5.

– 1, 2, 3 classes – open and closed compartments with seating;
– the sitting – an open compartment with seating;
– with numbered reserved seats – the open compartment with seats for lying;
– compartment – with four separate compartments with berths for lying;
– soft – with separate double 'SV' and triple compartment with seats for lying.

696. A passenger may be removed from the train in the following cases:

– if he is in explicit violation and drunk at the same time preventing other passengers calm;
– if he is suffering from disease and needs medical help. In this case, a passenger is removed with his belongings from the train with the obligatory participation of medical personnel;
– when determining the passenger transport prohibited items and substances and failure to remove them from the train. In this case, the travel documents are marked as 'invalid carriage of hand baggage'.

697. The estimated minimum weight of luggage (including lightweight) is 10 kg. The minimum declared value (including lightweight) is United States Dollars (USD) 10. The carry-on luggage includes items and things regardless of packaging that is easily transferred and its size is easily placed on the ground in coaches designed to accommodate hand luggage. Each passenger may carry a child free of charge in the compartment with a hand luggage weighing up to 36 kg.

698. Items deposited in the cloakroom may be stored there no more than two calendar days, and then are transferred to the general storage warehouse station. If within thirty days the owners do not take away their belongings, they will be removed in accordance with the laws of Ukraine.

699. When a late delivery of luggage or goods continues for not more than one day, the fine is not paid. The fine is also not paid in case when a passenger did not collect the luggage from the station according to the Rules. In case of transportation of objects that are forbidden for transportation, the owner pays a fine to the railways in the size of five times the cost of carriage of luggage or goods. A passenger is responsible for hand baggage which he carries with himself.

700. The carrier's liability for damage to life or health of passengers determined by the Rules is provided by the Civil Code, if the law or the contract of carriage does not provide the increased liability.

§4. Carriage of Goods

701. UkrZaliznytsya (railways) may act as subjects of foreign economic activity and carry it out on the basis of the current legislation of Ukraine and the international treaties ratified by Ukraine. To ensure foreign economic relations of Ukraine the railways carry out international transportations in direct railway transport, direct mixed and indirect international communications. During the international transportations railways have the right to be compensated for losses connected with additional services not envisaged by the international treaties at the expense of a shipper and a consignee on the basis of treaties (Article 9 of the Law of Ukraine on Rail Transport).

702. In addition to the CIM and the Agreement on International Railway Cargo Transportation (SMGS) the Ukrainian legislation on carriage of goods includes *inter alia* the Civil Code, Commercial Code, the Law of Ukraine on Transport, the Law of Ukraine on Rail Transport and subordinate regulatory Acts that govern the carriage of goods by railways in Ukraine. Form of the contract of carriage of goods by rail transport is established by the Rules on Carriage of Passengers, Luggage, Goods and Mail by Rail Transport of Ukraine.

703. As Article 7 of the Agreement on International Railway Cargo Transportation provides the contract of carriage according to SMGS Agreement is made in a form of SMGS waybill. The complete set of documents consist of five pages (original and duplicates). There is also a Regulation on Experiment with Using CIM/SMGS was approved by CMU dated 14 July 2006, No. 403-p in direction of two international transport corridors (No. 3 and No. 5).

704. Chapters 28 and 29 of the Statute of the Railways are devoted to the carriage of goods. Under the contract of rail carriage the carrier undertakes to deliver the goods entrusted to it by the consignor to the destination in due time and shall hand it over to the consignee (against the payment of a fixed fare by the consignor).[309] It is also provided that the consignor may insure the goods voluntarily. The obligations of a consignor include a duty to provide a loading station with a completed invoice (set of transport documents) for each shipping.[310] To witness the taking over of the goods for carriage, the station of departure shall issue a receipt to the consignor. The station of arrival shall issue a consignment note to the consignee together with the goods. The consignor shall be liable for wrongfulness, inaccuracy and incompleteness of the data stated in a consignment note.[311]

705. The railway is responsible to deliver the goods within the defined terms. The terms of delivery are established by the Rules on Carriage of Passengers, Luggage, Goods and Mail by Rail Transport of Ukraine. The goods are handed over to the consignee at the station of arrival specified in the invoice after making all appropriate payments. The consignee signs a waybill upon receipt of the goods. Other provisions on carriage of goods are contained in the above-mentioned Rules and include *inter alia* that the station of arrival shall not later than the day after the arrival of goods notify the consignee on arrival of the goods.[312] If the consignee notwithstanding the notification does not show up within thirty days from the day of

309. The Statute of the Railways, Art. 3, s. 22.
310. *Ibid.* s. 23.
311. *Ibid.* s. 24.
312. Rules on Carriage of Passengers, Luggage, Goods and Mail by Rail Transport of Ukraine, s. 29.5.

notification, the goods are considered unclaimed and are sold according to the legislation of Ukraine.[313]

§5. Liability of the Carrier

706. According to the provisions of COTIF-CIM, Article 35, the railway that accepted the goods for carriage with the consignment note shall be responsible for the carriage over the entire route up to delivery. The railway should also be liable for loss or damage resulting from the total or partial loss of, or damage to the goods between the time of acceptance for carriage and the time of delivery and for the loss or damage resulting from the transit period being exceeded. Article 36(3) of the COTIF defines the circumstances when railway shall be relieved of such liability when the loss or damage arises from the special risks.

707. In case of total or partial loss of the goods the railway must pay, to the exclusion of all other damages, compensation calculated according to the commodity exchange quotation or, if there is no such quotation, according to the current market price, or if there is neither such quotation nor such price, according to the normal value of goods of the same kind and quality at the time and place at which the goods were accepted for carriage.[314]

708. Article 30 § 2 of COTIF-CIM provides that compensation for loss shall not exceed 17 units of account per kilogramme of gross mass short.

709. The principles of insurance on liability of the rail carrier are the same as for the motor carrier. This type of insurance is not practically used in Ukraine because of monopolistic status of *UkrZaliznytsya.*

710. Circumstances which can serve as grounds for the liability of carriers, senders and recipients of cargo, luggage and passengers, shall be certified by Acts. Demands of consignees, passengers to the carriers in relation to violation of rights and legal interests are considered according to the claim and lawsuit procedure. The procedure and terms of drafting Acts, presentation and consideration of claims and lawsuits are determined by the Statute of the Railways in accordance with the legislation of Ukraine.

711. Pursuant to Article 23 of the Law of Ukraine on Rail Transport the carriers bear the liability for non-conservation (loss, defect, spoilage and damage) in the amount of the actually caused harm, unless they prove that loss, defect, spoilage damages arose out of the unpredictable circumstances.

313. *Ibid.* s. 29.8.
314. COTIF-CIM, Art. 40.

712. The limit of liability of railway is determined according to Article 13 of the Law of Ukraine on Transport and the Statute of the Railways. Claims and lawsuits must be brought to the Heads of Railways for settlement within six months.

713. The liability, the provisions set forth in the Statute of the Railways (section 116) establish that the railway pays a consignee the fine for non-prompt delivery of goods and empty carriages that belong to the legal entities, citizens being subject of commercial activity or leased by them (unless the railway proves that delay was not its fault) in the amount of:

- 10% of transportation fee – for two-day delay;
- 20% of transportation fee – for three-day delay;
- 30% of transportation fee – for four-day delay and more.

714. Thus, if a consignee does not collect the goods from the station within twenty-four hours after receiving the notification on arrival of the goods, the mentioned fine shall not be paid. The railway does not bear liability for violation of delivery terms, if such a violation happened due to the natural disaster or other circumstances not dependent upon the railway.

715. The Statute of the Railways (section 117) also regulates that consignee has the right to consider the goods as lost and demand compensation for loss, if the goods have not been handed over to him upon its request within thirty days from the moment of completion of delivery terms, and in case of through intermodal transport – upon termination of two months from the day the goods were taken over for carriage. If the goods arrived exceeding the noted terms, the consignee has to accept them and pay back the sum he received from the railway for the loss of the goods. In case the goods arrived in partly damaged condition, this amount is reduced regarding the loss (section 127).

716. The carrier is liable for loss, shortage, spoilage or damage to the luggage and the goods accepted for carriage and for the late delivery, if it can prove that the loss, shortage, spoilage, damage, delay was not attributable to it. The carrier is liable for shortage, loss, spoilage or damage of luggage and goods, in the following amounts:

- for luggage and goods accepted for carriage with the stated value – in the amount of the stated value, and if the railway can prove that the stated value exceeds the actual cost – in the amount of actual cost;
- for luggage accepted for carriage without the stated value – in the amount of actual cost of luggage, as set by the Rules;
- for spoilage and damage to luggage and goods – in the amount by which it reduced the cost. The railway pays a fine in the amount of 10% of the transportation fee for each day, but not more than 25% of transportation fee for late delivery of luggage and goods. Incomplete days shall be considered as complete.

717. Concluding this chapter it shall be pointed out that the claims arising from the carriage of goods by railways shall be brought to the railway of destination, while claims arising from the carriage of passengers are to be brought to the station of departure or destination. The time provided for bringing the mentioned claims shall cover six months.

Chapter 4. Carriage by Air

§1. Introduction

718. The following chapter covers the legal framework with respect to the carriage by air. It includes the national legislation in force, as well as international conventions. Additionally, the notion of the aircraft and the rules on registration and certification is provided. The authors explain the legal regime for carriage of goods and passengers in Ukraine and the liability regime and time-limits for claims and actions.

719. A due notion should be made to the Chicago Convention on International Civil Aviation (Chicago Convention 1944) that was an outcome of the 1944 Chicago Conference. The Chicago Convention was signed on 7 December 1944 in Chicago and was ratified by Ukraine on 10 August 1992. The aim of the Convention is to establish rules regarding the use of air territory of the states and to set the principle of absolute sovereignty of the state in its air territory. The International Civil Aviation Organization (ICAO) was established as a UN specialized agency by virtue of Article 43 of the Chicago Convention with a permanent seat in Canada. Moreover, the International Air Transport Association (IATA) exists in addition to ICAO which was created by a group of airlines. Today, IATA represents some 230 airlines comprising 93% of scheduled international air traffic.

720. The scope of application of the Chicago Convention 1944 is limited to the civil aircrafts, excluding state aircrafts. It is recognized in the Convention that the territory of a State shall have complete and exclusive sovereignty, suzerainty, protection or mandate of such State.

721. Similar provisions are restated in Article 1 of the Law of Ukraine on the State Border providing that the State border of Ukraine is a line and the vertical surface passing through that line which determines the limits of the territory of Ukraine – land, water, mineral resources and airspace. Article 1 states that Ukraine shall have full and exclusive sovereignty over the Ukrainian airspace that is a part of the Ukrainian territory. The Ukrainian airspace shall be a part of the air located over the Ukrainian mainland and waters, including its territorial waters (territorial sea).

722. Each Contracting Party of the Chicago Convention agreed not to use civil aircraft for purposes incompatible with it. It establishes the certain provisions for regular (irregular) international connections, cabotage, forbidden zones, facilitation to expedite aircraft navigation and air traffic rules, customs, immigration procedures and investigation of air accidents.

723. Further, the Law of Ukraine on the State Border sets forth that the take-off of the Ukrainian and foreign aircraft from the territory of Ukraine and the landing of such aircraft after flying into the territory of Ukraine shall be carried out at airfields (airports) that are open to international flights and at which there are admission checkpoints of the Border Forces for Ukraine and customs offices. Any other procedure for the take-off and landing of aircraft shall be permitted only with the consent of the competent authorities of Ukraine.[315] Moreover, the relevant provisions are also found in the Air Code of Ukraine.

724. The procedure for using the Ukrainian airspace shall be determined by the Regulation on Using the Ukrainian Airspace.[316] Adherence to this Regulation shall be ensured by the State system on airspace use.

725. Aviation flights on the territory of Ukraine may be performed by foreign operators that fully belong to foreign investors on the basis of a permit (license) for performing aviation services to be issued by the State Aviation Service of Ukraine.

§2. Legal Regulation

I. International Treaties

726.

The Convention for the Unification of Certain Rules Relating to International Carriage by Air (1929)	Ukraine joined the Warsaw Convention on 7 July 1992 as subsequently amended by the Hague Protocol, the Montreal Protocol No. 44 and the Guadalajara Protocol 1961
The Convention for the Unification of Certain Rules for International Carriage (1999)	The Law of Ukraine on Ukraine's Accession to Convention for the Unification of Certain Rules for Internal Carriage by air dated 17 December 2008, No. 685-VI.
The Transit Agreement of International Air Services (1944)	The Decree of President on Accession to the Agreement on Transit of International Air Services dated 4 June 1997, No. 490/97

727. Ukraine joined the Convention for the Unification of Certain Rules Relating to International Carriage by Air (Warsaw Convention 1929) and the Convention for the Unification of Certain Rules for International Carriage (Montreal Convention 1999). However, their application in Ukraine is not always clear from the legal point of view.

728. To fulfil the requirements of the ICAO, the EU, the European Civil Aviation Conference (ECAC), and the European Organization for the Safety of Air Navigation (EUROCONTROL), the *Verkhovna Rada* adapted a new the Air Code of Ukraine.

---

315. Law of Ukraine on the State Border dated 4 Nov. 1991, No. 1777-XII, Art. 10.
316. Regulation on Using Ukraine's Airspace approved by the Decree of the CMU dated 29 Mar. 2002, No. 401.

729. Integration into the Single Air Space that envisages adaptation of the aviation carriage to the European legislation is one of the priorities in the sector development. The Ukrainian air transport system is currently on the way towards integration to the European one. In order to introduce the concept of the *Single Sky* in Ukraine, the system of collection of the air navigation duties have been brought to consistency with the EUROCONTROL standards and all district centres for air traffic control have been automated.

730. Following the recent trends in the international air law, a conference under the auspices of the ICAO was held from 30 August to 10 September 2010 in Beijing and as a result two instruments for the suppression of unlawful acts relating to the civil aviation were adopted: the Convention on the Suppression of Unlawful Acts Relating to International Civil Aviation and the Protocol Supplementary to the Convention for the Suppression of Unlawful Seizure of Aircraft. The Convention was open for signature from 10 September 2010 and it requires twenty-two ratifications in order to enter into force. The Ukrainian delegation did not participate in the mentioned conference and did not sign the two instruments.[317]

731. Moreover, there are a number of bilateral agreements on international air service. Some of these treaties were signed by the Ukrainian SSR, and the others – after gaining its independence (e.g., between the governments of Ukraine and Latvia, Lebanon, Brazil, Hungary, Austria, Korea, Libya and others). Thus, these agreements provide that each Contracting Party shall establish regular international air transport on the routes specified in the annexes.

II. National Legislation

732. The Air Code of Ukraine[318] regulates using of the Ukrainian airspace with the purpose of meeting interests of Ukraine and its citizens and ensuring safe aviation. Adoption of the new Air Code of Ukraine was one of the priorities identified in the transport sector in 2010, specified in the Agenda Association between Ukraine and the EU. The Code provides the basic legal framework of civil aviation in Ukraine.

733. The Law of Ukraine on Liability for Carriage of Passengers by Air Crossing State Border Without Proper Documents for Entering or Leaving Ukraine dated 10 January 2002, No. 2920-III sets the administrative liability of the legal entities irrespective of ownership for carrying out international air carriage for passengers across the state borders of Ukraine without proper documents for entry into Ukraine and establishes the procedures for application of liability.

317. For more information, see at www.icao.org.
318. The Air Code of Ukraine dated 19 May 2011, No. 3393-VI.

734. According to the decision of the Constitutional Court of Ukraine dated 30 May 2001, No. 7-rp /2001, the Ukrainian legislation includes liability of administrative violations that applies only to individuals and therefore it is necessary to work out the procedural rules that regulate the issue brought to the financial liability of the entities. This Law provides liability for administrative violations by entities – air carriers.

735. The Rules on Carriage of Passengers and Baggage by Air[319] include the standards of rendering the services on air transport. The Rules include the legal provisions envisaged by the Montreal Convention and govern the carrier's liability and limits of compensation. These Rules also apply to foreign air carriers (which render their services on the territory of Ukraine) with regard to the obligatory informing the passengers pursuant to section XXXI of the Rules. Carrier may adopt its own rules on carriage of the passengers and luggage by air in Ukrainian language that shall be in compliance with the Rules on Carriage of Passengers and Baggage by Air, preliminarily coordinating them with the State Aviation Service of Ukraine.

736. State supervision over the safety of aviation shall be carried out by a State Aviation Service of Ukraine. Any legal entity or natural person engaged in using the object of civil aviation shall receive a certificate from the state certification and registration body (State Aviation Service of Ukraine) that confirms the level of technical skills are in accordance with the requirements of the relevant aviation rules of Ukraine.

§3. INSURANCE

737. The air carrier and the provider of air flight services shall insure the passengers, crew members and flight personnel being on board of the aircraft. The aircraft must be also insured as well as the liability of air carrier and the provider of air flight services for compensating the losses inflicted upon passengers, luggage, mail and cargo. Insurance shall not be below the level established by the Cabinet of Ministers and the international treaties ratified by the *Verkhovna Rada*. The Aviation Insurance Bureau (further – Bureau) shall coordinate activities of the insurers in the field of insuring aviation risks and represent their interests in the international insurer associations. The establishment and state registration of the Bureau shall be carried out according to the procedure set forth by the Cabinet of Ministers.

738. The procedure and the order of the compulsory aviation insurance of civil aviation were approved by the Cabinet of Ministries[320] with the purpose to ensure the interest of air carriers, providers of air flights, passengers, and third persons and include:

319. Rules on Carriage of Passengers and Baggage by Air approved by the Order of the MIU dated 30 Nov. 2012, No. 735, registered at the Ministry of Justice on 28 Dec. 2012, No. 2219/22531.
320. Regulation on Compulsory Aviation Insurance of Civil Aviation approved by the Decree of the CMU dated 12 Oct. 2002, No. 1535.

- insurance of liability of air carrier for damage caused to the passengers, baggage, mail and cargo;
- insurance of liability of aircraft operator for damage caused to third persons;
- insurance of crew members of an aircraft and other aviation staff;
- insurance of aircrafts;
- insurance of employees of the customer's aviation services and persons connected with providing the technological process during the performance of aviation services.[321]

739. The requirements determined by the Rules on Carriage of Passengers and Baggage by Air are also applicable to the foreign air carriers during performance of flights in the air space of Ukraine in part of liability for damage caused to the passengers, baggage, mail and cargo and third persons. With respect to the insurance of liability of air carrier for damage caused to the passengers, baggage, mail and cargo, an insurance fee is established by the contracts on compulsory insurance and should not be less than:

(1) for the damage caused to life and health of a passenger:
   (a) during the domestic flights – a sum which is equivalent to USD 20,000 for each passenger seat and regarding the number of passenger seats provided by the certificate of the aircraft operator. An insurer pays a compensation to each passenger or its successor;
   (b) during the international flights – within the limits stipulated by the international treaties or legislation of the country on which territory the passenger carriage is performed according to unified conditions of the London insurers' association or other conditions applicable in international practice;
(2) for loss or damage to baggage, mail or cargo – a sum which is equivalent to USD 20 for each kilogram of weight;
(3) for belongings (baggage) possessed by a passenger – a sum which is equivalent to USD 400 (section 13, of the regulation, see 746).

§4. Aircraft

740. In accordance with the Chicago Convention 1944, every aircraft that takes part in international aviation shall be provided with a certificate of airworthiness to be issued or granted by the country in which such vessel is registered. The pilot and other crew members of the aircraft shall also be provided with the certificates of competency and licenses issued or granted by the country in which the aircraft is registered. The State Parties to the Convention undertake to cooperate in this field in order to achieve the uniformity of rules, standards and procedures.

741. The Air Code of Ukraine defines in Article 38 that aircraft could be civil or state.

321. *Ibid.* s. 1.

742. In accordance with Article 39 of the Air Code the civil aircraft is subject to obligatory registration and must have a certificate of its type. It can be registered in one register only. By virtue of Article 17 of the Chicago Convention 1944, aircrafts shall have the nationality of the State in which they are registered. The Chicago Convention 1944 clearly forbids the aircraft to be registered in more than one state; however, it allows the change of registration from one state to another (Article 18). The Certificate of Registration is the fact of confession of the national affiliation (Article 25). From the moment of registry of the aircraft all the previous signs done before in relation to this aircraft in the registers of aircrafts of other states are not acknowledged in Ukraine.

743. Transportation of weapons, ammunition, explosive and toxic substances, nuclear fuel, radioactive substances and other cargoes that are especially dangerous shall be carried out with the permit of the competent bodies according to the special rules established by the State Aviation Service of Ukraine.

§5. Carriage of Passengers

744. There is no typical form established for air ticket in the Ukrainian legislation, but common provisions are provided by Article 3 of the Warsaw Convention. Hence, an air ticket shall contain the following particulars:

(1) the place and date of issue;
(2) the place of departure and destination;
(3) the agreed stopping places, provided that the carrier may reserve the right to alter the stopping places in case of necessity, and that if he exercises that right, the alteration shall not have the effect of depriving the carriage of its international character;
(4) the name and address of the carrier or carriers;
(5) a statement that the carriage is subject to the rules relating to liability established by this Convention.

745. According to the Rules on Carriage of Passengers and Baggage by Air (further – the Rules), Part IV, Chapter I, section 1, a passenger ticket and baggage check serve as confirmation of conclusion of the contract of carriage and represent its conditions. Absence, fallaciousness in registration or loss of ticket and baggage check, does not invalidate the contract. A ticket gives a passenger the right of flight and imposes an obligation on the carrier to transport the passenger and his luggage and also to render other services connected with transportation according to the conditions of the contract of carriage. Conditions of the contract of carriage added to the ticket must be in conformity with these Rules and the Warsaw and Montreal Conventions depending on which one of them is applicable.

746. The Air Code includes provisions on compensation in case of refusal, cancellation or long delays of the trip in Part XIII.

Article 103 of the Air Code clearly states that Part XIII applies to the passengers that depart from/to the airport located in Ukraine, as well as from/to the airport located in another country to/from the airport located in Ukraine.

747. In the rules with regard to the travelling to/from the EU airport, the following compensation regimes are established: if a passenger refused to be transported against its will, a carrier shall make compensation:

- EUR 250 – for flights at distance 1,500 km or less;
- EUR 400 – for flights at distance from 1,500 km to 3,500 km;
- EUR 600 – for flights at distance over 3,500 km.[322]

748. The air carrier has a right to decrease the size of indemnification marked above on 50%, if carrier offers replacement of the route of transportation to the place of destination by alternative trips and the time of arrival does not exceed the planned one on:

- two hours – in relation to all trips by distance to 1,500 km;
- three hours – for all trips by distance from 1,500 km to 3,500 km;
- four hours – for all other trips not marked in the first and second indentions of this point.[323]

749. When the flight is cancelled by the air carrier and a passenger still continues its trip with another flight it must be offered and provided free of charge:

- food and drinks (amount of which depends on the time of expectation for a new trip);
- rooms in a hotel in case if the passengers are forced to expect departure during one or more nights or if time of the additional expectation is longer than it was foreseen by the passenger;
- surface transfer (route: airport – hotel – airport);
- two phone calls, or telex-, fax-report, or e-mail.[324]

750. Part XVI, Chapter 4 of the Rules provides that in case of flight delay in one day, the carrier shall provide the passengers with the hotel rooms, meal and transfer airport-hotel-airport. This chapter covers domestic and international flights and provides similar conditions on compensation. The carrier's liability for damage caused by the delay in transport of the passengers of any flight is limited to 4,694 SDRs in respect of each passenger (see also Air code, Article 106).

322. Rules on Carriage of Passengers and Baggage by Air, Part XVI, Ch. 2(5), Air Code, Art. 104.
323. Rules on Carriage of Passengers and Baggage by Air, Part XVI Ch. 2, s. 6, Air code, Art. 104.
324. Rules on Carriage of Passengers and Baggage by Air, Part XVI Ch. 3, s. 1, 5, Air code, Art. 105.

§6. Carriage of Goods

751. The Warsaw- and the Montreal Conventions apply to international carriage by air that is defined by reference to the place of departure, place of destination and any 'agreed stopping places'. With respect to the contract of carriage, the Warsaw Convention contains a notion of 'air consignment note', whereas the Montreal Convention refers to the 'air waybill'.

752. The Warsaw Convention defines that the air consignment note is a document which every carrier has to receive from consignor. The air consignment is made out by consignor in three original parts and handed over with the goods. According to Article 6 of the Convention the first part shall be marked 'for the carrier' and shall be signed by the consignor. The second part shall be marked 'for the consignee'; it shall be signed by the consignor and by the carrier and shall accompany the goods. The third part shall be signed by the carrier and handed by him to the consignor after the goods have been accepted. The air consignment note is prima facie evidence of the conclusion of the contract, of the receipt of the goods and of the conditions of carriage (Article 11). The description and content of the air waybill are considered in Articles 5 and 7 of the Montreal Convention.

753. The Ukrainian legislation in force does not have the typical form for air waybill, but the airline members of IATA agreed to introduce a standard form air waybill for international carriage of cargo by air. This has become an international norm as its layout and wording enable the incorporation of all the particulars required by the various international air conventions. The airline members of IATA have also agreed on alternative form of the Conditions of Contract printed on the reverse of the standard form air waybill. The Conditions of Contract include the provisions required under the international air law conventions, as well as other terms applicable in cases where none of the conventions applies or dealing with the matters not regulated in the conventions. The terms cover such issues as limitation of the air carrier's liability, the liability of servants and agents of the carrier, written notice of complaint within a specified number of days, time limitation and related matters.

754. The Ukrainian legislation also includes the Rules on Carriage of Cargo by Air.[325] Pursuant to it, an air waybill is a document made out of by a cargo sender or on his behalf, including its electronic copy which serves as an evidence of the contract of carriage formation and acceptance of cargo for carriage upon the conditions specified in it. Under these rules air waybill shall also be deemed as a receipt for cargo. Since these Rules were adopted before Ukraine joined the Montreal Convention, the provisions of the later are not considered in the Rules. Part VI is specifically dealing with the air waybill. It states that the air waybill is issued upon carriage of cargo. It confirms the existence of the contract of carriage between a carrier and

325. Rules on Carriage of Cargo by Air approved by the Order of the State Service on Providing Safety of Aviation dated 14 Mar. 2006, No. 186, registered at the Ministry of Justice on 13 Jun. 2006, No. 705/12579.

a consignor who are specified in the contract and acceptance of cargo for carriage under the conditions provided in this document.

§7. Liability Provisions

755. Article 17 of the Montreal Convention defines that the carrier is liable for damage sustained in case of death or bodily injury of a passenger upon condition that the accident took place on board the aircraft or in the course of any of the operations of embarking or disembarking. The carrier is liable for damage sustained in case of destruction or loss of, or of damage to, checked baggage upon condition that the event took place on board the aircraft or during any period within which the checked baggage was in the charge of the carrier. Taking into account that Ukraine has implemented provisions of the Montreal convention into the national law, the Rules on Carriage of Passengers and Baggage by Air stipulate, that the carrier's liability is limited as follows:

- the carrier shall not be able to exclude or limit its liability for damage not exceeding 113,100 SDRs for each passenger; but the carrier may be liable for damage to the extent that they exceed this amount for each passenger, unless the carrier proves that (1) such damage was not due to its negligence or other wrongful act or omission of the carrier, its servants or handling agents, or (2) such damage was solely due to the negligence or other wrongful act or omission of a third party; the carrier is obliged to arrange advance payment immediately, but not later than fifteen days after identification of the natural person, who is entitled to receive compensation, in the amount not less than 16,000 SDRs;
- for damage caused by delay in carriage of passengers of any flights the liability shall be limited to the amount of 4,694 SDRs for each passenger;
- in case of destruction, loss, damage, or delay of checked baggage, the liability is limited to 1,131 SDRs for each passenger. The carrier's liability in case of carriage of baggage with declared value shall be defined by the amount of the declared value of baggage.

756. With respect to the cargo the Montreal Convention set in Article 22 that in case of destruction, loss, damage or delay in cargo, there is a limitation of 19 SDR per kg. The same limit of liability is stipulated in the Rules on Carriage of Cargo by Air. However, both the convention, and the rules stipulate that if the consignor has made, at the time when the package was handed over to the carrier, a special declaration of interest in delivery at destination and has paid a supplementary sum if the case so requires, the carrier shall pay a sum not exceeding the declared sum, unless it proves that the sum is greater than the consignor's actual interest in delivery at destination.

757. The Rules on Carriage of Cargo by Air shall apply to the agents, servants and representatives of the carrier and any person whose aircraft is used by the carrier and agents, servants and representatives of such person. The air carrier is liable for damage in case of destruction, loss, damage or delay in delivery of cargo if the incident that led to the damage occurred during the air transportation.

§8. Claims and Actions

758. The Montreal Convention set that the person entitled to delivery must complain to the carrier forthwith after the discovery of the damage, and, at the latest, within seven days from the date of receipt in the case of checked baggage and fourteen days from the date of receipt in the case of cargo. In the case of delay, the complaint must be made at the latest within twenty-one days from the date on which the baggage or cargo have been placed at its disposal (Article 31). The Ukrainian legislation includes similar provisions with respect to the Rules on Carriage of Cargo by Air (section 20.3).

759. It is to be noted that both the Warsaw and the Montreal Conventions established the fundamental principle of protection of the rights of parties of the contract of carriage.

760. In case of default of the obligations related to the carriage or improper discharge of such obligations a party can base its plaintiff on provision of the international treaties ratified by Ukraine and the national legislation. The plaintiff has the initial burden of proving the following matters:

- right and title to sue (i.e., as consignor, consignee or owner of the goods);
- receipt of the goods by the carrier in good order and condition (this is generally done through the air waybill which acknowledges receipt by the carrier in apparent good order and condition);
- failure to deliver or delivery by the carrier in a damaged condition and damages suffered by the plaintiff as a consequence.[326]

761. Under Chapter XXVIII of the Rules on Carriage of Passengers and Baggage by Air concerning claims and actions it is provided that during the transportation of passengers, luggage any claim regarding the damage, whatever its reasons or on the basis of the Montreal or Warsaw Convention (depending on which one of them is applicable), or agreement in connection with the offence or on any other basis, can be made only pursuant to the conditions and limits of liability provided by these Rules, without any prejudice to the persons entitled to claim and their respective rights. In the event of such suit, fines, penalties or any other payments not related to compensation of actual damage are not recoverable.

762. In accordance with Article 33(2) of the Montreal Convention an action for damage resulting from death or injury of a passenger may be submitted to a court referred to in Article 33(1), or in the State Party in which a passenger at the time the event has his/her principal and permanent residence.

326. Rules on Carriage of Passengers and Baggage by Air, Ch. XXVIII.

763. Under the Rules on Carriage of Cargo by Air in case of damage, a person entitled to receive the goods, shall send a claim to the carrier immediately after discovering the damage, but not later than fourteen days from the date of receiving the goods or from the date of signing of a respective act by the consignee. In case of delay, complaint must be sent within twenty-one days from the date when the goods passed in the order of the person who is entitled to receive it. In case of loss a claim must be sent within 120 days from the date of issuance of the air waybill (section 21.1.2). Any complaint must be made within the stipulated time frame (section 21.1.3).

764. Claims for liability must be submitted at the option of the plaintiff, to the court at the place of registration of the carrier, at the location of its head office or location of the office of the carrier, where the contact was concluded during the two years (section 21.3).

Chapter 5. Freight Forwarding Activity

765. The geographical location of Ukraine influences the formation and development of transport communication.

766. It should be observed that the Civil Code adopted in the USSR was in force in Ukraine until 2004. It did not provide the regulation of transport services and neither had a blanket rule nor the definition of the contract on transport forwarding. Nowadays the forwarding services and transport-dispatch activity is regulated by the Civil Code, Commercial Code and Law of Ukraine on Forwarding Activity. The definitions of the transport forwarding are contained in Article 929 of Civil Code in Article 316 of the Commercial Code. The Commercial Code of Ukraine recognizes the forwarding activity as an auxiliary type of activity associated with the carriage of goods. Considering the fact that the provisions on transport forwarding contained in the Civil Code are more elaborated than in the Commercial Code, it is reasonable to refer to the former.

767. The Law of Ukraine on Forwarding Activity[327] is the only special Law in this field that sets the legal regulation according to which application of sanctions to forwarders could be only on the ground of the Law. A Draft of Rules for Freight Forwarding Services is already examined by the Cabinet of Ministers.

768. On the initiative of more than a hundred of freight forwarding organizations of Ukraine, the AIFF was established in 1994 the main aims of which are coordination actions and solutions of professional problems. It is important to notice that this professional organization is a member of FIATA. Thus, for all members of the AIFF the Model Rules are obligatory. All AIFF members should mention Model Rules for freight forwarding services in the contract. According to the Law of Ukraine on Amending Certain Acts regarding the Terms of Delivery dated 5 July 2012, No. 5060-VI, the Law on Forwarding Activity was amended as well. According to Article 8 it is allowed to use international customs, recommendations and rules of international organizations unless it is explicitly prohibited by the laws of Ukraine. As regards the importance of implementation of FIATA Model Rules for freight forwarding services AIFF lobbies their interests in the governmental bodies and provides legal and informational support.

769. Chapter 65 of the Civil Code contains the definition of the contract of transport forwarding, its form, documents needed for the forwarding agent, regulates rights and obligations of the parties. It should be mentioned that the Ukrainian legislation in force contains a notion of *transport forwarding* and the person who undertakes the forwarding activity is known as a *forwarder.* According to the Civil Code a party – *forwarder* – shall undertake to perform or organize the carriage of the goods for reward and at the expense of the other party (consignor or consignee as a client) under the contract of transport forwarding. Moreover, the contract of

327. Law of Ukraine on Forwarding Activity dated 1 Jul. 2004, No. 1955-IV.

transport forwarding may provide for the forwarder's obligation to organize the carriage of the goods and along the route chosen by the forwarder or the client, the obligation of the forwarding agent to conclude a contract (contracts) for the carriage of the goods on behalf of the client or on his own behalf, to ensure the dispatch and receipt of the goods, and also other obligations for carriage. The rules of Chapter 65 of the Civil Code shall also extend to the cases when the forwarder's obligations are carried out by the carrier. The forwarder shall be liable to the client if he fails to fulfil his obligations under the contract of transport forwarding according to Chapter 82 of the Civil Code (Articles 1166–1167).

770. The Civil Code also sets in Article 929 that additional services such as operations necessary for the delivery of the goods as the receipt of documents required for export or import, the performance of customs and other formalities, the inspection of the quantity and condition of the goods, their loading and discharging, payment of duties, fees and other expenses to be incurred by the client, the storage of the goods, their receipt at the place of destination, and also fulfilment of other operations and provision of the services specified by the contract.

771. The Law on Forwarding Activity defines forwarding activity as a commercial activity of different ownership forms that for fulfilment of clients' commissions or according to working technologies may have warehouses, different types of vehicles, containers, production premises, etc. This commercial activity does not need special license. However, the *Verkhovna Rada* plans to consider a Draft of Ukraine on Amendments to Some Laws of Ukraine about Licensing of Commercial Activities for Freight Forwarding Services.

772. The scope of application of the Law on Forwarding Activity extends to the transportation of the goods by all means of transport, excluding the pipelines. The Law lays out the specifics of the contract of forwarding activity. The forwarding contract shall be concluded in a written form. In particular, the significant conditions of this contract shall be information about the parties of the contract; type of the service rendered by the forwarder; type and name of the goods; rights and obligations of the parties; liability of the parties, including damage due to force majeure; other conditions as determined by the law.

773. The types of forwarding activity are listed in Article 8 of the Law on Forwarding Activity. Transportation of the goods shall be accompanied by the transport documents which shall be in the international language depending on the chosen type of transport or in the official language, if cargoes are transported within Ukraine. According to Article 9 of the Law on Forwarding Activity these documents are air waybill, CMR, CIM, SMGS waybill, bill of lading, cargo manifest and other documents defined by the laws of Ukraine.

774. The forwarder's service is confirmed by a single transport document or a set of documents that present a route of carriage of cargo from the departure point to the final destination (Article 9 of the Law). A forwarder insures the goods and its liability according to the contract of transport forwarding.[328] The rights and obligations of a forwarder and a client are enshrined in the provisions of Articles 10–12 of the Law. The liability provisions under the Law refer to the provisions set by the Civil Code (Articles 1166–1167 of the Civil Code). The Law specifically mentions that a forwarder shall be liable for a number of places, weight, if control weighting was held at presence of a carrier's representative and certified by its signature. He is also liable for correspondence of packing to transport documents that are certified by a carrier's representative unless otherwise is provided by the contract.

775. Subject to Article 14 of the Law a forwarder shall also be liable for acts and omissions by third parties that it engaged to implement the contract of forwarding activity according to the same procedure as for its own actions.

776. The Law contains only general norms and does not pay any necessary attention to many other practical issues that the forwarders encounter on a daily basis. A Draft of the Rules Conducting the Forwarding Activity was brought to the Government in April 2010. It should be noted that a Draft Law amending Article 4 of the Law on Forwarding Activity proposes to complement Article 4 with a provision that a forwarder must create a guarantee fund in the amount no less than six thousand UMICs (see paragraph 630) with the purpose to provide fulfilment of the commitment. The mentioned proposal raised some concerns among the freight forwarders.

777. Few words must be said about the maritime agency service. The MSC contains the provisions on maritime agency service in Chapter 5 of Part IV (Articles 116–119). The maritime agents as permanent representatives of a ship owner operate in a sea port and beyond its territory and render the services subject to the contract of maritime agency service in the field of merchant shipping for reward (Article 116). Articles 117–118 deal with the rights and obligations of the parties to the contract.

328. Law of Ukraine on Forwarding Activity, Art. 13.

Chapter 6. Carriage by Inland Waterways

778. The Law of Ukraine on Transport stipulates that river transport[329] belongs to the unified transport system of Ukraine. It consists of legal entities that carry out the transportation of passengers, cargo, baggage, mail on inland waterways. It also includes ports and piers, shipbuilding and ship repairing yards, etc.

779. The Budapest Convention on the Contract for the Carriage of Goods by Inland Waterways (CMNI) entered into force 2005. Like CIM and CMR it is considered mainly as the European Convention.[330] Ukraine signed it on 20 June 2002 but has not ratified yet. However, Ukraine acceded to the European ADN on 28 January 2010 with a following reservation '... subject to the reservation that Ukraine does not consider itself bound by Article 15 of the Agreement with reference to paragraph 1 of Article 16 of the Agreement'. This reservation concerns the disputes between contracting parties.

780. Even though Ukraine has not ratified CMNI as yet, it is constructive to examine few provisions of the Convention. In accordance with Article 2 it applies to any contract of carriage according to which the port of loading or the place of taking over of the goods and the port of discharge or the place of delivery of the goods are located in two different states of which at least one is a State Party to this Convention. It provides that:

> If the contract stipulates a choice of several ports of discharge or places of delivery, the port of discharge or the place of delivery to which the goods have actually been delivered shall determine the choice.

Section 3 of Article 2 points out that the Convention will apply regardless of the nationality, place of registration or home port of the vessel or whether the vessel is a maritime or inland navigation vessel and regardless of the nationality, domicile, registered office or place of residence of the carrier, the shipper or the consignee.

781. The inland water transport is still mainly regulated by the Statute of Inland Waterways Transport of the USSR adopted in 1955 with the latest amendments in 1988.[331] It is a point of observation that it was adopted during the time of planned economics and state regulation of all economic activity, when Ukraine was a part of the USSR. Therefore, it is obvious that the legislation on inland water transport requires obligatory amendments and modernization to be in accordance with the legislation in force, market economy and the swift developments in the transportation and logistics industry.

---

329. According to the Draft Law of Ukraine on Navigation on Inland Waterways of Ukraine *river transport* will be updated with *inland water transport.*
330. P. Budgen & S. Lamont-Black, *Goods in Transit*, 2nd Edn (UK: Sweet and Maxwell, 2010), 313.
331. Statute of Inland Waterway Transport of the USSR dated 15 Oct. 1955, No. 1801.

782. The Water Code of Ukraine defines the bodies of executive power and local self-government in the field of management and control over use and protection of waters and reproduction of water resources. Here it should be mentioned that due to the administrative reform the State Committee on Water Sector of Ukraine was reorganized into the State Agency of Water Resources of Ukraine.[332]

783. The Code also defines the regime of river usage in Chapter 16. Part IV deals with protection of waters and Chapter 19 regulates the water objects of natural preservation fund. Violations of water legislation result in disciplinary, administrative, civil or criminal liability pursuant to the Ukrainian legislation.

784. In the meanwhile the *Verkhovna Rada* is considering a Draft Law on Navigation on Inland Waterways of Ukraine, No. 4319, which was adopted in the first reading on 02 November 2010, with necessary comments and propositions. During the development of the Draft Law the norms of the international law, in particular the European Agreement on Main Inland Waterways of International Importance (AGN)[333] dated 19 January 1996 and the European Code for Inland Waterways, 2002 were taken into account.

785. The goal of this Draft is a legal regulation of relations in the field of navigation on inland waterways. It determines the legal, economic and organizational grounds for activity of inland waterways. Implementation of the Draft's provisions undermines the amendments to a certain number of legal Acts of Ukraine. It is mentioned in Article 3 that the scope of application of this Draft covers the relationships associated with activity of inland water transport and usage of inland waterways. This Draft Law also governs the relations connected with functioning of seagoing vessels and vessels of mixed type 'river-sea' during their voyage through the inland waterways and fishing vessels during their stay on inland waterways in river ports.

332. Decree of the President on State Agency of Water Resources of Ukraine, dated 13 Apr. 2011, No. 453/2011.
333. Ukraine acceded to it on 5 Jan. 2010.

Chapter 7. Carriage by Pipelines

§1. Introduction

786. Pipeline transport is the most economical way to transport oil and natural gas, but the Ukrainian pipeline transport system meets changeable governmental regulations. The Government declared its main task – modernization of the pipeline system of Ukraine (Energy Strategy of Ukraine at the period until 2030).[334] Although the pipeline transport system equipment is maintained in a reliable condition, nevertheless it requires replacement or upgrading and additional operational costs.

787. In the times of independence the 674 km *Odessa-Brody* pipeline has been built in order to set another route to move the Caspian oil to the West and not to mix Azerbaijan and Kazakh crude oil, a high-quality blend with Urals blend. This pipeline was intended to transport the Caspian oil from the newly built *Pivdenny* terminal to the existing *Druzhba* pipeline for transport to the European refineries. The Ukrainian Government was encouraged by the EU and USA to build the *Odessa-Brody* pipeline. However, when it was completed, Ukraine did not have enough investments to fill it with the Caspian crude oil and none of the European states were willing to build the connecting pipelines needed to link *Odessa-Brody* to refineries. On 15 August 2008 the President signed the Decree adopted by the National Security and Defence Council of Ukraine on 28 July 2008 on Urgent Measures to Ensure the Operation of the *Odessa-Brody* Pipeline in the Direction as Designed, No. 716/2008. Later that year, the Government was tasked to complete the necessary organizational and legal arrangements by 1 September 2008, and to ensure that by the end of 2008 the *Odessa-Brody* pipeline operated in an averse regime. Pipeline *Odessa-Brody* plays a role of change in the political discussion between the government, parliament, president and owners of pipeline companies. The current situation centred in a possibility of pipeline *Odessa-Brody* to operate in averse regime to transfer oil to Belarus.

788. In March 2009 a new Agreement between Ukraine and the EU on the modernization of its gas transportation system was signed. However, following new presidential elections in 2010 the new priorities have been set in the field of pipeline transport system. Currently the Ukrainian Government is seeking closer cooperation with Russia, in particular, in creating a gas transport consortium to operate the national gas transportation system. *Naftogaz Ukrainy*[335] became a minority shareholder of *Gazprom*.[336]

---

334. Energy Strategy of Ukraine at the period until 2030 approved by the CMU Resolution dated 15 Mar. 2006, No. 145-p.

335. State company of the Ministry of Energy and Coal Industry of Ukraine.

336. Russian Company – extractor of natural gas, where the Russian government holds the controlling stake.

§2. LEGAL REGULATION

789. The legal provisions on pipeline transport are contained in the Law of Ukraine on Transport, the Law of Ukraine on Pipeline Transport,[337] the Law of Ukraine on Transit Cargo,[338] the Law of Ukraine on Oil and Gas.[339] It is submitted that at the moment the legal regulation of fuel and energy complex has a feature of non-systematic character and the absence of a framework law that would have determined the main principles and approaches to regulation of relations in energy, nuclear, coal, oil and gas complexes. Each of the mentioned aspects of fuel and energy complex has to be regulated by a separate law and subordinate regulatory Acts.[340]

790. The Law of Ukraine on Pipeline Transport defines the legal, economic and organizational principles of the pipeline transport. The Law applies to the relations in the field of pipeline transport designed for carriage of hydrocarbons, chemical products, water and other products and substances from the places of their location, mining, preparation or storage to the places of their processing or consumption, reloading and further transportation. Peculiarities of application of the Law regarding operation of industrial pipeline transport shall be defined by the Cabinet of Ministers.[341]

791. The pipeline transport system of Ukraine consists of major pipeline transport and industrial pipeline transport.[342] The pipeline transport system is a state property and privatization or any other change of ownership of the state enterprises of pipeline transport is prohibited. Change of ownership forms of industrial pipeline transport companies is to be made under the control of the special state authorities pursuant to Article 7 of the Law on Pipeline Transport. Liability provisions for the breaches of legislation on pipeline transport are contained in Article 20 of this Law.

792. The control in the field of pipeline transport shall be aimed at ensuring adherence to the requirements of legislation on pipeline transport by bodies of the state executive power, representative bodies and bodies of local self-government, as well as by the legal entities regardless of ownership forms and types of activity and by the citizens. The state control in the field of pipeline transport shall be conducted by the respective ministries and departments, state supervision and control bodies and others (Article 10). The Ministry of Energy and Coal Industry of Ukraine[343] reorganized the Ministry of Oil and Energy of Ukraine. It is a central authority in

337. Law of Ukraine on Pipeline Transport dated 15 May 1996, No. 192/96-BP.
338. Law of Ukraine on Transit Cargo dated 20 Oct. 1999, No. 1172-XIV.
339. Law of Ukraine on Oil and Gas dated 27 Nov. 2003, No. 1344-IV.
340. Energy Strategy, 6.1.4.
341. Law of Ukraine on Pipeline Transport, Art. 4.
342. Law of Ukraine on Pipeline Transport, Art. 2.
343. Presidential Decree on Optimization of the Central Executive Authorities System dated 9 Dec. 2010, No. 1085/2010.

the system of executive central authorities on implementation of state policy in energy, nuclear and oil and gas complexes.[344]

793. The Law of Ukraine on Oil and Gas dated 12 July 2001, No. 2665-III defines the legal, economic and organizational aspects of oil and gas industry of Ukraine and regulates the relations connected with the features of oil mineral resources' usage, extraction, transportation, storage and use of oil, gas and their products to ensure energy security of Ukraine, development of competitive relations in oil-gas branch, protection of rights of all subjects of relations arising in connection with the geological oil and gas reserve. This Law applies to the relations arising from the geological studies of oil and gas reserve, development of oil and gas reserve, storage, transportation and marketing of oil, gas and their products, regardless of ownership of business entities – participants of those relations. Ownership of natural resources of oil and gas that are within the territory of Ukraine, its territorial waters and EEZ belongs to the citizens of Ukraine.[345] Part VIII of the mentioned Law is devoted to the pipeline transport and transhipment complexes of oil, gas and their products. It is provided in Article 42 of the Law that commissioning and decommissioning of pipelines of oil, gas and their products is carried out in the manner prescribed by the Cabinet of Ministers.

794. Liability for violation of legislation governing the activities in the oil and gas sector is provided in Article 51 of the Law. It is enshrined in the mentioned Article that persons liable for those violations shall bear administrative, civil or criminal liability.

344. Regulation on the Ministry of Oil and Energy approved by the Decree of the Cabinet of Ministers of Ukraine dated 2 Nov. 2006, No. 1540.
345. Law of Ukraine on Oil and Gas, Art. 10.

Chapter 8. Transit of Goods

795. The Law of Ukraine on Transit of Cargo[346] defines the principles of organization and conducting of transit of cargoes by air, motor, rail, maritime and inland water transport through the territory of Ukraine. The mentioned Law determines free transit of cargoes which is ensured by:

- absence of any discrimination regarding participants of transit or transit cargo;
- free choice of transit services, works, their providers (performers), transit means as well as transit routes by the participants of transit;
- absence of groundless delays and limitations.

796. Control over the transit of cargoes shall be set exclusively by the laws of Ukraine and the international treaties. It is conducted in the admission points through the customs border of Ukraine. Tariffs on transit services are defined by state executive bodies or by the contracts. The settlements between cargo owners and other participants of transit are conducted according to these agreements (contracts). Transit of goods shall be performed on the respective motor, railway, inland, maritime and air communication routes passing through the admission points through the customs border of Ukraine. Pursuant to the Ukrainian legislation, the participants of transit are considered cargo owners and entrepreneurs (carriers, ports, stations, freight forwarders, maritime agents, etc.), who undertake the transit services. The Law on Transit of Cargo does not cover the transit of mail, luggage, arms, drugs, psychotropic substances, dangerous cargo, export and import of goods, transit of goods using pipeline transport and power lines.[347] Article 4 in its turn stipulates that the transit of goods may be carried out in through or combined transportation.

797. Transit of goods in combined transportation may be associated with transhipment from one means of transport to another, processing, sorting, packing, measuring, accumulation, forming and fragmentation, temporary storage, etc. Transit of goods in through transportation envisages a single transport document throughout the whole carriage. This Law does not mention the option of using a single document in combined transportation. The Law defines what goods shall be considered as transit. According to Article 6 of the Law on Transit the transit of goods shall be accompanied by the consignment note to be composed in the international language. Such consignment note may be an air waybill, SMGS waybill, SMGS/CIM, CMR consignment note, CIM consignment note, bill of lading.

798. It should be mentioned that there is the Law of Ukraine on the Comprehensive Programme for Consolidation of Ukraine as a Transit Country for

346. Law of Ukraine on Transit Cargo dated 20 Oct. 1999, No. 1172-XIV.
347. Law of Ukraine on Transit Cargo dated 20 Oct. 1999, No. 1172-XIV., Art. 2.

2002–2010.[348] The main goal of this Law is to ensure the optimal usage of available and further development of the Ukrainian transit potential by creating favourable conditions for participants in transit transportations, increasing foreign currency proceeds from exports of transport and other services. Additionally, this Programme undermines the strengthening of legal regulation of transit of cargo through Ukraine and adaptation of national legislation to the international one. It also envisages the development of *contrail* (combined) transportation.

799. The Ukrainian territory is crossed by four international transport corridors (No. 3, No. 5, No. 7 (sea), and No. 9), as well as the Baltic Sea – Black Sea (Gdinya/Gdansk – Odessa/Illichivsk) and Europe-the Caucasus-Asia (TRACECA) corridors.[349] Speaking on transit of goods, a few words should be said about TRACECA and its role in the Ukrainian development of maritime and multimodal transport. TRACECA is an interstate programme aimed at supporting the political and economic development in the Black Sea Region, Caucasus and Central Asia by means of improvement of the international transport. One of its objectives is to promote optimal integration of the international transport corridor Europe-Caucasus-Asia 'TRACECA' into the Trans-European Networks (TENs). Ukraine applied for a membership in TRACECA upon approval of the European Commission.

800. The Law of Ukraine on Transit of Cargo has been amended in 2010. Those changes concern Article 6 that was supplemented with the following:

Declaration of transit cargo that are transported by sea and river transport pursuant to the legislation of Ukraine is fulfilled provided the presence of bill of lading and cargo customs declaration to the custom bodies.

801. The cargo customs declaration is not required for the goods (excluding the excise duty goods) that are moving in transit by sea and river transport in containers and during the warehouse period remain within the borders of one point of admission. Similar amendments were introduced into the Customs Code of Ukraine dated 11 July 2002, No. 92-IV. In particular, Article 72 was supplemented by section 3, which reads as follows:

> Customs declaration of goods in transit that are transported by air transport within one point of admission and the custom declaration of goods in transit transported by sea and river transport in containers and during the warehouse period remain within one point of admission or customs control zone of sea port and performed considering the requirements of the Law of Ukraine On Transit of Goods.

802. Those amendments were presented to introduce transhipment into the Ukrainian container ports. By this the definition of transshipment that was absent in the national legislation, is introduced to the maritime activity of Ukraine for the first

348. Law of Ukraine on the Comprehensive Program for Consolidation of Ukraine as a Transit Country for 2002–2010 dated 7 Feb. 2002, No. 3022-III.
349. See at www.traceca-org.org.

time. Additionally, this will facilitate to attract more transshipment volumes to the Ukrainian container ports and consequently, more cargo movements which will increase additional profit to ports and to the state budget respectively. It is possible to predict that in future it might also increase the transportation of goods further to the river ports of Ukraine (so-called hub and spoke concept) by national vessels, including river vessels.

803. Important direction of the Ukrainian transport policy is development of the international transport connections, use and expansion of country transit potential and integration of the national transport system into the European one. Thus, the Cabinet of Ministers approved the Concept of Creation and Functioning of National Network of International Transport Corridors in Ukraine dated 4 August 1997, No. 821 that describes the basic principles of development to 2015. The first implementation phase of the Concept was the Programme of Creation and Functioning of National Network of International Transport Corridors in Ukraine approved by the Cabinet of Ministers dated 20 March 1998, No. 346 that foresees the complex of urgent measures directed at construction of the international transport corridors network for the period ending in 2005. The purpose of the Development Programme of National Network of International Transport Corridors in Ukraine for 2006–2010 is a further construction of the national network of international transport corridors, improvement of its condition and increase of traffic (carrying) capacity, improvement of international transportations technology by the logistic principles of goods delivery systems.

Chapter 9. Multimodal Transportation

§1. Introduction

804. This chapter consists of several sections. At the outset, a brief overview of multimodal transport[350] is submitted. A short observation of the Rotterdam Rules as a proposed solution to a multimodal problem is given. Further, the relevant provisions from the codes and other laws of Ukraine are analysed to give a broader picture of the current legal regulation of combined transport in Ukraine. Additionally, certain regional agreements concerning combined transport between Ukraine and other countries are overviewed.

805. Multimodal transport implies carriage of goods by more than one mode of transport where the whole transport operation is carried out by one multimodal operator under a single contract. The development of container transport from the middle of the twentieth century, modern logistics and technological developments facilitate to a great extent transportation of goods from one destination to another, in other words, from 'door-to-door' to meet the needs and expectations of the customer. The terms 'intermodal', 'multimodal' and 'combined' are sometimes used interchangeably when goods are carried by more than one mode of transport. The stages during which the goods are being transported from 'door-to-door' are called 'modes' or 'types' of transport. Therefore, the whole transport operation got a name *multimodal transport.*

§2. Legal Regulation

I. International Regulation

806. It should be admitted that at present there is no comprehensive international convention regulating multimodal transportation which includes a combination of all modes. Multimodal transport is mostly governed by unimodal conventions that, unfortunately, are unable to adequately respond to swift technological changes demanded by the transport industry. International efforts have been undertaken several times but these have not met with sufficient success. A definition of *international multimodal transport* was first introduced in Article 1.1 of the Multimodal Transport Convention 1980. It reads as follows:

> the carriage of goods by at least two different modes of transport on the basis of a multimodal transport contract from a place in one country at which the goods are taken in charge by the multimodal transport operator to a place designated for delivery situated in a different country. The operations of pick-up and delivery of goods carried out in the performance of a unimodal transport

350. Authors will use the notion *multimodal transport* as a generic term since there is no definition and generally accepted terminology. When referring to the national legislation, the authors literally translate the wording used in those laws and other legal Acts.

contract, as defined in such contract, shall not be considered as international multimodal transport.

807. The liability introduced by the Multimodal Transport Convention 1980 was based on uniform approach. In view of the fact that only thirteen States have signed it, the Convention is not likely to enter into force.

808. After the years of deliberation and debate on a global scale, the new Convention on international carriage of goods known as the Rotterdam Rules was adopted and signed by some twenty states. The fact that its application extends to the other modes beyond the sea leg is reflected in its official title, namely, 'United Nations Convention on Contracts for the International Carriage of Goods Wholly or Partly by Sea' (further – Rotterdam Rules). Twenty ratifications are required for its entry into force. It has been signed by twenty-four States and ratified by Spain and Togo.[351] One of the primary goals of the Rotterdam Rules is to cope with a patchwork of the existing international sea carriage regimes as well as the significant number of national hybrid regimes and replace all of them with a modern, contemporary convention that takes account of recent trends in the growth of containerized multimodal transport on a door-to-door basis and the corresponding impact of logistics on world trade.

809. While the Convention does not mention the term 'multimodal', it is apparent that door-to-door application is intended to be covered. An international sea segment is an obligatory requirement for the application of the Convention regime. Therefore, it has got a name *maritime plus* or *wet multimodal.* One of the reasons for adoption of such a regime was a practical reality of modern trade and transportation of goods, provided that the carriage of goods by sea constitutes by far the biggest mode of transport. In addition to maritime plus regime, a range of other novelties appeared in the convention such as electronic transport documents, volume or service contracts, maritime performing party, rights of control and some more. As stated in Article 5, section 2 of the Rotterdam Rules applies without regard to the nationality of the vessel, the carrier, the performing parties, the shipper, the consignee or any other interested parties. Besides, it deals to prevent the possible collisions with other international transport conventions currently in force by introducing several provisions in the text of the Convention. The success of the Rotterdam Rules remains to be seen in future.[352]

810. Ukraine did not sign the UN Multimodal Transport Convention 1980. As to the Rotterdam Rules Ukraine has not joined it either.

---

351. As on 1 Sep. 2013.

352. A great number of articles and few books are dealing with the various aspects of the new convention, including the multimodal aspects. For further information see also, *inter alia*, www.uncitral.org, www.comitemaritime.org, A. von Ziegler, J. Schelin & S. Zunarelli (eds), *The Rotterdam Rules 2008, Commentary to the UN Convention for the International Carriage of Goods Wholly or Partly by Sea* (Wolters Kluwer 2010), D.R. Thomas (ed.), *The Carriage of Goods by Sea under the Rotterdam Rules* (Lloyd's List 2010), M.F. Sturley, T. Fujita &G. van der Ziel, *The Rotterdam Rules* (Sweet and Maxwell 2010).

II. National Legislation

811. The Ukrainian legislation does not define *multimodal transport*; however, in a number of official documents and strategy plans this term is used together with intermodal and combined transport. One of the main impediments in development of multimodal transport in Ukraine is insufficient legislative regulation of multimodal transport and partial participation in international transport conventions. The number of companies who offer transport services, including multimodal transportation is growing and some of them have become active participants of international transport associations and contribute considerably to the development of transport services.

812. The Civil Code deals with through combined transportation (Article 913). It enshrines that transportation of cargo, passengers, mail might be carried out by several types of transport based on a single transport document. However, the Civil Code does not define the combined transport. The MSC contains a provision concerning claims arising out of the combined transport (Article 384).

A. Carriage by Road

813. The Ukrainian legislation on motor transport does not define multimodal transport, neither those provisions exist in the relevant Laws. However, it does contain some provisions on international transportation of goods and passengers in Part IV, Articles 53–59 of the Law of Ukraine on Motor Transport. International transportation of goods and passengers shall mean the transportation by motor transport with the intersection of the state border.[353] The multimodal provisions on cooperation of motor transport with other transport modes are maintained in the Statute of Motor Transport, Part VII. It provides that motor transport of general use performs the transportation of goods, passengers and luggage in close cooperation with other transport modes, such as rail, maritime, inland water and air transport, creating a system of through intermodal transport: motor–rail, motor–waterway, motor-waterway-rail, etc. The named transportation is carried out on the basis of single transport document issued for the whole voyage.

814. Ukraine has joined the CMR Convention[354] which is primarily a European Convention. It has the force of law in practically all European states.[355] It applies mandatorily to contracts for the carriage of goods by road and creates a uniform liability system for a certain kind of multimodal transport operations. This Convention shall apply to every contract for the carriage of goods by road in vehicles for reward, when the place of taking over of the goods and the place designated for delivery, as specified in the contract, are situated in two different countries, of which

353. Law of Ukraine on Motor Transport dated 5 Apr. 2001, No. 2344-III, Art. 1.
354. Law of Ukraine on the Accession of Ukraine to the Convention on the Contract for the International Carriage of Goods by Road dated 1 Aug. 2006, No. 57-V.
355. See at www.unece.org/trans/conventn/legalinst_25_OLIRT_CMR.html, 1 Sep. 2013.

at least one is a contracting country, irrespective of the place of residence and the nationality of the parties.[356] The CMR contains a well-known multimodal provision in Article 2; however, it applies only in cases when the goods are not unloaded from the transport vehicle and transported further by other modes of transport.

B. *Carriage by Rail*

815. At present the following combined transport trains are successfully operating in Ukraine: 'Viking' Illichevsk-Klaipeda, 'Yaroslav' Kiev-Slavkuv.[357] The provisions on combined transport are briefly contained in Part V of the Statute of the Railways on Through Intermodal Transport with the Participation of Railway and Other Types of Transport. Here the direct mixed transport is defined as transportation which is performed by railways and other types of transport according to the single transport document throughout the journey. It further provides that railways shall carry the goods, passengers, mail and luggage in cooperation with other types of transport through the system of combined transport. Railways are responsible for an uninterrupted and uniform delivery of wagons, ships and motor vehicles for the transhipment of goods at the transhipment points. Article 1 of the Law of Ukraine on Railway Transport[358] defines through combined transport as transportation carried out together with other types of transport provided that there is a single document issued for the whole voyage.

C. *Carriage by Air*

816. The Air Code of Ukraine does not consider cooperation between air transport and other modes of transport. The Montreal Convention, despite its application only to the international carriage by air, states in Article 18.4 that:

> carriage by air does not extend to any carriage by land, by sea or by inland waterway performed outside an airport. If, however, such carriage takes place in the performance of a contract for carriage by air, for the purpose of loading, delivery or transhipment, any damage is presumed, subject to proof to the contrary, to have been the result of an event which took place during the carriage by air. If a carrier, without the consent of the consignor, substitutes carriage by another mode of transport for the whole or part of a carriage intended by the agreement between the parties to be carriage by air, such carriage by another mode of transport is deemed to be within the period of carriage by air.

356. CMR, Art. 1.1.
357. See at http://liski.ua/container_trains.html, 1 Sep. 2013.
358. Law of Ukraine on Railway Transport dated 4 Jul. 1996, No. 273/96-BP.

817. In Ukraine the Rules on Carriage of Cargo by Air[359] regulate provisions of combined transport in Part XVI. Namely, it states that an air carrier will appear as a combined operator in case of combined transport carried out partially by air and other mode of transport. Such a combined transport will be performed in accordance with the contract of combined carriage.

D. Carriage by Sea

818. The MSC does not contain provisions on multimodal transport. However, it deals with presenting of claims in mixed transportation. It is stated in Article 384 of the MSC that the claims arising out of the carriage of goods by sea in through intermodal and through waterway connection shall be presented to a carrier by whose transport means the goods were delivered or should have been delivered. Further, in cases when the final point of destination is a rail station or road station or an airport, a claim is brought to the respective carrier pursuant to the rules established for this type of transport. Provided the Rotterdam Rules become effective in future, their provisions clearly establish the combination of sea leg with other modes of transport, upon the condition that the carriage is international. It is clearly stated in the name of the Convention *wholly or partly by sea* and in the intention of the drafters. Two Articles dealing with multimodal provisions are Articles 26 and 82. In contrast to its predecessor the Multimodal Transport Convention 1980, the Rotterdam Rules introduced the so-called network liability or modified network liability. Article 26 stipulates that:

> When loss of or damage to goods, an event or circumstance causing a delay in their delivery, occurs during the carrier's period of responsibility but solely before their loading onto the ship or solely after their discharge from the ship, the provisions of this Convention do not prevail over those provisions of another international instrument.

E. Carriage by Inland Waterways

819. Neither the Statute on Inland Waterways 1955 nor the Draft Law of Ukraine on Navigation by Inland Waterways of Ukraine mentions about multimodal transportation. However, the Law of Ukraine on Transit of Cargoes applies *inter alia* to the transit of goods by inland water transport.

§3. Regional Agreements on Multimodal Transport

820. Several bilateral agreements on combined transport are concluded between Ukraine and other countries at the regional level. One of them is the Agreement on

359. Approved by the Order of the State Aviation Administration dated 14 Mar. 2006, No. 186, registered at the Ministry of Justice of Ukraine on 13 Jun. 2006, No. 705/12579.

Development of Carriage of Goods in the Destination Baltic Sea-Black Sea, which among others includes activation of combined transport of goods. The parties to this Agreement are Ukraine, Belarus and Lithuania.

821. Ukraine is also a party to the CIS and CIS's Agreement on Coordinated Development of International Transport Corridors, Passing through the Territory of Member States that was adopted on 20 November 2009. This Agreement underlines the importance of harmonization of the legal basis of the CIS' Member States with the international legal norms enshrined in the multilateral agreement and international conventions on transport and customs tariffs with the purpose of further integration of different types of transport in the European and Asian transport network.

822. Additionally, Ukraine is one of the Member States of GUAM – Organization for Democracy and Economic Development (ODED). The Agreement among the Governments of Member States of the ODED – GUAM on International Multimodal Transportation of Goods was adopted on 19 June 2007. Article 1 provides that:

> The present Agreement shall govern relations among transport organizations, multimodal transportation operators, consigners, consignees, other natural and legal persons representing the owner of goods during transportation of goods, multimodal transportation utilizing rail, sea, river, road transport and ferry service. It set forth rights, obligations, and liability of each participant of transportation.

823. It does not affect rights and obligations arising from other international instruments to which ODED-GUAM Member States are Parties. Its scope of application covers the international multimodal transportation of goods among ODED-GUAM Member States and transit through their territories carried out by carriers incorporated in the territory of a Party with origin and destination in their territory and utilization of rail, river, sea, and road transport. Article 5 defines rights, obligations, and liability of the multimodal transportation operator, whereas, Article 6 defines the rights, obligations, and liability of the cargo owner (consignor). It recognizes the advantages of such transportation in Article 9 and calls on the promotion of multimodal transportation of goods in Member States and urgent measures to support and develop it at the national level. Since the Agreement does not have a binding legal force for the States Parties it provides that multimodal transportation of goods shall be governed by the Parties' domestic laws (Article 3(2)).

824. Concluding this chapter, it should be highlighted that the national legislation on multimodal transport is rather undeveloped. As mentioned above, the scarce provisions contained in the national legal Acts do not fully address various aspects of multimodal legal regime and liability. There was a discussion to adopt a new Law on Multimodal Transport suggested by the *UkrZaliznytsya*; however, no draft has been registered yet. It should also be reiterated that absence of uniform terminology and definitions in the national legislation does not contribute to a common understanding and approach to this problem. As it has been already mentioned, the beneficial geopolitical location at the crossroads of international corridors and growing multimodal transport and freight forwarding in the country urgently requires an updated and adequate legal regulation in this field and harmonization with international legal instruments.

Selected Bibliography

Brodie, P.R. *Dictionary of Shipping Terms*. 5th edn. London: Informa, 2007.

Brylyov, O. 'Admiralty Courts in Ukraine – To Be or Not to Be'. *Jur.Gazeta.* www.yur-gazeta.com/oarticle/218/, 20 October 2003.

Butler, E.W. *Russian Law.* 3rd edn. Oxford: Oxford University Press, 2009.

Budgen, P. & S. Lamont-Black. *Goods in Transit*. 2nd edn. London: Sweet and Maxwell, 2009.

Cartner, A.C.J., R.P. Fiske & T.L. Leiter. *The International Law of the Ship Master.* London: Informa, 2009.

Chuah, C.T.J. *Law of International Trade: Cross-Border Commercial Transactions.* 4th edn. London: Sweet and Maxwell, 2009.

Churchill, R.R. & A.V. Lowe. *The Law of the Sea*. 3rd edn. Manchester: Juris Publishing, Manchester University Press, 1999.

Evans, D.M. *International Law.* 3rd edn. Oxford: Oxford University Press, 2010.

Falillev, P. 'Commentary to the Chapter XXII of MSCRF'. www.fortisjuris.ru. Falkanger, T., H.J. Bull & L. Brautasset. *Scandinavian Maritime Law*. 2nd edn. Oslo: Cappelen akademisk forl., 2008.

Fitzpatrick, D. & M. Anderson (eds). *Seafarer's Rights*. Oxford: Oxford University Press, 2005.

Garner, A.B. (ed.). *Black's Law Dictionary.* 9th edn. USA: WEST, 2009.

Hill, C. *Maritime Law*. 5th edn. London, Hong Kong: LLP, 1998.

John, F.W. *Carriage of Goods by Sea.* 6th edn. Essex: Pearson, 2008.

Kritzer, M.H. (ed.). *Legal Systems of the World, a Political, Social & Cultural Encyclopaedia*, vol. IV. Santa-Barbara: ABC CLIO, 2002.

Mallayev, V. 'Ship Arrest in Ukraine'. www.shiparrested.com/ship-arrest-inukraine-by-vagif-mallayev-chechel-mallayev-partners-law-firm.html, 2006. Mukherjee, K.P. *Maritime Legislation*. Malmö: WMU Publications, 2002.

Oude Elferink, G.A. 'Russian Federation Maritime Boundary Delimitations'. *Int'l J. Marine and Coastal L.* 11. Kluwer Law International, 1996, 563. Owen, R.D. 'The Origins and Development of Marine Collision Law'. *Tulane Law Review* 51, No. 4 (June 1976–1977).

Power, V. *EC Shipping Law.* 2nd edn. London, Hong Kong: LLP, 1998.

Prescott, V. & S. Clive. *The Maritime Political Boundaries of the World*. 2nd edn. Leiden, Boston: Martinus Nijhoff Publishers, 2004.

Rose, F.D. (ed.). *Kennedy and Rose, the Law of Salvage*. London: Sweet & Maxwell, 2002.

Rowbotham, J.M. *Introduction to Marine Cargo Management*. London: Informa, 2008.

Shemyakin, A. *Morskoe Pravo*. 2nd edn. Odessa: VMV, 2006.

Stebelsky, I. & I. Teslia. *The Internet Encyclopaedia of Ukraine,* vol. 4 (1993).

www.encyclopediaofukraine.com/land.asp. Tetley, W. *Maritime Liens and Claims*. 2nd edn. Montreal: International Shipping Publications, 1998. Shaw, N.M. *International Law*. 5th edn. Cambridge: Cambridge University Press, 2003.

Tetley, W. 'Reform of Carriage of Goods – the UNCITRAL Draft and Senate COGSA'99'. *Tulane Maritime Law Journal* (Winter 2003).

Tiberg, H. & S. Johan. *On Maritime and Transport Law in Sweden 2nd ed.* Axel Ax:son Johnson Institute for Maritime and Other Transport Law, 2009.

Thomas, D.R. (ed.). *The Carriage of Goods by Sea under the Rotterdam Rules*. London: Lloyd's list, 2010.

Thomas, D.R. (ed.). *A New Convention for the Carriage for the Carriage of Goods Wholly or Partly by Sea – The Rotterdam Rules.* Witney: Lawtext Publishing Limited, 2009.

Treitel, H.G. & F.M.B. Reynolds. *Carver on Bills of Lading*. 2nd edn. London: Sweet & Maxwell, 2005.

Von Ziegler, A., J. Schelin & S. Zunarelli (eds). *The Rotterdam Rules 2008, Commentary to the UN Convention for the International Carriage of Goods Wholly or Partly by Sea*. The Netherlands: Wolters Kluwer, 2010.

Table of Cases

Constitutional Court of Ukraine

Decision of the Constitutional Court of Ukraine dated 11 March 2010, No. 1-1/2010.

Decision of the Constitutional Court of Ukraine dated 15 December 2004, No. 1-17/2004.

Decision of the Constitutional Court of Ukraine dated 30 May 2001, No. 7-rp /2001.

Supreme Courts

Ruling of the Supreme Court of Ukraine dated 22 May 2007 (no number).

Ruling of the Supreme Court of Ukraine dated 17 April 2007, No. 3-1058k07.

Ruling of the Supreme Commercial Court of Ukraine dated 18 March 2008, No. 9/338-07-9047.

Ruling of the Supreme Commercial Court of Ukraine dated 27 February 2007 on the case No. 6/165.

Ruling of the Supreme Commercial Court of Ukraine dated 20 March 2007, No. 14/26273.

Ruling of the Supreme Commercial Court of Ukraine dated 22 March 2007, No. 9/361-IIH-06.

Other Courts

Decision of the Primorskiy Court of the city of Odessa dated 11 December 2007, No. 2-7562/07.

Decision of Illychivsk City Court of Odessa Region dated 23 April 2010, No. 2-434/2010.

Decision of Odessa District Appellate Court dated 08 January 2009, No. 6/497/08.

Decision of the Skadovsk Regional Court of Kherson Region dated 10 June 2010, No. 2-403/10.

Other cases

ECJ decision in *Commission v. France*, Case 167/73 [1974] ECR 359.

Index

The numbers here refer to paragraph numbers.

www.ingramcontent.com/pod-product-compliance
Lightning Source LLC
Chambersburg PA
CBHW071441230926
51846CB00001B/302
9789041154286